D1173885

BIOG HEN

Kidd, Thomas S.

Patrick Henry

**Please check all items for damages
before leaving the Library.
Thereafter you will be held
responsible for all injuries
to items beyond reasonable wear.**

# PATRICK HENRY

## Also by Thomas S. Kidd

*God of Liberty*

*American Christians and Islam*

*The Great Awakening: The Roots of Evangelical*
*Christianity in Colonial America*

*The Great Awakening: A Brief History*
*with Documents*

*The Protestant Interest*

# PATRICK HENRY

## First Among Patriots

### THOMAS S. KIDD

BASIC BOOKS
A Member of the Perseus Books Group
New York

Copyright © 2011 by Thomas S. Kidd

Published by Basic Books,
A Member of the Perseus Books Group

Books published by Basic Books are available at special discounts
for bulk purchases in the United States by corporations, institutions,
and other organizations. For more information, please contact the Special
Markets Department at the Perseus Books Group, 2300 Chestnut Street,
Suite 200, Philadelphia, PA 19103, or call (800) 810-4145, ext. 5000,
or e-mail special.markets@perseusbooks.com.

Cover illustration: Painting by Peter Rothermel of Patrick Henry
delivering a speech before the House of Burgesses, March 23, 1775
(Photo by Fotosearch/Getty Images)

Designed by Linda Mark

The Library of Congress has cataloged the hardcover as follows:
Kidd, Thomas S.
Patrick Henry : first among patriots / Thomas S. Kidd.
p.   cm.
Includes bibliographical references and index.
ISBN 978-0-465-00928-2 (hardcover : alk. paper)   ISBN 978-0-465-02810-8 (e-book)
1. Henry, Patrick, 1736–1799. 2. Virginia—Politics and government—1775–1783.
3. United States—Politics and government—1775–1783. 4. United States—
Politics and government—1783–1789. 5. Legislators—United States—Biography.
6. United States. Continental Congress—Biography. I. Title.
E302.6.H5K53 2011
973.3092--dc23
[B]
2011025656

10 9 8 7 6 5 4 3 2 1

306p.

M 330

*In memory of my father, Michael S. Kidd,*
*a native of southwest Virginia and*
*graduate of Emory and Henry College*

# CONTENTS

*Contents*

# INTRODUCTION

# "The Nefarious and Highly Criminal" Patrick Henry

*Patrick Henry in American Memory*

Patrick Henry's career was celebrated the most for his speeches. His performances summoned the memory of ancient heroes of the Greek and Roman republics who rallied their citizens to a noble and urgent cause with orations that changed history and made history themselves. But one of Henry's speeches thunders above his others in American patriotic memory: the address to the Virginia Convention at St. John's Church in Richmond in 1775, when he shamed reluctant colonial delegates into taking defensive measures against the British. Tension between crown and colonists was at a historic high, and many Americans expected war to begin shortly. Some Virginia delegates continued to push for reconciliation with Britain, which to Henry seemed cowardly. "We must fight! I repeat it, sir, we must fight! An appeal to arms and to the God of hosts, is all that is left us!" he declared, his voice echoing in the rafters of the white clapboard church, the only building in Richmond large enough to hold the delegates. "Is life so dear, or peace so sweet, as to be purchased at the price of chains and slavery? Forbid it, Almighty God!" With this, Henry raised his arms and bellowed, "I know not what course others may take, but as for me, give me liberty, or give me death!"[1]

The speech represented Henry as "his pure self," said future Virginia governor Edmund Randolph. "It blazed so as to warm the coldest heart. In the sacred place of meeting, the church, the imagination had no difficulty to conceive, when he launched forth in solemn tones various causes of scruple against oppressors, that the British king was lying prostrate from the thunder of heaven." Without a doubt, Henry's rousing call to arms was the most electrifying speech of the Revolution.[2]

There was, however, another, lesser-known speech that framed Henry's remarkable career, a speech that revealed a different but no less fervent aspect of Henry's belief in political liberty. It came thirteen years later, at the Virginia convention tasked with evaluating the new U.S. Constitution, and accepting or rejecting the charter that would bind Americans into a firmer union. The vote among the delegates for ratification would be very close. Henry warned that in his mind's eye he could see angels watching, "reviewing the political decisions and revolutions which in the progress of time will happen in America, and consequent happiness or misery of mankind—I am led to believe that much of the account on one side or the other, will depend on what we now decide."[3]

But here is the surprise: Henry was an anti-federalist. He believed that Americans would secure their own destruction if they *ratified* the Constitution.

With its stirring summons to "liberty or death," Henry's 1775 oration fits easily into American patriotic history. It is more difficult to account for Henry's opposition to the Constitution, because it leads us to confront a less familiar, and more problematic and enduring question raised by the American Revolution: Now that the people had won liberty, how might it be preserved? No one deserved more credit for the Revolution than Henry, and that fact alone makes his life a compelling one to study. But by 1788, Henry had begun to fear that the Revolution was in deep trouble. For him, the Constitution was no culmination of the Revolution. Ratifying the Constitution betrayed the Revolution because it threatened to forfeit America's freedom.

Some Federalists—supporters of the Constitution—truly loathed Henry for his opposition to the Constitution. The French writer St. John de Crèvecoeur, a longtime resident of New York and vehement Federalist, wrote to a friend from Virginia that the "nefarious and highly criminal P. Henry" was trying to destroy the incipient Union. "Now is the critical hour and which in Virginia remarkable from the opinion of Mr. Henry the fate of America seems now to depend." If the Constitution failed there, Crèvecoeur believed, "the flames of civil war I am persuaded will be first kindled in your country, for both parties are and will be still more incensed against each other."[4]

The fifty-two-year-old Henry was used to these kinds of accusations. He had heard them for most of his adult life, beginning with his legislative resolutions against the Stamp Act in 1765, the action that inaugurated the Revolutionary crisis with Britain. "Twenty-three years ago," Henry mused, "I was supposed a traitor to my country: I was then said to be a bane of sedition, because I supported the rights of my country." And here he was again—a man first among patriots, denounced as a turncoat.[5]

In his final speech at the Richmond ratifying convention, Henry evoked a vision of monitory angelic figures, to emphasize the gravity of Virginia's decision. The vote over ratification was an epochal moment in the history of human liberty, Henry declared. "I see the awful immensity of the dangers with which it is pregnant.—I see it—I feel it.—I see *beings* of a higher order, anxious concerning our decision." As he pleaded with his colleagues not to shackle themselves by consenting to this powerful new government, a howling storm arose outside the hall. Thunder crashed; delegates took cover under tables. Henry's first biographer wrote that the "spirits whom he had called, seemed to have come at his bidding." And yet when the vote was cast, Henry lost. Virginia—and the United States—embraced the Constitution.[6]

Patrick Henry always wondered whether Americans had the moral and political fortitude to safeguard the American Revolution. To him, the Revolution promised a return to the best kind of republic: a virtuous society with robust local governments. In his view, and the view of many other patriots, moral dissipation and consolidated political power set the stage for tyranny. From his own education in the classics, he knew that republics had fallen many times throughout history. Henry had witnessed, and eloquently decried, the tyranny that had threatened the American colonies from 1765 to 1775 and incited a revolution. In 1788, with the war for independence won, Henry believed that the new republic was in peril again. Although he would reconcile himself tentatively to the outcome of ratification, Henry never got over the feeling that when Virginia approved the Constitution, the Revolution was lost. This patriot believed that he had helped America win its independence, only to find the legacy of the Revolution forsaken by the likes of Thomas Jefferson, James Madison, and Alexander Hamilton.

Can we still place Henry in the pantheon of leading Founders if he opposed the Constitution? Can a sincere patriot question the Constitution itself, the document that has ostensibly become the bedrock of national freedom? Whatever we think of his resistance to the "more perfect union" embraced by other patriots, Henry's opposition to the Constitution was born out of the cause that defined his career, an unshakeable commitment to liberty.

# 1

## "IF YOUR INDUSTRY BE ONLY HALF EQUAL TO YOUR GENIUS"

## Patrick Henry and Backcountry Virginia

P ATRICK HENRY WAS WORKING as a part-time barkeeper when Thomas Jefferson first met him. It was Christmas 1759, and the seventeen-year-old Jefferson was going to college at William and Mary, spending the Christmas holidays at the Hanover, Virginia, home of a family friend, Captain Nathaniel West Dandridge. Hanover, the midway point on the journey from Jefferson's Albemarle County home to the college at Williamsburg, was also the new home of Patrick Henry, who was twenty-three years old, and his young family.

Henry was also a good friend of Dandridge's; five years later, he would become Dandridge's lawyer. But that association seemed improbable in 1759: Henry had already failed twice as a shopkeeper, he had recently lost his family home in a fire, and his prospects appeared uncertain at best. Neither he nor Jefferson came from elite families, but Jefferson's parents at least had the means to send him to college. Unlike Jefferson, Patrick would never receive any formal higher education. That Christmas, he was just trying to feed his family, which is what had brought him to work at his father-in-law's tavern and inn, just across from the Hanover courthouse. Patrick served drinks and tended to the needs of lodgers who had traveled by horse and carriage to address grievances and settle accounts in the bustling county seat on the edge of Virginia's farm frontier. On court days, little Hanover took on the festive air of a carnival, attracting all kinds of peddlers and performers. Men took bets on cockfights, horse races, and boxing matches, and hooted at convicted criminals sentenced to stand in the wooden pillory outside the courthouse. As he poured hot toddies and home-brewed beer for the guests and watched them play backgammon, dice, and cards, he pondered the future. He could not tend bar forever. Thomas Jefferson was young enough and well-off enough to enjoy years of contemplative study and political reflection. Henry, older, poorer, with two young children and a needy wife, had to find his calling in life as soon as possible; he needed a good career.[1]

Despite the difference in their age and situation, Jefferson and Henry became friends during Henry's daily visits to the Dandridge home. During the twelve days of Christmas, they enjoyed the "usual revelries of the season," as Jefferson put it. Henry undoubtedly joined in the fun, playing the violin and taking turns in the dances that animated a household like Dandridge's in eighteenth-century Virginia. His wife, Sarah, a quiet, dutiful twenty-one-year-old, might also have joined in the reels down the length of Dandridge's parlor. And of course there was food: the colonists' celebrations from Christmas to Twelfth Night (January 5) featured gastronomic delights bordering on the gluttonous. For example, in 1771, the Christmas menu for the Fairfax family of northern Virginia included "six mince pies, seven custards, twelve tarts, one chicken pie, and four puddings."²

Although Jefferson observed Henry to be a bit coarse, he also found him charming. "His passion was music, dancing, and pleasantry," Jefferson recalled. "He excelled in the last, and it attached everyone to him." Patrick Henry had not proved himself successful in farming or business, but he won people's affections with his joyful embrace of the life he shared with other rural Virginians. He would find his vocation through the bonds that his conviviality created with his fellow citizens. Over the next five years he would move from behind his father-in-law's bar to join the bar—the legal profession— and rapidly rise in local politics. Yet he would remain close enough to the people among whom he lived to understand and represent their hopes and anxieties. Personality and place formed Patrick Henry's politics.³

WHEN PATRICK HENRY'S FATHER, John, arrived in America in 1727, Virginia was 120 years old, the oldest of England's surviving North American colonies. The original Jamestown settlers had dreamed of gold and quick riches, but they found colonizing this new land much harder than they could have imagined. They endured famine and disease, and engaged in brutal conflicts with local Native Americans affiliated with the great chief Powhatan. One starving settler killed and ate his wife, for which he himself was burned at the stake.

By the late 1610s, Virginians began to turn to tobacco as their economic salvation. Native Americans had smoked tobacco long before Europeans arrived in the New World, and in the sixteenth and seventeenth centuries European colonists began to ship the crop back to Europe. When smoked or chewed, tobacco releases the powerful compound nicotine, a drug that produced just as pleasant, potentially addictive sensations then as it does today. Virginia had excellent soil for growing tobacco, and once cured by drying, the crop would easily ship to European markets. The growth of tobacco output from the Chesapeake colonies not only rescued the new colony from disaster but also brought prosperity to its growers, expanding from sixty thousand pounds in 1620 to twenty-eight million pounds by the 1680s.[4]

Who would undertake the hot and blistering work of growing and harvesting the brown gold of tobacco? Virginians needed workers to man its fields, but the tobacco barons did not originally rely on the labor of African slaves. In early seventeenth-century Virginia, whites came as indentured servants, with relatively small numbers of African-Americans serving as slaves. The white servants accepted indenture in exchange for passage to the New World, hoping that if they lived beyond the term of their contracted labor, they might even acquire land themselves. The black slaves had no such hope.

But for many, even hope turned to horror. Early Virginia was a charnel house. Neither whites nor blacks could expect to live long after their arrival. They died in droves from disease and in fights with local Native Americans. In time, as tobacco became profitable and conditions in the colony's fields became less deadly, more poor whites in England scrambled to get on ships bound for Virginia, drawn by the illusory promise of wealth. So many destitute whites poured in that some elite settlers feared that the colony had become "a sink to drain England of her filth and scum," as one Virginian put it in 1676.[5]

The white servants who lived long enough to earn freedom from indenture (usually a term of seven years or less) often found themselves unable to achieve their dream of independence. Pushed farther and farther into the backcountry to find available land, they normally lived in windowless, dirt-floor shacks and tended hastily cleared fields dotted with burned stumps of trees. The poor farmers resented the tidewater "planters," as the tobacco nobles became known. Yet they hated Native Americans even more, because they perceived the region's original settlers to be standing in the way of security and prosperity. Compounding the predicament of small tobacco farmers, in the 1660s tobacco prices began to drop precipitously, thanks to the growing number of producers, but British-appointed authorities still maintained high taxes on their small plots of land. Callous British officials in London aggravated the situation with the Navigation Acts, which required farmers to ship their tobacco only to England, on English ships, and made tobacco surpluses even more acute. The colony began to boil with instability.

In 1676, a hundred years before America's independence, Virginia erupted into a civil war known as Bacon's Rebellion. Angry white settlers found a leader in young Nathaniel Bacon, a recent arrival from England and a relative of Virginia's governor, William Berkeley. Though most members of the elite sided with the Virginia government, Bacon sympathized with the plight of the poor colonists; he viewed Berkeley as a weak leader and saw an opportunity to gain power for the oppressed farmers and himself at the expense of Native Americans. Bacon and his followers—a "Rabble Crue," Berkeley's supporters called them—began indiscriminately attacking Native Americans, both foes and former friends. When Bacon refused to end the unsanctioned attacks, Berkeley declared him a rebel against the colony. Bacon then turned his forces against Berkeley and the capital at Jamestown, which he burned to the ground in September 1676. But when Bacon abruptly died of the "bloody flux," or dysentery, the rebellion fizzled. Thereafter, Virginia stabilized and flourished, partly because the colonial assembly significantly reduced taxes on the poor farmers. Indentured servants spurned Virginia and increasingly gravitated to newer English colonies, such as Pennsylvania, making the problem of the landless poor whites less severe.[6]

The shrinking pool of white workers had tragic consequences. Virginia planters began to import more African slaves to work the tobacco fields. In 1700, the 13,000 Africans in Virginia represented 13 percent of the colony's population, but by 1750, their numbers were up to 150,000, or 40 percent of its inhabitants. (The white population in Virginia also grew rapidly, from 90,000 in 1700 to 225,000 in 1750.) Whites now perceived slaves, land, and tobacco as the keys to economic success and personal independence. Race divided eighteenth-century Virginia in a way that it had not a century earlier.

Young Patrick Henry, a child of the mid-eighteenth century, grew up in a world of relatively new, yet deep-seated racism. To the white planters, the burgeoning black population—the very people whose captive presence ensured the elites' prosperity—seemed to them alien and menacing: they arrived from west Africa not speaking English, they were not Christians (aside from a handful of whom had already been converted to Roman Catholicism, which Virginia Protestants did not count as Christianity), and they often had filed teeth, plaited hair, and ritual scarring. As never before, whites were now deeming blacks to be intrinsically inferior to their owners, suitable only for the servile labor to which they were condemned. A host of new laws codified the cultural separation between whites and blacks. For example, interracial marriage was explicitly banned, as was sex between white women and black men. (The law remained significantly silent on sex between white men and black women.)

By the 1720s, the planters dominated all aspects of political and economic life in Virginia, even as new European immigrants sought to penetrate the ranks of the colony's aristocrats. The elite gentry represented a tiny fraction of the population—maybe no more than 5 percent of whites—yet that social stratum was in fact permeable at its bottom, open to those with good luck and connections. Scots like John Henry (as opposed to the masses of Scots-Irish from Northern Ireland) came in relatively small numbers to America in the colonial era, and most were professionals and businessmen who could realistically aspire to entrepreneurial success. Some Scots sought opportunity in the Virginia backcountry, usually related to the burgeoning tobacco trade. Scottish merchants played a major role in shipping tobacco, which by the 1760s accounted for more than 80 percent of all Scottish imports from mainland North America.[7]

John Henry was one of the early Scottish immigrants to recognize the opportunities in Chesapeake tobacco farming. He came from Aberdeen, Scotland, where he attended but failed to graduate from college. The reasons that John left college are lost to history, but certainly the pull of prosperity in America helped lure him away from his books. Soon after leaving the university, he secured passage to Virginia, arriving in Hanover County because of a connection there with John Syme (pronounced "sim"), an influential planter.

The American backcountry was not so far back in those days. Hanover County was about sixty miles inland from the new colonial capital at Williamsburg, and just north of the future capital at Richmond, founded in 1737, a year after Patrick's birth. Hanover lay in the Piedmont region of Virginia, well to the east of the Blue Ridge Mountains and Shenandoah Valley, both of which were true nether regions of Virginia where European settlers had just begun to trickle in. The original residents of the area encompassing Hanover County were Pamunkey and Chickahominy Indians, who, like most Native Americans, faced calamity from European diseases and dislocation from English settlements.

Hanover County was carved out of New Kent County in 1720 and named for the family of Britain's King George I. When Queen Anne died in 1714, the Hanovers, Protestant Christians originally from Germany, rescued the British monarchy from the prospect of a Catholic ruler. Anne had no surviving children, but British law required that the crown be held by a Protestant, which led the government to pass over more than fifty Catholics with closer blood relations to Anne and make George the king of England. The county received the name of the house of Hanover as a sign of affection for England and its Protestant king. At this time, there was no hint of the anti-monarchical sentiments that Patrick Henry, Hanover County's favorite son, would trumpet a generation later.

The county that became John Henry's new home was fertile and hilly, prime terrain for tobacco and many edible crops. An American Continental soldier visiting Hanover in 1781, hungry from marching, was delighted to forage on the county's abundant watermelons, "the best and finest I have ever seen. This country is full of them; they have large patches of two and three acres of them." He observed that African-American slaves had small garden plots in Hanover, with "great quantities of snaps and collards." Tobacco became the economic mainstay staple of the county, as it was for the colony itself. Patrick Henry would grow up during another boom period in the crop, with the total volume of tobacco exported to Britain rising more than 250 percent between 1725 and 1775. Already by the 1720s, the average person in England smoked about two pounds of tobacco per year.[8]

For several years John Henry toiled on Syme's plantation. Then in 1731, his fortunes changed. Syme died, widowing his attractive young wife, Sarah. In 1734, John married Sarah, winning not just the widow's hand but also Syme's estate and Sarah's connections to the gentry. Now possessed of over 7,000 acres of land, John Henry became an up-and-coming figure, connected to the old Virginia aristocracy. He continued to acquire land throughout central Virginia, and held a variety of political and military posts. A man who had left Scotland seven years earlier with little more than an incomplete education and a strong ambition now was a fully rooted member of the burgeoning colony. For his son Patrick, John Henry's success would represent the possibilities America availed to an individual with drive and dreams. At times, his father's success would also be something of a reprimand.

ON MAY 29, 1736, Sarah Henry gave birth to Patrick, the second of eleven children born to the Henrys. Patrick was named for John's older brother, who had become a Church of England parson after graduating from college in Scotland. The Reverend Patrick Henry had also emigrated from Scotland to Virginia, and in 1736 he became the rector of St. Paul's Parish in Hanover County; his brother John became a vestryman, a member of the council that governed the affairs of the parish and levied local taxes to support it. They exercised considerable power over those under their watch. Publicly supported religion meant a great deal to the Henry family. They were convinced that a virtuous society required tax-funded churches and the vigilance of parsons and vestrymen like the Henry brothers.[9]

Patrick Henry received an education that was, for a scion of the new gentry, modest. He learned to read, write, and count at a small common school he attended until he was ten years old. Thereafter, he received no other formal schooling at all—no preparatory academy existed in Hanover until 1778—but as he began his teenage years, he learned Latin, Greek, and advanced mathematics from his father. An autodidact like many of his day, Patrick read deeply in ancient and modern history, no doubt focusing on the heroes of Greek and Roman antiquity and their counterparts in British and European history since the Protestant Reformation. He was hardly uneducated, especially in the liberal arts, but the relative informality of Henry's home education did not herald the emergence of a great statesman. Nevertheless, the close attention he received from his father made him sensitive to the great principles of the British and Western traditions that defined themselves around Christian faith, the liberty espoused by well-known British opposition figures such as John Trenchard and Thomas Gordon, and the concept of virtue, which for an eighteenth-century Anglo-American meant a moral disposition committed to the public good. At his death, Henry possessed about two hundred books—an impressive number for a man of the era—on law, Christianity, and history, with some classical texts in Latin and Greek.[10]

From this array of sources—literary, cultural, and religious—Henry derived a worldview that was pervasively Christian, with a heavy dose of ancient Greek and Roman influences. Among the foundational beliefs of this worldview was the imperfection of mankind. His King James Bible repeatedly affirmed that (in the words of Paul's letter to the Romans) "there is none righteous, no, not one." Likewise, Henry knew that, in a classic lesson of man's flawed nature, the golden era of the Roman republic had disintegrated into political intrigue, chaos, and civil war. Julius Caesar (assassinated by rivals in 44 BCE) was only the best known casualty of the republic's fall. Rome's turmoil had led inexorably to the rise of the emperors, including notorious tyrants such as Caligula and Nero. Concentrated power could not be trusted in the hands of fallible men. Henry knew that he, too, was fallible. Throughout his life, as family man, farmer, lawyer, and politician, he earnestly sought—not always with complete success—to stay on the path of uprightness.

From his reading, from absorbing his father's principles, and through the very air he breathed in a Virginia populated by people who had escaped an Old World rife with conflict, oppression, and lack of individual opportunity, Patrick Henry believed that the imperfection of men made fragile the kind of liberty he and his family enjoyed. It was in the nature of human beings, he learned, always to grasp for what was not theirs, seeking dominion over others in a way that threatened the common good and undermined the stability of the state. Good government took the realities of human nature into account by balancing power between the interests and branches within it, yet even the best government was subject to corruption. To young Patrick Henry, the men of a republic (in his era, women would normally not have been included in this political

such extremists, repeatedly charged the evangelicals with holding unauthorized meetings. To the elite Virginia Anglicans who dominated colonial and local government, the revivalists threatened their church and the sanctity of its parish system. Virginia's governor, William Gooch, insisted that the state suppress these ministers who were "under the pretended infatuation of new light, extraordinary impulse, and such like fanatical and enthusiastic knowledge." In the eighteenth century, "enthusiasm" implied religious frenzy.[10]

Pastor Henry's consternation at the Great Awakening climaxed when George Whitefield himself visited Hanover in 1745 and requested permission to preach at St. Paul's Church. Henry tried to force Whitefield to meet with him before giving his approval, presumably to inquire about the itinerant's intentions, but Whitefield refused. Instead, the preacher simply showed up at the church Sunday morning, bringing a huge crowd with him. Henry decided to let Whitefield preach, as long as he also performed the Anglican liturgy. Whitefield agreed. Henry worried that if he refused to let Whitefield preach, he would have simply gone out to the churchyard. "All the people to a man had a great desire to hear the famous Whit[e]field," Henry lamented. Anglican clerics had never faced this kind of treatment before, with Whitefield bypassing them and colonial officials to appeal directly to the people for support. The Great Awakening in Hanover County, as in many places in America, stirred a profound change not only in the locus of faith but in the nexus of political action. The center of authority slowly moved from politicians and parsons to the people.[11]

THE ARRIVAL OF SAMUEL DAVIES in Hanover County in 1747 gave heft to the fledgling evangelical movement in Virginia. Like Francis Makemie nearly fifty years before, Davies secured a license from the government to preach in several Virginia counties. Nevertheless, Parson Henry tried to paint him as a subversive fanatic. To him,

Davies and the other revivalists were simply trying to "screw up the people to the greatest heights of religious frenzy." Although some of the early Presbyterians in Virginia's Great Awakening did manifest a frighteningly radical style, Davies sought to cast himself as an unobjectionable moderate to win the favor of the Virginia authorities.[12]

Davies became the Virginia dissenters' most articulate defender, arguing that the Act of Toleration required the colonial governments to provide licenses to preach wherever the people demanded it. After local Anglicans like Parson Henry accused him of "intrusive schismatical itinerations," Davies appealed to the bishop of London in 1752 to vindicate himself and his dissenting colleagues. Davies denied that he denigrated the Anglican clerics or recruited Anglicans to become Presbyterians. He only preached the essentials of the gospel, he declared, and the light of truth drew new converts to his churches. Could the bishop blame him for this? The colonial government, after granting him licenses to preach in four Virginia counties, balked at his requests to preach more widely and to open new churches. Davies insisted that his followers were spread over several counties and needed meetinghouses close to them. How could Virginians claim to tolerate the dissenters, if they would not allow them to meet? Davies stayed in Hanover for eleven years, from the time Patrick Henry was twelve to twenty-three years old—during his transition into maturity and marriage until just before he embarked on his legal career. In 1759 Davies became the president of the College of New Jersey, where he replaced Jonathan Edwards, who had died of smallpox shortly after his tenure in Princeton began. Davies would not live long as college president, either, dying in 1761 at the age of thirty-eight.[13]

The influence on Patrick Henry of Davies and other evangelicals would become clearer as his career developed. Although Henry never abandoned the Anglican denomination (which, in America, later came to be called the Episcopal Church), he proved himself a foe of Anglican political power in the colony, and a friend to the dissenters' liberty. Unlike the more radical evangelicals, however, Henry could not accept the full disestablishment of the Anglican Church; he believed that a godly republic had to support religion. He was content with distributing taxes to multiple denominations but could not countenance Virginia's rejection of public support for religion altogether.

Henry also came to follow the model of Davies and George Whitefield in his method of popular appeal. Just like the instigators of the Great Awakening, Henry and other populist patriot leaders of the American Revolution challenged established authority by employing direct appeals to the people in their own language. Other patriots would root their arguments in the new philosophy of the Enlightenment, but Henry relied on simpler emotional persuasion that roused the people with moral fervor. Some observers thought Patrick Henry the patriot spoke like a gospel preacher.[14]

But what of Henry's own faith? Later in life Henry wondered whether he had adopted all the style of Davies and the revivalists but not enough of the substance of their preaching. It is difficult to discern how passionately Henry held his own faith as a young adult, because (as was typical of many of his Virginia colleagues, including George Washington and James Madison) he was reticent in defining his own devotion to Christ. We may certainly conjecture, given his background in the Great Awakening and career-long emphasis on religion and virtue, that Henry's own piety was quiet but steady, and a source for his fundamental beliefs about human dignity, rights, and virtue.

Like many of the other founders of the American nation, Henry may have emphasized the social effects of religion more than his own practice of it. He did not attend church consistently as an adult. Nevertheless, he was an avid reader of religious books and pamphlets, and even personally distributed some Christian texts later in life. One of these, Soame Jenyns's *A View of the Internal Evidence of the Christian Religion*, offered an Enlightenment-style defense of traditional Christianity by appealing to the ethical excellence of Jesus's teachings. Jenyns, a lawyer and member of the British Parliament, did not deny the legitimacy of the Bible's prophecies and miracles, but he thought that the ethics promulgated by Jesus were the firmest basis on which to make a case for the supernatural origins of Christianity. Such a perfect system of virtue could not have been invented by mere men, Jenyns argued, but "must have been effected by the supernatural interposition of divine power and wisdom." Henry was one of many Americans who regarded Jenyns's method as a sure way to defend Christianity in an enlightened age; *A View of the Internal Evidence of the Christian Religion* went through many editions in the 1780s and '90s, including two in Richmond, Virginia. As governor, Henry would arrange for hundreds of copies of Jenyns's book to be printed and distributed at his own expense.[15]

Henry's brother-in-law also recalled that Patrick's favorite book on religion was Philip Doddridge's *The Rise and Progress of Religion in the Soul*. Published in London in 1744, *The Rise and Progress of Religion* was one of the most influential evangelical texts of the eighteenth and nineteenth centuries. In advising his readers on how to know whether they had experienced a saving conversion, Doddridge prayed that his book would rescue readers from "the madness of a sinful state" and bring them to a true knowledge of God. Patrick Henry's esteem for this book would suggest that evangelical faith made a deep, personal impression on him. Perhaps Henry privately experienced something like the kind of conversion that Doddridge, Davies, and Whitefield advocated, but we do not know for sure. It is clear from Henry's reading habits, however, that he was no deist or skeptic like Thomas Jefferson. He accepted a traditional form of Christianity that was woven into the culture of eighteenth-century Anglo-America.[16]

Given Henry's background, we may readily understand his brother-in-law's assessment that Henry was "through life a warm friend of the Christian religion. He was an Episcopalian, but very friendly to all the sects—particularly the Presbyterian." Henry never accepted his uncle Patrick's doctrinaire, ugly hostility toward non-Anglicans. He valued Christian devotion across denominations. Henry and most of the Revolutionary generation believed that a republic needed religion to preserve virtue, honesty, and independence lest it trespass into amoral individualism and a degenerate complacency. An ethically directionless people would eventually succumb to the enticements of a tyrant, Henry feared.[17]

Even as he would espouse state support for religion, he would also evince growing doubt about Anglicanism as the exclusively established church of Virginia. Henry remained committed to his Anglican faith, but he became convinced that religion could be used as a political tool to oppress not only Presbyterians, but all Virginians. His growing concern prepared him for his first episode of public resistance against encroaching British power: defending Hanover County in the Parsons' Cause.

BECAUSE HE BELIEVED in the public importance of religion, it may seem strange that Patrick Henry's first great political cause involved reducing the parsons' publicly supported income. But Henry reflected an increasing hostility toward the Anglican clergy among the lay leaders of the church. During the Great Awakening, Anglican vestrymen became increasingly frustrated with ineffective clergy, who seemed unable to counter the surge of evangelical fervor. Virginia also struggled to recruit native-born parsons, leading it to accept a number of ministers from Scotland, such as Patrick Henry's uncle. A number of these British-born parsons appeared to be as concerned with financial gain as pastoral care. Some ministers were also exposed for gross immorality, which further damaged the standing of clergy in Virginia society.

Conflict between Anglican clergy and laymen intensified in the mid-1750s because of disputes regarding the parsons' salaries. Virginia had taken the lead in the Seven Years' War, beginning with George Washington's ill-fated expedition in 1754, and suffered financially as a result. Nevertheless, the clergy felt they deserved more compensation for their services, and in 1755 some of them brought a petition to the legislature, the House of Burgesses, asking for a pay raise. The petition was summarily rejected.

Far from raising the priests' salaries, the House of Burgesses passed the first Two Penny Act in 1755, which temporarily substituted a cash payment of two pence per pound of tobacco for the priests' normal supply of actual tobacco. (Tobacco was commonly used as currency in Virginia.) But in 1755 tobacco was valued at more than two pence per pound, so this represented a pay cut. Parsons' salaries were not the only cost-saving casualties of the Two Penny Act, but they did seem an easy target because of the public animosity toward the clergy. Some parsons tried to organize official protests against the 1755 act, but the populace largely approved of the reduction and felt it was justified due to the colony's military and financial crises—a situation exacerbated by poor tobacco harvests. James Maury himself wrote that although the Two Penny Act caused him serious financial hardship, he thought that "each individual must expect to share in the misfortunes of the community to which he belongs."[18]

Tensions between the clergy and lay authorities continued to escalate in the late 1750s. The behavior of the clergy riled many of the Anglican faithful. They clashed with the governor in 1757 over the status of the Reverend John Brunskill of King William County, who was reported to have committed "monstrous immoralities" in his parish. According to the governor, Brunskill had engaged in many bizarre acts, including tying up his wife "by the legs to the bed post, and cutting her in a cruel manner by knives." It was uncertain whether this kind of disciplinary case fell under political or religious jurisdiction, but Virginia's governor decided to act. After a trial, he removed Brunskill from his pastorate. Other ministers came to Brunskill's defense, not necessarily because they believed him to be innocent, but because they rejected the governor's authority over church affairs. Their assertion of clerical independence did not improve the parsons' standing before a skeptical public, however. Virginians thought the parsons had defended Brunskill to protect their own power, despite his grievous offenses.[19]

The conflict between lay Anglicans and the parsons came to a head with the passage of a second Two Penny Act in 1758. A convention representing about half of the colony's seventy ministers commissioned an appeal to London authorities to overturn the pay cut. The clergy complained that the act created "distressful, various, and uncertain" circumstances for them, while also more provocatively asserting that the act "interferes with the royal prerogative." The Crown had instructed Virginia's popular governor, Francis Fauquier, not to alter any royally approved laws, such as the one establishing clerical salaries, without permission. The bishop of London aggravated tensions when he characterized the Two Penny Act as treason against the Crown.[20]

The parsons' appeal and bishop's tirade raised the stakes of the Two Penny Act above mere finances and made it an issue of imperial authority, convincing the Privy Council to annul the act. The Crown's decision produced a sharp reaction from Virginia's defenders. Open verbal and physical assaults on the clergy and the bishop of London commenced with Landon Carter's *A Letter to the Right Reverend Father in God, the Lord B—p of L—n.* Carter was a prominent planter of Richmond County, and an Anglican layman, but he had fallen out with his own parish minister, William Kay, who claimed that Carter had bullied him over his sermons. After a particularly pointed homily decrying spiritual pride, Carter denounced Parson

Kay, claiming that the jeremiad was a thinly veiled attack on him. Carter cursed at Kay and tried to beat him. Carter reportedly swore he would take revenge against Kay and go on to "clip the wings of the whole clergy, in this colony."[21]

The controversy over the Two Penny Act steeled Carter's resolve to assert the authority of Virginia's laymen over the clergy. The planter maintained that the Two Penny Act was a just reaction to the humanitarian crisis in the colony, a set of dire economic conditions for which the clergy apparently had no sympathy. His pamphlet excoriated the bishop of London, warning Virginians that the bishop intended to take Britain back to the time, prior to the Glorious Revolution of 1688, when "priesthood and cruelty were the inseparable enemies of British liberty." (The colonists had viewed James II, who was deposed in the Glorious Revolution, with particular fear and disdain, because he tried to tighten imperial control over the colonists, and because he was Roman Catholic.) Carter believed God had given Britain its Protestant monarchs, beginning with King William and Queen Mary, the successors to James II, to protect Britons from "diabolical schemes of merciless bigotry." He did not blame the aging King George II (who died in 1760, to be replaced by his grandson King George III) for misunderstanding the nature of the dispute: officials like the bishop, he asserted, meant to deceive the king into violating the colonists' liberties, as the clergy did in annulling the Two Penny Act.[22]

Richard Bland's *Letter to the Clergy of Virginia* also presented the clergy as plotting against the colonists' liberties. Bland, a planter and Anglican vestryman from Prince George County, had his share of controversies with the clergy, including one that resulted in the dismissal of the Reverend John Camm from the faculty of the College of William and Mary. Camm, whom Governor Fauquier described as a "turbulent man who delights to live in a flame," represented the Virginia clergy in London in their appeal of the Two Penny Act.

When Camm returned, proudly bearing the veto of the Two Penny Act to the governor's palace in Williamsburg, Fauquier was disgusted. The governor was appointed by the Crown, to be sure, but like many royal governors before him, he still felt that he needed flexibility to respond to local conditions. He did not want to wait on approval from London to make moves such as the Two Penny Act. As Camm waved the veto in his face, Fauquier summoned his slaves and pointed at the intruder: "Look at that gentleman and be sure to know him again," he said, "and under no circumstances permit him to revisit the palace." Camm and the clergy had exacerbated their bad reputations, even among those closest to the Crown.[23]

In his pamphlet excoriating the clergy, Richard Bland represented Camm and his fellow ministers as "Romish Inquisitors" who "carry on their insidious practices in the dark, lest the daylight should discover the iniquity of their transactions." Both Bland and Carter drew on deep cultural wells of anti-Catholicism that dated back to the Protestant Reformation. Virginia Protestants responded readily to the notion that Roman Catholicism represented the epitome of corrupt spiritual power, and the parsons' appeal to the king seemed tainted with that kind of venality. Bland bristled at the notion that the Two Penny Act evidenced disloyalty to Britain. Ironically, he believed the clergy were pushing the colonists toward "a thought of withdrawing their dependency from the British throne." To Bland, enforcing royal supremacy would reduce the colonists to political slavery. But he speculated that they might declare independence before that happened.[24]

The House of Burgesses, for its part, saw London's nullification of the Two Penny Act as more evidence of the British government's insensitivity to the colony's needs. Swiftly changing economic conditions, such as fluctuations in the price of tobacco, required nimble responses from the Virginia government. Getting approval from London could take months, long after action was required. "Many unavoidable changes in our circumstances do frequently happen," the Burgesses protested, "which require the immediate assistance of the legislature before it is possible for us at so great a distance to make any application to your Majesty." But the king's counselors rejected their petition on appeal—this was just the way the colonial system worked, Virginia's legislators were told. The Burgesses did not have the discretion to change royally sanctioned laws.[25]

A year before Henry took on the case, the furor over the Parsons' Cause became more intense when priests began suing in Virginia county courts to recoup salary lost under the Two Penny Act. Parson Alexander White sued in King William County in 1762, but the court struggled to seat a proper jury. In the end, so many of the gentry refused to appear for service that the jury "consisted at last of ordinary planters some of whom we found after had declared beforehand what they would do," reported an Anglican official. White lost the case.[26]

The court in Maury's case also encountered problems in assembling a qualified jury, much to Maury's dismay. Several gentlemen declined to serve, so the sheriff, in Maury's words, "went among the vulgar herd" to corral jurors. Maury complained that not only had he not heard of many of the jurors before, but that several of them were dissenters "of that denomination called New Lights." One of these New Lights was Samuel Morris, the bricklayer who had originally started the evangelical meetings in Hanover County. The parson knew that these evangelicals would oppose him, but when he protested the composition of the jury, Patrick Henry rose to its defense; these jurors were honest men, he insisted. From the start, Reverend Maury thought the case was rigged against him.[27]

The trial took place at the Hanover County courthouse, a distinguished brick building less than twenty-five years old. Earlier Virginia courthouses had often amounted to little more than wooden shacks, but Hanover's edifice reflected the growing sophistication and prestige of Virginia's legal system. Its most distinctive feature was the brick arcade across its front and sides. On court days the courthouse became a hive of activity, as did the adjacent tavern of Henry's father-in-law, where the new lawyer had labored until recently.

The courtroom for the Parsons' Cause case was packed. An early nineteenth-century rendering of the scene shows Henry addressing the clerk and jury from a slightly raised lawyers' bar, with the rest of the chamber jammed with observers, including a couple of mischievous-looking children. It was a standing-room-only event, perfectly suited for Henry's oratorical tastes. Now the young attorney would test the potential of his rhetorical powers.[28]

Maury thought Patrick Henry's behavior in the case was revolting. The parson's account is the best contemporary record of the trial, even though he may have exaggerated Henry's legal pyrotechnics. Henry seems to have come into the trial prepared, or even recruited by the vestrymen, to do the "dirty Jobb" (as Maury called it) of accusing the Anglican clergy of helping the Crown expand imperial power. At one point, Henry addressed the court for almost an hour on the ominous implications of the king's annulment of a legitimate law.

Henry's attack on the clergy illuminated his view of what the state's proper establishment of the church should represent. State-supported clergy should encourage obedience to good civil laws, he argued. In this case, Henry declared, the parsons not only failed to perform their duty, but also actively disobeyed the law themselves—which gave the state the right to strip clergy of their civil appointments. Henry thundered that Maury deserved not reimbursement but punishment for undermining the colony's assembly. If the jury did not wish to "rivet the chains of bondage on their own necks," he thundered, then they should make an example of Maury. Such a judgment would make other clergymen think twice before challenging the true legal authority over the people of Virginia: their colonial government.[29]

Henry's appeal worked wonderfully, and the "vulgar herd" relished the chance to throw's Maury lawsuit back in his face. When the verdict came, the jury awarded James Maury a grand total of one penny in damages.

Maury dubiously claimed that Henry had apologized to him after the trial, saying that he had given his juror-rousing speech only to "render himself popular." Whatever Henry actually said to him, Maury concluded that the fiery-tongued young lawyer had chosen celebrity over honor, pandering to the people who relished his trampling of church and crown.[30]

A disgusted John Camm publicly skewered Henry and Richard Bland in the aftermath of the trial, accusing Bland of attacking the king's integrity; if such an established politician would dare challenge the Crown, he thought, it was no wonder an "obscure lawyer" from Hanover would tell a jury that the king "had forfeited the allegiance of the people of Virginia." For Camm, Maury's trial was a farce, and no doubt he felt the same when the General Court of Virginia—which handled cases related to imperial law—decided against Camm himself in a similar case. Camm, always eager to defend the clergy's prerogatives, appealed to London's Privy Council to overturn the General Court's decision. He found no sympathy from them the second time around. By that time, in 1767, the British government had bigger problems to deal with in America than John Camm's salary.[31]

WHATEVER HENRY'S MOTIVATIONS in the Parsons' Cause, he had begun to position himself for a political career. With his genial manner and his orations defending the liberty of common-folk Virginians, he was developing a following in the backcountry counties, and in 1764 he began to gain more attention in Williamsburg. That year he represented Nathaniel West Dandridge in a case against James Littlepage, who had recently replaced Dandridge in the House of Burgesses. Dandridge had accepted the position of coroner for

Hanover County but apparently had second thoughts about leaving the House when Littlepage was elected. Dandridge accused Littlepage of bribing voters to win his seat, and when a House committee heard the case in late 1764, Henry represented Dandridge.[32]

Bribery was not unusual in Virginia elections prior to the Revolution. Indeed, voters expected candidates to give them gifts, especially alcohol. This practice was called "swilling the planters with bumbo." (Bumbo was rum punch.) In one typical case, when George Washington ran for the House of Burgesses in 1758, he distributed 160 gallons of alcoholic beverages to 391 voters and "unnumbered hangers-on." The libations included fifty gallons of rum punch, forty-six gallons of beer, thirty-four gallons of wine, twenty-eight gallons of straight rum, and two gallons of hard cider.[33]

In 1762, the House banned such practices in electioneering, but the law was hardly enforced. Most House members had, themselves, employed such tactics in their own campaigns. Henry used the 1762 law to make his case against James Littlepage before the Burgesses, but because bribery was so pervasive, Henry's argument was weak. True, Littlepage's friends had bought gifts for his supporters, and at one function the candidate himself ordered more rum when the supply ran out, but most of his "treating" was undertaken by intermediaries. On Election Day, for example, a freeholder named Grubbs appeared at Hanover Courthouse offering to vote for the candidate who bought him a "dram." A friend of Littlepage's purchased him a drink, and Grubbs obliged him by voting for Littlepage. The House committee found this evidence unpersuasive and dismissed Dandridge's case as "frivolous and vexatious." Later recollections of the case portrayed Henry as dazzling the House with an oration on the rights of voters, but we do not actually know what he said. In any event, the case gave Henry an opportunity to present himself again to the political leaders in Williamsburg, if not endear himself to them; the committee members who heard the arguments included such luminaries as Richard Bland, Peyton Randolph, George Wythe, and Richard Henry Lee. The Dandridge case also revealed Henry as something of an opportunist. His dramatic accusations did not translate into victory this time, but maybe a negative outcome was worth the price for the up-and-coming attorney.[34]

Even though Patrick Henry had not yet held public office, people were now mentioning his name as a candidate for the House of Burgesses. Although most Virginia politicians first served in county-level positions before entering the legislature, Henry capitalized on his expanding landholdings and political connections to make the jump straight to the House. In 1765, he received from his father a 1,700-acre parcel of land called Roundabout in Louisa County. When that county's delegate to the House resigned his office, friends of the Henry family from Louisa promoted the twenty-eight-year-old Patrick as a candidate in the special election. Even though Patrick did not live in Louisa County, he was qualified to run for office because he owned land there. Even some residents of Hanover who owned land in Louisa traveled to Louisa's courthouse to vote for their local hero, who entered the House on May 20, 1765.[35]

For a man who had been polishing beer glasses in his father-in-law's tavern just five years before, Henry's ascension to the House of Burgesses was a dramatic reversal of ill fortune. His newfound political success arose from a variety of factors: his family's connections, an increasing legal caseload, his passionate oratory modeled in the evangelical style, an eagerness to seize political opportunities, and a keen sense of the popular mood in the backcountry. Henry had developed a prodigious aptitude for creating a political sensation, as he had enthusiastically demonstrated in the Maury case. He deeply appreciated the anxieties of Virginians. His fellow colonists never believed that the empire took them seriously as full British citizens, and they worried that the powerful government in London wielded too much power over them. British officials, they increasingly believed, could easily turn Americans into slaves of the imperial system. Henry perfectly articulated the slowly escalating unease of Americans with that subservient status.

Henry's electoral success also undoubtedly came from lucky timing. Circumstances allowed him to make his mark in the Parsons' Cause just as his legal career was taking off. But even more critically, he had won a delegate's seat at the outset of the imperial crisis in America. Having proved himself a man who never shied away from controversy, Henry introduced resolutions protesting Parliament's new Stamp Act only nine days after entering the House.

# 3

## "IF THIS BE TREASON"

## The Stamp Act Crisis

ATRICK HENRY'S 1765 SPEECH denouncing the Stamp Act is shrouded in myth and embellishment. Accounts of his famous address rely on ill-remembered retellings given decades later, after Henry had entered the pantheon of patriotic heroes. But one person in attendance, an anonymous French traveler, did record the scene for posterity: "One of the members [of the House of Burgesses] stood up and said he had read that in former times Tarquin and Julius had their Brutus, Charles had his Cromwell, and he did not doubt but some good American would stand up, in favour of his country." The speaker's implication was unmistakable, radical, even treasonous: Patrick Henry was implying that the king should be assassinated.

When Henry made that outrageous assertion, murmurs from members sitting on straight-backed benches floated across the wood-paneled chamber. The Speaker of the House, John Robinson, instantly grasped the gravity of the freshman Burgess's statement. He stood from his canopied armchair and declared that Henry had spoken treason. Henry immediately recanted his not very oblique call to kill the king, but he did not shirk from his central assertion—the need to defend liberty. He would, he said, "show his loyalty to his majesty King George the third, at the expense of the last drop of his blood, but what he said must be attributed to the interest of his country's dying liberty which he had at heart." The Speaker accepted his apology and the grumblings in the chamber abated, though eyebrows presumably remained raised.[1]

A dubious tradition holds that Henry defiantly responded to the speaker's charge of treason with the rejoinder that "if this be treason, make the most of it!" The line, the second–most famous utterance that history has ascribed to Patrick Henry, is almost certainly apocryphal. Its original source is uncertain, but the motive behind the myth is understandable: the words seemed like something the Patrick Henry who is known to history would indeed have said. Yet we do not need to insert this line to appreciate the audacity of Henry's oration. Opposing the Stamp Act's edict that Americans would have to pay taxes on a host of printed goods, he sought to push the legislators further than they would go, then halfheartedly retracted his brazen words, citing his overwrought passion for America's liberty. Some thought Henry had cleverly played "on the line of treason, without passing it," as Edmund Pendleton would later write to James Madison. Without a doubt, at a time when Americans were just starting to articulate opposition to the Crown's aggressive laws, if not to the Crown itself, Patrick Henry's deep sensitivity to threats against liberty had already radicalized him, well before most other Revolutionary leaders.[2]

Present that day for Henry's incendiary, history-making speech was Thomas Jefferson. The twenty-two-year-old William and Mary law student stood at the door of the chamber and watched "the splendid display of Mr. Henry's talents as a popular orator. They were great indeed; such as I have never heard from any other man." Jefferson remembered vividly how the cry of treason rang through the chamber, and how Henry cleverly backed away from his comparison of George III to Julius Caesar, and thus "baffled the charge [of treason] vociferated." Jefferson regarded him with admiration and perhaps trepidation. This man, he thought, could say nearly anything and get away with it.[3]

HOW HAD AMERICA AND BRITAIN arrived at this unprecedented level of tension? The crisis over the Stamp Act emerged from wrenching changes brought about in both Britain and America by the Seven Years' War. That conflict had begun eleven years earlier, in 1754, when George Washington unwillingly presided over the massacre of French troops in western Pennsylvania. The Seven Years' War had saved British American colonists from the French threat in North America. But it had created a crushing debt for the British government. Such paralyzing obligations can lead to drastic measures. The national debt in Britain soared from 72 million pounds sterling in 1755 to 130 million in 1764.

In the aftermath of the war, the British also maintained an expensive standing army in America, to fend off possible new attacks from the French as well as from Native Americans. In 1763 an outbreak of violence associated with Pontiac's Rebellion—attacks by the Ottawa Indian leader on British installations—showed the wisdom of the continuing British military presence. With the end of the French political influence in the Great Lakes region, the British had adopted a more belligerent policy toward Native Americans, curtailing the "gift giving" of essential supplies that had traditionally soothed relations between Native Americans and Europeans in the backcountry. The reduction pushed some Indians into desperate measures. Allied Indian forces attacked British forts across the Great Lakes region. Pontiac's forces besieged Fort Detroit, slaughtering men, women, and children they found nearby. In one battle, the Indians shot a British commander dead, then cut out his heart, decapitated him, and placed his head on a pike in their camp. Such killings steeled the British determination to keep an army in America to face these fearsome threats—even as the 10,000 troops required would drain an additional 220,000 pounds sterling a year from British coffers.[4]

British officials understandably looked to the American colonists to share some of the financial burden. Historically, the colonists had largely owed only customs duties, not taxes, to Britain. Through bribery and smuggling, Americans often evaded those duties on imported goods. Resistance to British taxation had already been building for some years. Before the Seven Years' War, the colonial assemblies (including the House of Burgesses) developed independent streaks. They did not take kindly to parliamentary mandates, especially regarding money—an attitude that pointed to how much the nature of the British government had changed since the founding of the earliest colonies, especially Virginia, in the seventeenth century. Most notably, the Glorious Revolution of 1688–89 had affirmed Parliament's supremacy in England, but Parliament's authority in the colonies was never as clear. Decades of relative inattention by the British government had allowed the American legislatures' pride and stubbornness to grow unchecked.

The funding crisis left by the Seven Years' War brought into the open the latent tensions between Parliament and the colonial assemblies. British Prime Minister George Grenville, convinced that Americans were not paying their fair share for the protection and upkeep of the colonies, tried to shut down the elaborate system of corruption existing within the customs network. In the Sugar Act of 1764, Parliament imposed a new set of duties on imported cloth, sugar, coffee, and wine. The act's biggest effect was to reduce the duty on West Indian molasses from sixpence to threepence a gallon. Grenville anticipated that the lower duty on molasses, combined with effective enforcement of the law, would discourage smuggling and generate revenue for the British treasury.

Although the Sugar Act was explicitly intended to raise tax revenue, colonists interpreted this legislation as a regulation of trade across the empire, a power that most of them would agree belonged to Parliament, not to colonial legislatures. But Parliament was also considering a stamp tax—that is, a duty on all manner of printed goods used in the colonies, including court documents, college diplomas, land deeds, contracts, playing cards, pamphlets, newspapers, and almanacs. Each of these would now have to be produced on paper bearing a stamp of the British treasury. That paper would be sold by stamp agents.

This prospect elicited the cry of "no taxation without representation": colonists from New Hampshire to Georgia declared that only their representatives, in their own assemblies, had the right to tax them. The House of Burgesses, for example, asserted in messages to the king and Parliament in 1764 that "it is essential to British liberty that laws imposing taxes on the people ought not to be made without the consent of representatives chosen by themselves." Despite the moderate protests against the Sugar Act, Grenville and British politicians did not appreciate the colonists' obstinacy. The Americans showed insensitivity to the budget crisis, and resistance to Parliament's supremacy. Yet while rumblings of resistance had begun, in 1764 the reaction to the Sugar Act remained relatively quiet. Grenville suggested that the colonists might avert a direct tax in 1765 if their assemblies raised sufficient revenue on their own, but he doubted the colonies would follow through on their obligation to help. By 1765, the stamp tax had become as much a test of British authority as a way to address the empire's budget deficit. Ben Franklin, recently arrived in London as an agent for Pennsylvania, commented that "we might well have hindered the sun's setting" as prevented the act's adoption.[5]

The colonists had defenders in Parliament. One of the most articulate, Colonel Isaac Barré, replied indignantly when another member suggested that the colonists were acting like ungrateful children. Barré, a veteran of the Seven Years' War, declared that the American "Sons of Liberty" had established flourishing colonies in America despite Britain's neglect of them. "They have nobly taken up arms in your defense," he proclaimed, "have exerted a valor amidst their constant and laborious industry for the defense of a country, whose frontier, while drenched in blood, its interior parts have yielded all its little savings to your emolument. And believe me, remember I this day told you so, that same spirit of freedom which actuated that people at first, will accompany them still." Barré represented a minority opinion in the chamber, however, and in early 1765 Parliament easily passed the Stamp Act.[6]

The consequences of the act would reverberate throughout the colonies, with most people feeling the pinch. The Stamp Act's rates were not extraordinarily high, but they were intrusive, a literal and daily mark reminding the colonists of Parliament's authority over their finances. The act also provided for enforcement of taxation through British admiralty courts, which had no juries. Parliament was asserting the right to tax the colonists without their direct consent, and to try them without the benefit of a jury of peers if they refused to pay. Many colonists, after enjoying decades of relative independence, saw the Stamp Act as a disturbing assault on their rights. A headline in a Boston newspaper screamed "THE STAMP ACT!!!!!!" with a notice below it demanding that all persons with outstanding debts to the paper's publisher pay up before the act went into effect in November.[7]

As the storm approached, the staid House of Burgesses slumbered. In theory, the colonies' most venerable elective assembly represented the interests of the people of Virginia—or at least the planters—against the power of the British government, an authority embodied in the person of Virginia's royally appointed governor, but by 1765, it had become something of a clique with a select number of wealthy planters typically dominating the chamber's proceedings. Its elite were not inclined to challenge the authority of another legislative body, especially a House of Commons whose procedural rules and very meeting hall were the model for their own. Sometimes the chamber's business was less than scintillating: among the first statutes the House passed when Patrick Henry entered the body in May was a bill "to prevent the raising of hogs, and suffering them to run at large, in the town of Richmond." But the House was starting to simmer with new political talent, as well: from northern Virginia, Richard Henry Lee and George Washington, both four years older than Henry, were elected to the House in 1758. In the coming years, the two men would develop enduring (though not untested) political friendships with Henry, as they all helped lead Virginia—and the nation—forward against Britain.[8]

In the House, Henry dove right into controversy over the prospect of new taxation and the issues it presented. Even before the Stamp Act was debated, he opposed a plan offered by the Speaker to establish a public office that would offer low-interest loans to financially strapped tobacco farmers. Henry viewed the loan office as an attempt to bail out rich planters who had recklessly gotten themselves in debt by spending on luxuries. "Is it proposed, then," Henry asked, "to reclaim the spendthrift from his dissipation and extravagance, by filling his pockets with money?" According to Thomas Jefferson, Henry attacked the idea with "bold, grand and overwhelming eloquence," but the upstart delegate was unsuccessful in blocking the bill. Henry saw no need for reticence, despite his freshman status in the august body. To him, the public loan office represented corruption and cronyism, just at the time when Virginia needed the moral courage to stand against the Stamp Act.[9]

HENRY RECALLED THAT HE WROTE Virginia's resolutions against the Stamp Act "alone, unadvised, and unassisted, on a blank leaf of an old law-book." He introduced them on his twenty-ninth birthday, May 29, 1765. Strangely, no one knows exactly how many resolutions Henry wrote against the Stamp Act, but we can be sure of at least five. During his lifetime, Henry made little attempt to preserve most of his personal papers, but presumably because he proudly recognized their role in inciting the American Revolution, he did leave behind a copy of the five resolutions, preserving them alongside his will. The first four, which are also recorded in the journals of the House, essentially restated the colonists' opposition to taxation without representation. The two initial resolutions asserted that the colonists enjoyed the same "liberties, privileges, franchises, and immunities" as the people of Britain. Their colonial status did not imply inferior rights, the document declared. The third and fourth resolutions argued that accepting levies enacted by one's own representatives alone "is the only security against a burdensome taxation, and the distinguishing characteristic of British freedom." To Henry and the colonists, not only did the Stamp Act impose a burdensome tax, but it also represented an offense against their liberty as Britons.[10]

Henry's fifth resolution, which appears to have passed the House of Burgesses by the narrowest of margins, was more provocative. It contended that "the General Assembly of this colony have the only and sole exclusive right and power to lay taxes and impositions upon the inhabitants of this colony and that every attempt to vest such power in any other person or persons whatsoever other than the General Assembly aforesaid has a manifest tendency to destroy British as well as American freedom." This assertion of the House's supremacy in tax law was so bold that it generated second thoughts among the delegates, and the legislature subsequently rescinded it.

All of Henry's resolutions faced opposition from the established leaders of the House, including Speaker John Robinson, Richard

Bland, and George Wythe, who apparently felt that the first four resolutions were unnecessary because they restated arguments made in the petitions of 1764; the fifth resolution they may have viewed as too inflammatory. They also resented Henry's brash leadership. As the governor of Virginia wrote, Henry had led the "young hot and giddy members" to overwhelm the old-time gentry, at least for the moment.[11]

The senior leaders of the House managed to repeal the fifth resolution the day after it passed, when Henry had apparently left Williamsburg to return home. The freshman legislator may have assumed, naively, that the debate was settled. The House also considered two other resolutions by Henry and other radicals, but they were not adopted, probably because even the fifth had proven so difficult to pass. But all the resolutions, including the sixth and seventh, ended up reported in regional newspapers, which tallied differing numbers of resolutions introduced by the young delegate: five, six, or even seven.

The sixth and seventh resolutions Henry put before the House, as reported in the *Maryland Gazette*, were nothing short of revolutionary. The sixth asserted that the colonists were "not bound to yield obedience to any law or ordinance whatsoever, designed to impose any taxation upon them, other than the laws or ordinances of the General Assembly." The seventh declared in capital letters that anyone who promoted the right of Parliament to tax the colonists should be "deemed, AN ENEMY TO THIS HIS MAJESTY'S COLONY." The resolutions called for open resistance against the Stamp Act, and called the act's defenders traitors.[12]

Henry's resolutions electrified the colonies, especially when newspapers printed all seven of them. Most of the other colonies crafted resolutions similar to those that Virginia adopted or considered. In Massachusetts, the Virginia resolutions shamed the colony's radical patriots into assuming a more assertive stance. A Boston editorial praised the Virginians and denounced Massachusetts's pro-British conservatives: "The people of Virginia have spoke very sensibly, and the frozen politicians of a more northern government say they have spoke treason. . . . These dirty sycophants, these ministerial hacks, would fain have us believe that his sacred Majesty, ever loved by his American subjects, would be displeased to hear their murmurs at the sight of chains!" Many Americans like this radical Boston editorialist blamed the crisis on bureaucrats within the British government, not the king. They believed that colonial protests would elicit sympathy from George III, who was still widely revered among Americans in 1765.[13]

The organized outcry against the Stamp Act ultimately led delegates from nine of the thirteen colonies, inspired by hope of relief from the king, to meet in New York City in October 1765, in what historians call the Stamp Act Congress. Henry did not attend. Indeed, Virginia did not send delegates at all, because the governor refused to convene the House of Burgesses to elect representatives to the Congress. Even as protests arose in colonies from Massachusetts to the Carolinas, the thirteen resolutions the Stamp Act Congress issued took a relatively moderate tone, affirming the colonies' allegiance to King George and their "due subordination" to Parliament. At the same time, they asserted that the colonists had the same rights as the people of Britain, saying that no one should impose taxes on them but their own representatives, and called for the repeal of the Stamp Act.[14]

The Stamp Act Congress exhibited nearly unprecedented unity among a majority of the colonies. But the Congress also reflected a broad, restrained consensus, not Henry's revolutionary zeal. And the Stamp Act Congress did not force the repeal of the Stamp Act. The Americans' most effective resistance to the act came through violence and rioting in the cities, instigated by new patriot organizations called the "Sons of Liberty," a name derived from Isaac

Barré's speech in Parliament. In August, a mob in Boston burned in effigy the newly appointed stamp agent, Andrew Oliver, and destroyed his home. Because the act was not scheduled to take effect until November 1, Oliver had not even begun his duties yet. Oliver was no fool; he promptly informed London that he would not collect the taxes.[15]

Virginia's experience with the collection of the stamp tax was similar to that of Massachusetts. Colonel George Mercer, the stamp agent, was a native Virginian with deep connections to George Washington; he had been an aide-de-camp to Washington during the Seven Years' War and was wounded at the Battle of Fort Necessity in 1754. Mercer also served in the House of Burgesses in the early 1760s, but he resigned to work as an agent of the Ohio Company in London, where he was living when the Stamp Act was passed.[16]

Apparently perceiving the post of stamp collector as a path to political advancement, Mercer accepted the job and returned to Virginia on October 30, just before the act was to take effect. His arrival coincided with a meeting of the General Court, the colony's high court, so Williamsburg was filled with merchants and lawyers. Governor Francis Fauquier, a native Englishman who strongly supported the Stamp Act, would report later that a crowd assembled when word came of Mercer's arrival. Fauquier wrote that he would have called the group a "mob, did I not know that it was chiefly if not altogether composed of gentlemen of property in the colony." The throng met Mercer in front of the capitol and demanded that he resign instantly as stamp agent. He tried to put them off and went to a local coffeehouse, where he met the governor and Speaker John Robinson. The crowd followed, surging at the steps of the coffeehouse, yelling, "Let us rush in!" Governor Fauquier found himself in the unnerving position of having to stand at the "top of the steps, knowing the advantage our situation gave us to repel those who should attempt to mount them." A few bold souls threatened to drag down the governor, but Fauquier's grave, aristocratic presence seemed to calm most of the crowd. Mercer promised that he would answer demands for his resignation the next day, and the governor personally led him through the muttering host to his house. "I believe I saved him from being insulted at least," Fauquier wrote.[17]

The governor urged Mercer not to resign unless he feared for his life. But the prospective stamp agent's hostile reception in Williamsburg had accomplished its purpose; Mercer quit the next day. As for the governor, he despaired of the colonies' future and believed that "disorder, confusion and misery are before us, unless this poor unhappy deluded people in the colonies in general, should change their plan." But the colonists did not change their plan. From New Hampshire to Georgia, stamp agents were systematically intimidated; a number resigned and fled the colonies. By the end of the year, the Stamp Act had become unenforceable.[18]

When news of the unrest in America reached England, the Stamp Act's architect, George Grenville, had already been removed from the prime ministership because of personal animosity between him and the king. Into his place came Charles Watson-Wentworth, the Marquis of Rockingham. The Marquis thought the Stamp Act was a foolish scheme—harmful to both the colonists and the British economy—and he banded with British merchants to work for its repeal. The Stamp Act had hurt many merchants with transatlantic business, particularly when the colonists implemented voluntary nonimportation agreements to get around the tax. British businessmen sent petitions to Parliament calling for the Stamp Act to be repealed.[19]

In London, Benjamin Franklin was summoned to testify before Parliament against the Stamp Act. Franklin had initially advised colonial compliance with the tax, a stance that almost ruined his reputation in America. By early 1766 he had reversed course and begun to work against the tax. His testimony, published in England and America, succinctly articulated the enormous change in colonial attitudes brought about by the controversy. Franklin asserted that the Stamp Act had wrecked decades of goodwill toward England in America:

QUESTION: What was the temper of America towards Great-Britain before the year 1763?

FRANKLIN: The best in the world. They submitted willingly to the government of the crown. . . . They were governed by this country at the expense only of a little pen, ink and paper. They were led by a thread.

QUESTION: And what is their temper now?

FRANKLIN: Oh, very much altered.

QUESTION: And have they not still the same respect for parliament?

FRANKLIN: No; it is greatly lessened.

QUESTION: Don't you think they would submit to the Stamp Act, if it was modified, the obnoxious parts taken out, and the duty reduced to some particulars, of small moment?

FRANKLIN: No; they will never submit to it.

Americans cheered Franklin's denunciation of the act. He became recognized as America's key defender in England, and besides representing Pennsylvania, he soon also became the agent for Georgia, New Jersey, and Massachusetts.[20]

Faced with an act unenforceable in the colonies, and strong pressure from business interests and a new administration at home, Parliament reluctantly repealed the Stamp Act in February 1766. But they sought to establish their legal authority by passing the Declaratory Act, which asserted that the king and Parliament had the right to "make laws and statutes of sufficient force and validity to bind the colonies and people of America, subjects of the crown of Great Britain, in all cases what-soever." Although this statement did not explicitly refer to taxes, the debate in Parliament suggested that the body meant to claim its right to tax the colonies again in the future.[21]

Colonists rejoiced at news of the repeal; they saw it as a victory not only for their economic welfare but for liberty as well. Americans were not sure, however, how to interpret the Declaratory Act's assertion of authority "in all cases whatsoever." Some argued that their claim referred not to taxation, but only to legitimate parliamentary actions, such as regulating trade. Some felt that the Declaratory Act evinced England's patronizing attitude toward the colonies, as did warnings from British merchants that the colonists should not gloat over the repeal. Patrick Henry's fellow Virginian George Mason parodied the tone of the British, as if they were parents addressing a child: "we have, with infinite difficulty and fatigue got you excused this one time; pray be a good boy for the future, do what your papa and mama bid you, and hasten to return them your most grateful acknowledgements for condescending to let you keep what is your own; and then all your acquaintance will love you, and praise you, and give you pretty things."[22]

The repeal pleased the colonists, but the Declaratory Act worried them. Nothing had been solved with regard to Parliament's right to tax the colonists. That issue would in fact never be solved peacefully.

PATRICK HENRY'S ROLE IN THE later stages of the revolt against the Stamp Act is largely unknown. He did not want to make politics a full-time career, so he often labored at home at times we might have expected the historical record to show him as being in Williamsburg. Indeed, we do not know whether Henry was in the crowd that confronted Colonel Mercer and Governor Fauquier in October 1765. He probably was not there, because his presence certainly would have warranted mention.

In the short time he had been in the House of Burgesses, Henry's boldness had won him celebrity in Virginia and notoriety in the broader Anglo-American world. The anonymous French traveler who had witnessed his speech in May passed through Louisa County the following month and found the place abuzz with talk of the "noble patriot Mr. Henery." Some of his constituents declared that "if the least injury was offered to [Henry] they'd stand by him to the last drop of blood." Henry's bold stance against the Stamp Act had begun to spur a revolutionary way of thinking among ordinary Virginians. Yet even as he was becoming an avatar of the emerging movement for American liberty, Henry remained preoccupied in maintaining his livelihood as lawyer and planter. His concern for his own financial welfare partly accounts for his lifetime of comings and goings from the political stage.[23]

Henry might have won the admiration of the voters in Louisa and Hanover Counties and liberty-minded Americans in all thirteen colonies, but the Anglican authorities in Virginia lamented his leadership in denouncing the Stamp Act, which they connected to his attack on the clergy in the Parsons' Cause. Anglican Commissary William Robinson wrote to London in August 1765 to explain that Henry had become a hero in the backcountry because of his disdain for royal and clerical authority. Since his speech in the House that May, Robinson wrote, Henry had "gone quietly into the upper parts of the country to recommend himself to his constituents by spreading treason." Robinson feared that Virginians like Henry intended to create "an arbitrary aristocratical power of [Virginia's] own with the name of liberty." Based on the evidence of letters like Robinson's, even authorities in England had begun to hear of the young lawyer's agitation against parliamentary power.[24]

What led Henry to make his inflammatory stand against the Stamp Act? Certainly he was disposed to view encroachments against the colonists' liberties in the worst possible light. Throughout his career, Henry's brilliant speeches would paint grim scenarios of the desolation awaiting those who would not stand up for their freedom. Patriots must act while they still could, he proclaimed. For him, accepting small infractions against fundamental rights represented a headlong path toward tyranny.

Henry himself saw his stand against the Stamp Act as a defense of both liberty and virtue. On the back of his copy of the resolutions against the Stamp Act, he wrote that resisting the tax galvanized the colonists against taxation by Parliament, where they had no representatives. This fundamental disagreement with Parliament, which Henry first exposed to public controversy, would ultimately lead to war and independence. Henry did not know whether Americans would finally benefit from their independence, however; it was up to succeeding generations to avail themselves of "the blessings which a gracious God hath bestowed upon us. If they be wise, they will be great and happy. If they are of a contrary character, they will be miserable." Citing a well-known Bible passage from the book of Proverbs, Henry concluded that "righteousness alone can exalt them as a nation." A virtuous people would resist—even to the point of blood—those who sought to undermine their liberty.[25]

In the prelude to the Revolution, Patrick Henry embodied the emerging American zeal for independence and integrity that he helped kindle during the middle decades of the eighteenth century. Those years saw both the maturation of the House of Burgesses as a semiautonomous legislature and the spiritual fires of the Great Awakening. The era summoned heroic personalities like his, men who were called to defend America's liberties with political and moral fervor. In 1765, the twenty-nine-year-old Patrick Henry responded, ultimately becoming one of the greatest patriots of all.

# 4

## "THE FIRST MAN UPON THIS CONTINENT"

## Boycotts and the Growing Crisis with Britain

A FTER THE FAILURE OF THE STAMP ACT, Britain imposed a new round of taxes, the Townshend Duties, in 1767. Two years later, in 1769, Massachusetts continued its protests by instituting a boycott of British goods—a measure that Virginia Governor Norborne Berkeley had warned the House of Burgesses not to follow. When the delegates defied him by passing a resolution supporting Massachusetts's position, Berkeley told them bluntly, "I have heard of your resolves, and augur ill of their effect: you have made it my duty to dissolve you; and you are dissolved accordingly."[1]

Having anticipated their dismissal by the governor, the Burgesses immediately left the governor's council chamber and hurried down the street to reconvene at Williamsburg's Raleigh Tavern. Led by George Washington (a member who usually preferred a quieter role), the legislators adopted a version of the nonimportation agreements that had been circulating in the colonies. Virginia's agreement was probably written by George Mason, with whom Washington had been discussing nonimportation as a means to resist the British duties. Washington told Mason that "at a time when our lordly masters in Great Britain will be satisfied with nothing less than the deprivation of American freedom, it seems highly necessary that something should be done to avert the stroke and maintain the liberty which we have derived from our ancestors." The Virginia agreement required subscribers to avoid importing goods taxed by the Townshend Duties. Displayed prominently at the top of the list of the agreement's signers was the name of Patrick Henry.[2]

The repeal of the Stamp Act had not clarified Parliament's uncertain authority in the colonies. In 1767 Charles Townshend, Britain's new chancellor of the exchequer (the finance minister), tried to raise revenues again by enacting levies on trade goods imported into the colonies. The British government simultaneously took steps to enforce its authority in America. It established a new Board of Customs in Boston, and the British army withdrew from the American frontier and redeployed in towns of the East Coast. This move raised fears that the army was actually in America to control not Native Americans but the colonists themselves. In Virginia, leaders such as Patrick Henry interpreted Townshend's reforms as the latest attempt to assert parliamentary dominance.

In its 1768 session, the House of Burgesses passed a remonstrance—a statement of grievances—reemphasizing its opposition to taxation without representation. Henry, still torn between tending to his personal affairs and representing Louisa County in Williamsburg, did not attend. He was apparently surveying lands in western Virginia he had recently acquired from his father-in-law.

Over the course of the next year, the colonists' resolve to stop importing British goods escalated the conflict over the Townshend

Program. Massachusetts circulated a letter among the other colonial legislatures calling for concerted action against the duties, which the British secretary of state for the American colonies ordered revoked, but the colonial legislature in Boston overwhelmingly rejected the directive. The imperial governor of Massachusetts subsequently dissolved the legislature, and the British insisted that the other legislatures ignore Massachusetts's "flagitious attempt to disturb the public peace," or face dissolution themselves.[3]

Patrick Henry and his fellow Burgesses refused to comply with the British administration's order. In May 1769, four years after the Stamp Act resolutions, the legislature (with Henry now in attendance) adopted resolutions that would frustrate the efficacy of the Townshend Program. In addition to protesting taxation by any legislature other than the Burgesses, the House passed a resolution supporting Massachusetts's circular letter. Anticipating retribution from London, they also opposed Parliament's proposed new extension of treason laws to the colonies, which might have brought accused traitors from America to England for trial.

A committee of delegates, including Patrick Henry and Richard Henry Lee, quickly drafted a remonstrance against the Townshend Program, which the House unanimously adopted. The declaration reiterated the colonists' continuing devotion to the king, and their hope that George III would intervene on America's behalf against a despotic Parliament. In the fawning yet sincere rhetoric of the era, the Burgesses presumed to "prostrate ourselves at the foot of your royal throne, beseeching your majesty, as our king and father, to avert from your faithful and loyal subjects of America, those miseries which must necessarily be the consequence of such measures."

The Burgesses closed their entreaty by reminding the king that Americans prayed for him daily, wishing "that your Majesty's reign may be long and prosperous over Great Britain, and all your dominions; and that after death your Majesty may taste the fullest fruition of eternal bliss, and that a descendant of your illustrious house may reign over the extended British empire until time shall be no more." At this point in their conflict with Britain, Virginians assumed their devotion to the monarchy would eventually assuage the conflict between the colonists and Parliament. Appeals to the king did not cool this feud, however, and Virginia's governor dissolved the defiant Burgesses immediately after they passed Henry and Lee's remonstrance.[4]

Although Henry's most spectacular acts as a political instigator would occur in 1765 and 1775, the Burgesses' stubborn denunciations of the Townshend Program showed how in the intervening years his radicalism had spread even to previously reticent members such as Washington. In the lead-up to the Revolution, Henry's zeal opened up possibilities never before imaginable for his fellow colonists, from denouncing the king as a tyrant to calling for a military struggle against the empire. But the time for war had not yet arrived. As it had with the Stamp Act, Parliament eventually repealed most of the Townshend Duties, but the underlying crisis of authority festered.

HENRY CONTINUED TO HAVE PLENTY to do beyond his duties in Williamsburg. Like most American officials in the colonial era, he never intended to make government service a career. Henry had high political ambitions that drove his pursuit of office and fueled his penchant for controversy, but he also remained an active lawyer, land speculator, and family man, and would return to those roles repeatedly in life, often forgoing opportunities for greater political involvement in favor of tending to private business. Henry was very devoted to his children—his third child, William, was born in 1763, and his fourth, Anne, in 1767. He would maintain an engaged paternal relationship with the children even after they became adults, keeping up an avid correspondence with them about family matters. Henry could never envision himself serving continuously in office; like Washington, he viewed political life with ambivalence. It was noble to serve, but it caused difficulty for his family and his finances.

By the early 1770s, practicing law seemed the most promising way for Henry to bolster his finances. Ever since his star-making turn in the Parsons' Cause, Henry had developed a sizeable legal practice in Hanover and Louisa Counties. In 1769, he began practicing before the General Court of Virginia, a more prestigious venue than the county courts. Working in the General Court also gave him even more access to the established political leaders of the colony, such as Robert Carter Nicholas, a longtime Burgess, and since 1766, the treasurer of the colony, who would turn over his law practice to Henry in 1773 when his duties as treasurer prevented him from maintaining his caseload. Nicholas initially offered the work to Thomas Jefferson, who declined. The General Court did not always provide a steady income, however. Jefferson, Henry, and other lawyers who worked in the General Court apparently found it difficult to make ends meet there; they published a notice in the *Virginia Gazette* in 1773 announcing that they would no longer accept cases from clients who did not pay their whole fee in advance.[5]

Henry loved arguing cases before a jury. Sometimes he could win marginal cases just by appealing to the hearts of jurors. Even though he and Jefferson were still friends at this point, Jefferson thought that Henry's courtroom pyrotechnics evaded the hard principles of the law. In comments on a marriage case concerning an annulment and dowry rights in 1773, Jefferson wrote that "Henry for the plaintiff avoided, as was his custom, entering the lists of the law, running wild in the field of fact." Yet Henry won the case. There was more than a hint of jealousy in Jefferson's dismissive comment: he could never stir a jury's emotions like Henry. The differences in sensibility and legal values between the two men would not fracture their friendship, however, until well into the Revolutionary War, when Jefferson's questionable behavior as governor, and a subsequent legal investigation initiated by Henry, would nearly ruin Jefferson's reputation.[6]

In retrospect, real estate seemed a more risky path to financial security than law, but Henry followed the lead of his father and father-in-law in buying and selling land in the west. (The "west," to Henry, was central and western Virginia.) Often the lands were in locations uncertain to their sellers and buyers, encompassing territory traditionally used by Native Americans. Nevertheless, up-and-coming colonists like Henry believed that western land deals offered the potential for significant profits. Land was traditionally associated with independence in British culture. Tobacco also depleted soils quickly, requiring access to new areas for cultivation.

In 1765, the year of the Stamp Act crisis, Henry received 1,700 acres in Louisa County from his father as repayment of a loan. This land, on Roundabout Creek, became the Henry family residence for six years; he built a modest home of one and a half stories there, with three rooms downstairs and one upstairs. John Shelton, his father-in-law, also became a source of major land acquisitions for Henry. In 1766, Henry helped save Shelton from bankruptcy by purchasing about 3,400 acres of land from him on separate tracts in southwest Virginia. Henry bought the land unseen and had difficulty locating the tracts when he went surveying. When he did find them, he realized that Cherokees occupied them, but eventually he arranged for the government to acknowledge his claims to that acreage. Aggressive American attempts to remove the Cherokees from their traditional lands would not culminate until seventy years later, with the Trail of Tears. As governor of Virginia during the Revolution, Henry repeatedly assured the Cherokees that Virginia wanted to ally with them against their Native American rivals and that "his heart and the hearts of all the Virginians are still good toward the Cherokees." Henry's assurances did not keep Virginia out of a vicious war with the Cherokees, a conflict that would begin in 1776.[7]

Henry sensed the opportunities waiting for land speculation in America's interior, especially in the Ohio River valley region. Henry and his business associates were planning to settle English families in the Kentucky territory, negotiating to relocate Native Americans when necessary. In one of his earliest surviving letters, written to the Scottish immigrant William Fleming, who was surveying lands in Kentucky where the Ohio and Mississippi Rivers met, Henry encouraged Fleming to keep a diary while on his journey, so that detailed information on the characteristics of that vast region could be "printed in order to invite our countrymen to become settlers. The task is arduous, to view that vast forest, describe the face of the country and such of the rivers, creeks, etc., as present themselves to view is a work of much trouble, hazard, and fatigue, and will in my judgment entitle you to the favorable notice of every gentleman engaged in the scheme." Henry and other leading Virginians, such as Washington, continued to acquire land in the west, even as that region descended into chaotic violence between new colonial settlers and Native Americans in the early 1770s.[8]

By 1771, Henry's land speculations and legal work allowed him to move up from the modest home at Roundabout to a genteel mansion at Scotchtown, in Hanover County. He apparently acquired the house and 1,000-acre tract from John Payne, the father of Dolley Madison; the future First Lady had lived briefly at the plantation as a young girl. The house had sixteen rooms and several outbuildings. It was one of the largest mansions in Virginia at the time.[9]

An ad describing Scotchtown said it was "remarkable for producing the finest sweet scented tobacco. . . . The soil is also exceeding good for wheat, and there are several swamps and parcels of low grounds on it, that will suit for meadows. There is on it a large commodious dwelling house with eight rooms on one floor, and a very large passage, pleasantly situated, and all convenient outhouses, also a good water grist mill; and there are three plantations cleared sufficient to work twenty or thirty hands, under good fences, with Negro quarters, tobacco houses, etc." Henry's purchase of this estate was a sign that he fully belonged to the gentility.[10]

At Scotchtown, Henry continued working to establish his financial independence. He increasingly grew grain along with tobacco, following the lead of planters such as Washington, who had already switched the fields of Mount Vernon from tobacco to wheat, hemp, and flax by 1766, and by the mid-1780s Washington was planting as many as sixty different crops. Tobacco had become less appealing and lucrative, and not only because it exhausted the soil. The planters' debts to the English tobacco merchants and creditors escalated across Virginia in the 1760s, convincing many that agricultural diversity was in order. Wheat seemed a more virtuous crop than tobacco, anyway. Jefferson wrote that tobacco was "a culture productive of infinite wretchedness. Those employed in it are in a continued state of exertion beyond the powers of nature to support. Little food of any kind is raised by them, so that the men and animals on these farms are badly fed, and the earth is rapidly impoverished." Wheat required less labor, and thus fewer slaves. Altogether, it seemed like an advantageous change for Virginia's economy and society.[11]

Yet Henry did not always find wheat a guaranteed moneymaker—sometimes thanks less to the vagaries of the crop than the irresponsibility of a family member. In 1776, just before the promulgation of the Declaration of Independence, he would sell almost four hundred bushels of wheat to his financially delinquent half-brother, John Syme. But Henry discovered later that Syme had not given him credit for at least half of his wheat deliveries, making "most gross errors in crediting my crop's wheat." In 1785, the accounting problems with Syme lingered, and Henry noted in a financial memo that

"I think certainly I owe him nothing. . . . I am willing to be even, but owing nothing." Meanwhile, Syme continued to enjoy the life of the Virginia gentleman, racing horses and consuming luxury goods. If even his half-brother was willing to cheat him, Henry mused, how could he ever hope to achieve financial security?[12]

HIS INCREASING LAND, POWER, AND WEALTH—and his persistent pursuit of personal independence—led Henry to acquire more slaves. Sarah's dowry had included six slaves, and by the late 1780s Henry owned sixty-six African-Americans on his various properties. Anglo-Americans, particularly in the southern colonies, largely took slavery for granted and did not blink at its scenes of human bondage and severe punishments. The day of Henry's Stamp Act speech in the House of Burgesses, for instance, the bodies of three African-Americans convicted of robbing a leading politician were hanging outside on Williamsburg's gallows. They served as a grisly reminder to slaves of their subservient place in Virginia society.[13]

Planters like Henry knew that keeping slaves was an invitation to violent resistance. Members of the southern elite incessantly worried about how to maintain power over their slaves, and prevent them from revolting or running away. Their fear often led them to inflict lurid and grotesque punishments against unruly slaves, especially runaways. A 1705 slave code allowed masters to apply to county courts for permission to cut off body parts of repeat offenders. The Virginia assembly hoped that these punishments would dissuade other African-Americans from thinking of running away. Masters and their overseers meted out vicious punishments with some regularity. The village of Negro Foot near Henry's Roundabout plantation, for example, apparently got its name when someone put a slave's dismembered foot on a pike in the area in 1733. Placing body parts on pikes was not new in English history. As early as the conquest of Ireland, the English had routinely displayed the heads and other appendages of their vanquished enemies as a warning not to revolt. The gruesome cautionary punishments could make for some harsh contrasts: the tiny hamlet of present-day Negro Foot lies on Patrick Henry Road in Hanover County.[14]

White Virginians' occasional recourse to the dismemberment of slaves had not abated in 1769—the year the Propositions and Grievances Committee in the House, of which Patrick Henry was a member, considered an amendment to a 1748 act controlling the behavior of servants and slaves. That act had reauthorized the county courts to "direct the [non-lethal] dismembering of slaves, who are notoriously guilty of going abroad in the night, or running away, and laying out, and who cannot be reclaimed by the common methods of punishment." In 1769 the House decided to amend the act, having decided that its enforcement was "often disproportioned to the offence, and contrary to the principles of humanity." But the new law provided only one new restriction on dismembering: a ban on castration, except in the case of attempted rape of a white woman by a slave.[15]

Virginia planters knew they had to keep a tight rein on slaves, who could rise up at any moment in localized violence or massive insurrection. Large-scale rebellion was highly uncommon—the task of organizing far-flung slaves and the threat of crushing retaliation made such revolts unlikely. But Virginia whites had witnessed enough slave uprisings to be scared into imposing draconian punishments. In 1730, hundreds of blacks participated in an insurrection around Norfolk, resulting in the hanging of thirty or more slave leaders. The slaves reportedly timed the revolt to begin on Sunday morning, when many whites would be in church and unarmed. Subsequently the governor ordered that when attending church, the colony's militiamen should "carry with them their arms to prevent any surprise thereof in their absence when slaves are most at liberty." Even during worship, white masters could not quite find relief from the fear of slave insurrection.[16]

Local fights could also turn into minor revolts. In 1769, a newspaper report recounted how slaves on the Hanover County plantation of Bowler Cocke turned against a demanding overseer and his assistant, who was attacked with an ax and severely beaten. After escaping, the assistant summoned an armed posse of whites, who confronted the defiant slaves at a barn. The slaves, said the article's white author, "rushed upon them with a desperate fury, armed with clubs and staves; one of them knocked down a white man, and was going to repeat the blow to finish him, which one of the [white] boys seeing, leveled his piece, discharged its contents into the fellow's breast, and brought him to the dust . . . the battle continued desperate, but another of the Negroes having his head almost cut off with a broad sword, and five of them being wounded, the rest fled." We cannot know to what extent the white men involved had provoked these attacks, but reports like this one confirmed white Virginians' conviction that by keeping slaves, they were sitting on a powder keg. Too many violent punishments—such as dismemberments—might elicit rebellion, but too much leniency might open the door for runaways or outright resistance.[17]

Many Virginia elites viewed slavery as a threat not only to their safety but to their own virtue as well. By the late 1760s, some of the colony's leaders had also begun to fear that the colonists' dependence on slave labor might breed lazy, debauched tendencies among the planters. Beyond such concerns, the rising number of slaves was also negatively affecting the economy. Virginians had begun to accumulate a surplus of slaves, some of whom they sold to planters of the lower South. Restricting further imports could both limit the slave population, which would offer some protection against possible slave revolts, and raise the prices for slaves at market. The Burgesses knew they could not ban the importation of slaves without London's approval, however, and in 1772 they petitioned the king directly for permitting such a ban.

The petition revealed not only the Burgesses' growing reservations about the slave trade but also their continuing devotion to the king. Their confidence in the monarch's tender care for the colonies, they wrote, led the Burgesses to "look up to the throne, and implore your Majesty's paternal assistance in averting a calamity of a most alarming nature." The delegates, most of them slave owners, however benevolent, did not linger on the contradictions inherent in the inhuman nature of the transatlantic slave trade—the very commerce that had always delivered the slaves whose continuing arrivals they now sought to curtail. They expressed fear that continued importations could threaten the security of the colonies. They also noted that more slaves meant fewer "useful inhabitants," or free white workers whose incomes would support the empire. The Burgesses, including Patrick Henry, unanimously approved the petition, complete with its affirmation of Virginia's loyalty to the "best of kings," George III.[18]

In 1772, even as the colonies stood at the edge of the second, more acute phase of the revolutionary crisis, most Americans remained convinced of George III's fatherly kindness toward them, and could present such appeals to him wholeheartedly. The corrosion of George III's reputation soon accelerated, assisted in part by the king's lack of attention to petitions like this one. The king's failure to reply to the House's appeal would merit notice in Jefferson's draft version of the Declaration of Independence in 1776. In a long section on slavery (subsequently deleted by the Continental Congress), Jefferson wrote that the king had suppressed "every legislative attempt to prohibit or to restrain this execrable commerce" in slaves. The Crown's refusal to allow the colonies to restrict the importation of slaves gave colonists some basis for the otherwise dubious claim that Britain had forced slavery on white Americans.[19]

PATRICK HENRY VEHEMENTLY SUPPORTED the restriction on the slave trade. Like many Virginia slave masters, he expressed frank personal reservations about slaveholding in a supposed land of liberty. Soon after the Burgesses sent their petition against the slave trade to the king, Henry received an antislavery book by the Quaker abolitionist Anthony Benezet as a gift from Virginia Quaker leader Robert Pleasants. In reply to Pleasants, Henry wrote a remarkable reflection on slavery:

> It is not a little surprising that Christianity, whose chief excellence consists in softening the human heart, in cherishing and improving its finer feelings, should encourage a practice so totally repugnant to the first impression of right and wrong. What adds to the wonder is that this abominable practice has been introduced in the most enlightened ages. . . . Is it not amazing, that at a time, when the rights of humanity are defined and understood with precision, in a country above all others fond of liberty, that in such an age, and such a country we find men, professing a religion the most humane, mild, meek, gentle and generous; adopting a principle as repugnant to humanity as it is inconsistent with the Bible and destructive to liberty. . . .
>
> Would any one believe that I am a master of slaves of my own purchase! I am drawn along by the general inconvenience of living without them, I will not, I cannot justify it. . . .
>
> I believe a time will come when an option will be offered to abolish this lamentable evil. Every thing we can do is to improve it, if it happens in our day, if not, let us transmit to our descendants together with our slaves, a pity for their unhappy lot, and an abhorrence for slavery. If we cannot reduce this wished for reformation to practice, let us treat the unhappy victims with lenity, it is the furthest advance we can make toward justice.[20]

Henry believed that the principles of the Bible, as well as new ideals of liberty becoming popular in Europe and America, contradicted slaveholding. He hoped that Americans' commitment to liberty would put the institution on a path to extinction. Ever concerned with the moral character of Virginia society, Henry worried that slavery prevented the development of a republic of independent, virtuous freeholders. James Madison shared this concern, privately calling slavery "unrepublican." Slaveholding encouraged vicious behavior by the planters against their weaker, victimized laborers. Henry commended the Quakers for leading this moral cause. He took personally their fervent injunction against slavery, worrying that he was hypocritically keeping slaves for his convenience when every moral gauge told him it was wrong.[21]

Henry so heartily applauded the Quakers for their abolitionism that Pleasants and others believed that the famous orator might serve as their political champion. Radical Quakers had long promoted antislavery principles, much earlier than most other Christians in Britain and America, and were often scorned by other colonists for their controversial views. Pleasants recommended a number of Virginia politicians, including "particularly our friend Patrick Henry," to Anthony Benezet in 1774, when Henry was going to Benezet's Philadelphia for the meeting of the Continental Congress. Another Quaker correspondent was even more effusive in his 1774 description of Henry as "a real half Quaker . . . in religious matters a saint but the very devil in politics—a son of thunder— Boanerges." This writer portrayed Henry as a serious Christian who practiced politics with such religious zeal that he was like the disciples James and John, whom Jesus renamed Boanerges—the "Sons of Thunder"—in the Gospel of Mark.[22]

With the Continental Congress so focused on resistance to the Intolerable Acts, harsh measures that came in 1774 in reaction to the Boston Tea Party, Henry did not advocate in Philadelphia for the abolition of slavery, but Quaker activists continued to hope that the "half Quaker" would join their cause. New Jersey Quaker Samuel Allinson wrote to Henry in late 1774 to argue that the slavery issue had never deserved more attention "than at a time when many or all the inhabitants of North America are groaning under unconstitutional impositions destructive of their liberty." Allinson speculated that the crisis with Britain might represent divine judgment on America for the practice of slavery; he warned Henry that God would not bless the colonists' fight for their political liberty if they continued to deny the slaves the more basic right of freedom from chains. After Henry became governor of Virginia, Robert Pleasants continued to correspond with him, asking Henry to consider a plan for the gradual abolition of slavery in the state.[23]

The Quakers may well have been disappointed with Henry. He never freed his own slaves—not even at his death—much less became an abolitionist. When the Revolution began, Henry grew more concerned with controlling the slave population of Virginia than promoting abolition. The Quakers also tended toward Loyalism, which created a wedge of suspicion between them and patriot leaders. In 1778, Henry had to mediate between Congress and a group of Pennsylvania Quakers detained in Winchester, Virginia, because of suspected treachery against the American cause. Whatever sympathies Henry ever had for antislavery sentiment certainly dissipated with the onset of hostilities with Britain.[24]

Although Henry's poignant letter to Pleasants may surprise us because of its candor, his sentiments against slavery reflected those of several other leading Virginians of the time, including Thomas Jefferson. Jefferson declared in *Notes on the State of Virginia* that human liberty was a gift from God and, like the Quakers, suggested that Americans provoked God's wrath because of their embrace of slavery. "I tremble for my country when I reflect that God is just," Jefferson wrote, and "that his justice cannot sleep forever." At the same time, however, Jefferson feared the consequences of emancipation, believing that it might unleash a horrific race war in the South. For Jefferson, freedom for slaves might have represented a long-term ideal, but the logistical difficulties, financial disruptions, and potential violence he anticipated prevented planters like him from taking emancipation seriously or, ultimately, enacting it in their own lives.[25]

At the Constitutional Convention in 1787, Henry's fellow Virginian George Mason would deepen the contradiction inherent in the position of southern slave masters who lamented American slavery. In a debate over Congress's power over slavery, Mason warned that slavery would cause God to curse America: "Every master of slaves is born a petty tyrant. They bring the judgment of heaven on a country. As nations can not be rewarded or punished in the next world they must be in this. By an inevitable chain of causes and effects providence punishes national sins, by national calamities." Like Henry and many other patriots, Mason saw a direct relationship between a nation's moral characteristics and its future welfare. Yet, like Henry and others, Mason never liberated any of his slaves. At the time these founders lived, it was conventional for leading southerners to criticize slavery, but those kinds of sentiments would no longer be acceptable in the proslavery white South sixty years later. If indeed the Revolution presented an opportunity to phase out slavery in the South, that window closed because planters like Henry indulged fears, rationalizations, and racial prejudices that barred the consistent application of the ideal of universal liberty they espoused.[26]

THE PLANTERS MIGHT NOT SEEK immediate freedom for their slaves, but they zealously agitated for freedom from parliamentary taxation. Their efforts were successful, at least in the short term. The colonial boycotts of the late 1760s helped convince royal officials to repeal most of the Townshend Duties. Five months after dissolving Virginia's assembly for endorsing Massachusetts's effort to resist the Townshend Program, the imperial governor reconvened the House of Burgesses. He informed them that the taxes would soon be re-pealed and that the Parliament did not intend to pass any new taxes for raising revenue from the colonists. The Burgesses responded with a conciliatory address to the governor and king, expressing gratitude for the policy change and renewing "the strongest assurances of our uninterrupted and most inviolable attachment to the sacred person and government of our royal sovereign."[27]

In early 1770, Parliament did repeal most of the Townshend Duties, except for the tax on tea. This action dulled resistance in the col-onies, even though the Virginia boycott was renewed in June 1770 with the promise that its adherents would continue to refuse to im-port British goods until the Townshend Duties were "totally re-pealed." The boycott in Virginia lost much of its force during 1770, however, and it did not reenergize even after news of the Boston Massacre that March, when tensions over the presence of the stand-ing army in Boston finally boiled over and redcoats opened fire on a crowd of colonists, killing five. Ironically, for about three years after the massacre, Massachusetts, Virginia, and the rest of the col-onies entered a season of relative quiet, even though none of the fundamental constitutional problems between the colonists and the Crown had been resolved.[28]

As the colony enjoyed a brief respite from imperial controversy, the rest of the key players in Virginia's rebellion were coming into place. In 1769, the twenty-six-year-old Jefferson joined Henry as a member of the House of Burgesses. Born seven years after Henry, Jefferson had also become a planter and lawyer. Jefferson grew up in Albemarle County, some seventy miles to the west of Hanover. His family was more deeply connected to Virginia's elite gentry than Henry's, and he received the best education possible, including a degree from the College of William and Mary. As a postgraduate student, Jefferson was studying law at William and Mary when he witnessed Henry's Stamp Act speech in 1765. Jefferson had inherited significant land holdings in Albemarle County when his father died in 1757, including the land on which Jefferson would build his famous home, Monticello. But like Henry, Jefferson did not restrict himself to farming, so he began practicing law in 1767, and in late 1768 Albemarle County elected him to the House of Burgesses. The two men were very different lawyers. In court, the contrasts in their personalities shined through, as Edmund Randolph remembered: "Mr. Jefferson drew copiously from the depths of the law, Mr. Henry from the recesses of the human heart." Jefferson believed in the power of ideas, Henry in the power of persuasion.[29]

We know relatively little about the activities of Henry—or of Jefferson—during the early 1770s, except that for Henry it was a time of significant personal reflections on slavery, because of the 1772 petition to the king and the 1773 letter to Robert Pleasants. In late 1770, Virginia's relatively congenial governor, Norborne Berkeley, died and was replaced by John Murray, the Earl of Dunmore, who would preside over the colony as its relationship with Britain disintegrated. The assembly met once in 1771, and again in 1772, and dealt primarily with local affairs, except for the petition on slave imports. Jefferson did not even attend the February 1772 session, having just married his wife, Martha, a month earlier, on New Year's Day.

But in early 1773, when the Burgesses gathered in Williamsburg, open tension between Britain and the colonies resurfaced. Local problems between Governor Dunmore and the assembly were themselves combustible, but the chief event igniting tensions between Britain and the colonies was the 1772 burning of the British schooner Gaspee in Rhode Island. This aggressive customs vessel had been harassing merchant ships off the New England coast, trying to catch smugglers. When the Gaspee ran aground during a pursuit, unidentified Rhode Islanders boarded the ship under the cover of night, removed the crew—shooting the ship's lieutenant in the groin during the scuffle—and burned the boat.

The *Gaspee* affair opened another critical front in the contest over British constitutional authority in the colonies. Furious, the British government commissioned an investigation of the brazen attack. Although they could not determine who had burned the vessel, London officials gave the commission authority to send any suspects back to England for trial. To colonists, this move jeopardized their time-honored right to trial by a jury of peers.

As it had in 1765, Virginia led the resistance in this phase of the imperial crisis. Thomas Jefferson recalled that the news of the *Gaspee* commission had roused some of the more radical members of the assembly to action. "Not thinking our old and leading members up to the point of forwardness and zeal which the times required," Jefferson, Henry, Richard Henry Lee, and others met in a private room at the Raleigh Tavern and drafted a proposal to form a committee of correspondence to monitor the British government's actions. In resolutions the young men got the House of Burgesses to adopt in March 1773, the legislature declared that in light of ominous reports of designs to deprive them of their constitutional rights (referring obliquely to the *Gaspee* commission), it would appoint a committee to "obtain the most early and authentic intelligence of all such acts and resolutions of the British Parliament, or proceedings of administration, as may relate to, or affect the British colonies in America." The committee would also correspond with other American colonies on shared imperial concerns. Although the group included such cautious senior members as chairman Peyton Randolph, it also featured the instigators: Henry, Jefferson, and Lee.[30]

Massachusetts used a similar committee of correspondence to stir resistance in its hinterlands, and Virginia's committee helped build intercolonial cooperation. Richard Henry Lee had proposed the idea of such an organization as early as 1768 to John Dickinson of Pennsylvania, recommending that "a private correspondence should be conducted between the lovers of liberty in every province." The creation of Virginia's committee set the plan in motion. It would be the first step toward framing a separate American government.[31]

Shortly after the Burgesses formed the committee of correspondence, Parliament miscalculated colonial sentiment by passing the 1773 Tea Act. The measure was primarily intended to rescue the struggling East India Company by giving it a monopoly on the tea trade in America. The net effect would be to lower the price of tea in the colonies, but sensitive colonists interpreted it as another attempt by Parliament to assert the right to tax the colonies, and many American merchants realized they would lose their right to sell tea because of the East India Company's monopoly. In Boston, the furor over the act led to the Boston Tea Party of December 1773, in which radicals raided ships and dumped about £10,000 of tea into Boston Harbor.

When the Virginia assembly met again, in May 1774, Parliament had already retaliated for the Tea Party by passing the Boston Port Bill, which closed the port to commercial traffic until the value of the destroyed tea had been recovered. Open attacks on the Port Bill would be reserved until the end of Virginia's legislative session; the Burgesses knew that any official complaints would lead to their dissolution by the governor. George Mason told a friend that as plans proceeded behind the scenes to protest the Port Bill, Henry reasserted himself as Virginia's chief patriot orator. In a vivid description of Henry's role, Mason wrote:

> Matters of that sort here are conducted and prepared with a great deal of privacy, and by very few members; of whom Patrick Henry is the principal. At the request of the gentlemen concerned, I have spent an evening with them upon the subject, where I had an opportunity of conversing with Mr. Henry, and knowing his sentiments; as well as hearing him speak in the house since, on different occasions.

Mason had come to know Henry well. He was awed by Henry's rhetorical talents and portrayed him as a man of classic public virtue (and Mason would seem to have no reason to be obsequious in a personal letter not directed to Henry):

> He is by far the most powerful speaker I ever heard. Every word he says not only engages but commands the attention; and your passions are no longer your own when he addresses them. But his eloquence is the smallest part of his merit. He is in my opinion the first man upon this continent, as well in abilities as public virtues, and had he lived in Rome about the time of the first Punic War, when the Roman people had arrived at their meridian glory, and their virtue not tarnished, Mr. Henry's talents must have put him at the head of that glorious commonwealth.[32]

For a patriot like Mason, comparing Henry to the leading citizens of ancient Rome was the highest form of praise. To him, Henry's courageous oratory revealed his commitment to both freedom and virtue.

Jefferson would recall that he, Henry, and other radical members of the assembly met privately to discuss resistance to the Port Bill, and decided to call for prayer and fasting on the day the Port Bill went into effect. This was a clever move, for what Christian gentleman could argue—except perhaps the imperial governor—against holding a day of prayer? In the decade since the Seven Years' War, Virginians had grown unaccustomed to holding such solemn days, so Jefferson, Henry, and the others rummaged through old Puritan precedents and crafted a declaration "to implore heaven to avert from us the evils of civil war, to inspire us with firmness in support of our rights, and to turn the hearts of the King and parliament to moderation and justice." The instigators recruited the moderate, notably religious Robert Carter Nicholas to introduce the resolution, which passed unanimously.[33]

Predictably, Governor Dunmore did not appreciate this action and promptly dissolved the assembly. The Burgesses took another stroll down the street to the Raleigh Tavern, where they adopted a plan for the boycott called the "association." The association asserted that the Boston Port Bill evidenced a plot "for reducing the inhabitants of British America to slavery." Slave-owning Burgesses such as Henry and Jefferson saw no irony in their own fear of bondage to the British. They readily employed such metaphorical language to articulate their dread of becoming economic pawns of the empire.[34]

The boycott proposed by the association applied to most goods produced by the East India Company, but not all British trade items. Members decided against a general boycott to cause the least damage to British merchants and manufacturers, whom colonial leaders viewed as potential allies in the contest with the empire, just as they had been in the battle over the Stamp Act. Making their solidarity with Massachusetts clear, the Burgesses proclaimed that an attack on one colony represented an attack on all of British America. They also called for a general congress of the colonies to discuss resistance to the British threat. Beyond the system adopted by the association, the Virginia committee of correspondence also worked to promote extralegal resistance and cooperation with other colonies. Shortly after the dissolution of the assembly, they approved a New York plan for a general American congress, and they called for a convention in Williamsburg in August 1774 to nominate delegates to attend the congress.

Virginia's counties followed through with the appointed day of prayer and fasting on June 1. Jefferson wrote that the day was like a "shock of electricity," focusing the colonists' attention on the gravity of the crisis. In Williamsburg, Peyton Randolph assembled a solemn audience at the courthouse, from which they proceeded to the Bruton Parish Church, where the Reverend Thomas Price, chaplain of the House of Burgesses, preached on the text "the Lord hath prepared his seat in heaven, and his kingdom ruleth over all." To the colonists, God's providence presided over the trouble with Britain, and God's law was sovereign over the arbitrary acts of men. Surely providence would vindicate the righteousness of their lawful cause.[35]

THE UNREST IN THE COLONIES only escalated in the summer of 1774, as news arrived of more parliamentary moves against Massachusetts and the colonies. Known in America as the Intolerable Acts, these laws included the Massachusetts Government Act, which dramatically reduced the power of the colony's elected officials; the Administration of Justice Act, under which royal officials charged with capital crimes could be tried in England; and a revised Quartering Act, which gave the British power to take over private buildings— even homes—for the quartering of British soldiers. The British viewed these measures as necessary responses to Massachusetts's recklessness, while many colonists saw the laws as the unfolding of the newest stages in Britain's plan of tyranny.

In Virginia, the Intolerable Acts generated a surge of popular anxiety, and a host of petitions from the counties. In Hanover County, citizens appointed Patrick Henry and his ne'er-do-well half-brother, John Syme, as delegates to the Williamsburg convention in August. Then they adopted a resolution, which may have been drafted by Henry and Syme, assessing the imperial crisis. It called for the repeal of the Intolerable Acts and united colonial action against them. It also declared that the Atlantic slave trade was "dangerous to the virtue and welfare of this country" and advocated that it be banned.[36]

The convention that assembled in Williamsburg in August adopted a stringent new association vowing to ban all imports (except for medicine) from Great Britain. They also resolved to stop importing slaves. Declaring that since tea represented "the detestable instrument which laid the foundation of the present sufferings of our distressed friends in the town of Boston, we view it with horror," they went so far as to ban not only the importation of tea, but even the brewing of any remaining tea in homes.[37]

The convention also appointed seven delegates to attend the American colonial congress, scheduled to assemble in Philadelphia the following month. The delegation's members ranged from the zealous to the grave. Among them were Peyton Randolph, Richard Henry Lee, Edmund Pendleton, Richard Bland, George Washington, and Patrick Henry. Thomas Jefferson was absent from the convention due to illness, and was not chosen. Edmund Randolph recalled that Lee and Henry were selected because of their reputation for eloquence, while Washington was chosen in case the congress decided to raise an army.[38]

On the evening of August 30, Henry and Pendleton rendezvoused at Washington's Mount Vernon estate, on the banks of the Potomac River. On the 31st, Washington jotted in his diary "with Colo. Pendleton, & Mr. Henry I set out on my journey for Phila." The party arrived in Philadelphia on September 4. The Virginians had stepped onto a bigger American stage.[39]

# 5

## "LIBERTY OR DEATH"

## Arming for Revolution

PHILADELPHIANS RECEIVED HENRY, Washington, and Pendleton as heroes. Hundreds of officers, militiamen, and a troupe of musicians met them several miles outside the city and escorted them through the streets to "great applause." Philadelphia was the largest town in America at the time, with about 34,000 residents. Though just under a hundred years old, it had already become one of the most economically developed cities in the British Empire. To many of the delegates—including Patrick Henry—the sights of the metropolis must have been a bit overwhelming.[1]

The residents of Philadelphia were packed chiefly into eight blocks running from the Delaware River waterfront to Eighth Street. At the docks, ships from across the Atlantic loaded and unloaded their cargo. Philadelphia stood at a fine natural port on the river, which widened farther south into Delaware Bay, and finally the ocean. Some ships at the docks trafficked in slaves, despite the historic resistance of

Pennsylvania's Quakers to slavery. In 1774, thousands of slaves still lived in Pennsylvania; not until 1780 would the state put in place a plan for gradually abolishing slavery. As Henry and the other delegates made their way to Carpenter's Hall on Chestnut Street, Philadelphia offered them a startling mix of refinement and crudeness: it featured such renowned institutions as the American Philosophical Society and the Library Company of Philadelphia, both founded by Ben Franklin, but packs of pigs and mangy dogs also roamed freely. Residents complained about the vile practice of leaving dead horses and other carcasses in the streets.[2]

Thanks to his eloquence, boldness, and charm, Henry quickly cemented his reputation among the delegates as a dynamic advocate for American rights. But other Virginians also influenced the debates and actions of the Congress, among them Peyton Randolph, who was unanimously chosen as its chair. A dazzling cast of characters from beyond Virginia was present, too, many of whom would lead their states through the Revolution and the adoption of the Constitution. Roger Sherman, a devout Christian and lawyer from Connecticut, went on to become the only person to sign all four of the great state papers of the American founding: the Continental Association (which the Continental Congress adopted as a means to enforce the boycott of British goods), the Declaration of Independence, the Articles of Confederation, and the U.S. Constitution. Massachusetts sent the dynamic Adams cousins, Samuel and John. John Adams, older than Henry by only seven months, was one of the great political thinkers among the Americans. Though they never became particularly close friends—Adams moved in national political circles while Henry mostly remained in Virginia—the two men certainly shared a radical commitment to American liberties, and a deep respect for each other's convictions. As Adams wrote to Henry in 1776, "I esteem it an honor and a happiness, that my opinion so often coincides with yours."[3]

In his first speech to the Congress, Henry argued for proportional representation in Congress—the distribution of voting power to each colony based on its population. Some delegates charged that he was trying to give the large colonies power over the small ones. According to John Adams, Henry declared that a delegate's loyalty to his specific colony should take second place to the imperative of continental unity. "Government is dissolved," he proclaimed, meaning that the upheaval over taxes had already annulled the old colonial system. He heralded the advent of a new American nation. "Fleets and armies and the present state of things show that government is dissolved. Where are your landmarks, your boundaries of colonies? We are in a state of nature. . . . The distinctions between Virginians, Pennsylvanians, New Yorkers, and New Englanders, are no more. I am not a Virginian, but an American." Charles Thomson, the secretary of the Congress, remarked that Henry spoke more like a Presbyterian pastor than a politician. Evangelical fervor was continuing to infuse power into Henry's speeches.[4]

Henry's soaring rhetoric masked a complex agenda, at least on this occasion. On one hand, he clearly believed that Anglo-Americans had common interests to protect against the tyrannical encroachments of empire. On the other, Henry struggled to accept the notion that an emerging political entity—America—should command a higher allegiance than his home colony, even as the radical patriots felt impelled to advocate for unprecedented American union.

In the interest of concerted action, Henry maintained a harmonious tone in his relations with the other colonies. In one concession, he did abandon hope that the Congress would count slaves for the purpose of representation—an effort that anticipated a similar controversy over slaves at the Constitutional Convention of 1787. Southern planters were not seeking political rights for their slaves, but they did want them to count as residents to boost their states' population numbers and thus increase their legislative muscle. But in 1774,

Henry knew this position would not earn him favor among north-erners in the Congress, and he dropped the idea rather than risk a debate over slavery.[5]

Among the Congress's most provocative actions was the adoption of the Suffolk Resolves, which were originally passed in Suffolk County, Massachusetts, and introduced to the Congress by Samuel Adams, and which declared that colonists should resist the Intolerable Acts "as the attempts of a wicked administration to enslave America." The Congress also denounced the recently announced Quebec Act, a parliamentary measure that allowed the open practice of Roman Catholicism in Canada. To anxious colonists and congressional dele-gates, the act evidenced a sinister religious plot. The Quebec Act, the resolves asserted, endangered the Protestant religion in America, and "therefore as men and Protestant Christians we are indispensably obliged to take all proper measures for our security." When the Con-gress adopted the resolves, John Adams declared it one of the happi-est days of his life.[6]

With the approval of the Suffolk Resolves, it might have seemed as if radical delegates had won control of the Congress. Later that month, however, Joseph Galloway of Pennsylvania introduced a proposal for a modified political union between Britain and America, which featured a grand council of the colonies that would handle intercolonial issues but remain subservient to Parliament. As recorded in John Adams's notes, Henry argued against this new, more moderate plan, insisting that the "original constitution of the colonies was founded on the broadest and most generous base. The regulation of our trade was compensation enough for all the protection we ever experienced from her. . . . We are not to consent by the representatives of representatives. I am inclined to think the present measures lead to war." The moder-ates' proposal failed, when what Galloway called the "violent party" of Henry and Samuel Adams convinced a slight majority of Congress not to use halfway political measures to stave off a looming confrontation with Britain. Henry resented the moderate faction. When John Adams met privately with him on October 11, 1774, Henry railed against Galloway, John Jay, and others whose conciliatory plans would "ruin the cause of America." But Henry publicly tempered his voiced opinion of the moderates to preserve congressional harmony.[7]

Henry had impressed Adams and a number of the other delegates with his passionate oratory in defense of American liberty. Silas Deane, a delegate from Connecticut, wrote that Henry was the "compleatest speaker I ever heard . . . but in a letter I can give you no idea of the music of his voice, or the highwrought yet natural elegance of his style and manner." Deane noted that some had begun calling Henry the Demosthenes of America (and Richard Henry Lee the Cicero). The moniker was a significant one; the patriots revered the memory of the ancient Greek and Roman republics, and Demosthenes was a heroic defender of Greek liberty against the powerful empire builder Alexander the Great. Keenly aware of historical precedents in their struggle for liberty, Americans had begun to associate their champions with the republican heroes of old.[8]

A WEEK BEFORE HIS DEPARTURE from Philadelphia, Henry's sister Anne Christian wrote a letter revealing some of Henry's personal circumstances during these months. "My brother Pat is not returned from Philadelphia yet," she wrote. "His wife is extremely ill." This letter evinces the friendly informalities of Henry's family, as they sometimes called him "Pat"—even as its contents revealed Sarah Henry's declining health. Little specific information exists about her condition, but by late 1774 Sarah seems to have descended into what we might characterize as extreme depression or perhaps even a violent and unpredictable form of insanity. Whatever her diagnosis, she now lived her life confined to the basement of the mansion at Scotchtown. The records are uncertain even about the details of her fate, but it is known that she died, apparently in early 1775.[9]

As was typical of women in colonial families, Sarah had spent much of her married life pregnant and tending to small children. At the time of her death, she and Patrick had six children. The oldest, Martha, was already twenty years old and married, the second, John, was eighteen, but the other four were young; all were born in the twelve years between 1763 and Sarah's passing. Patrick was a devoted father, a commitment no doubt intensified by Sarah's illness and death. He later developed a particularly close relationship with his daughter Elizabeth, who was born in 1769. Their sixth child—and their only one born at Scotchtown—was Edward (called "Neddy"), born in 1771.[10]

Memories recorded long after the fact recalled that Sarah had become deranged, suicidal, and perhaps violent toward others, maybe even toward her young children, which would explain her confinement to an isolated portion of her home. Few other options would have existed at the time for treating or housing the mentally ill. A state mental hospital had just opened in Williamsburg, but it was tiny, with twenty-four beds, and meant primarily for patients whose only other alternative was jail. Although the opening of this hospital represented a progressive step toward recognizing the medical realities of mental illness, the treatments offered there were, by modern standards, barbaric. Mostly doctors attempted to balance patients' bodily "humors"—a balance that, in Hippocratic medicine, would supposedly produce health by routines of bleeding and vomiting. It is unlikely that Henry would have even considered the hospital as an option. Though it is difficult to assess Sarah's condition or the nature of her confinement, there is no reason to think Patrick's treatment of her was negligent or cruel. We will never know quite what happened in Sarah's declining months, but it seems likely that Henry arranged for her to be as comfortable as possible, without harming herself or others.[11]

HENRY MUST HAVE EXPERIENCED great personal turmoil during his wife's illness, but during her decline and death, he managed to maintain his involvement in political affairs. He traveled to Richmond in March 1775 for the second session of the Virginia Convention at St. John's Church, which would be the scene of his "Liberty or Death" speech. The freeholders of Hanover County had once again chosen him and John Syme as their delegates, instructing them to support the collection of the colonial taxes required to secure their liberty. They also encouraged the delegates to explore measures to provide for the families of Virginians killed or wounded in a 1774 war against Native Americans in western Virginia. This second injunction suggested the emerging belief among Virginians that the convention constituted an independent provincial government, which would care for veterans' families, among other tasks.[12]

At the convention, the combustion among the delegates began when Edmund Pendleton offered a resolution endorsing a 1774 petition from the legislature of Jamaica (which, like Virginia, was a British colony). The Anglo-Jamaicans had strongly protested recent British actions as a "plan almost carried into execution, for enslaving the colonies, founded, as we conceive, on a claim of Parliament to bind the colonies in all cases whatsoever," even as they struck a moderate tone by affirming George III's right to veto colonial legislation. Endorsement of this sentiment would have communicated Virginia's desire for a "speedy return of those halcyon days, when we lived a free and happy people."[13]

A perturbed Henry struck back against Pendleton with amendments calling for Virginia to assume a defensive posture against Britain—that is, through the raising of a militia that would hopefully replace British regular troops. Moderates balked at this bold statement, because it assumed that armed conflict with Britain was unavoidable. Henry would not back down, however. He rose to call Virginia to arms.

There are many moments in Henry's life for which we might wish for better documentation. The "Liberty or Death" speech is probably the most significant of those points. Amazingly, we do not have a contemporary text of it, even though it is one of the most celebrated and stirring orations in American history. One of Patrick Henry's charms was an apparent lack of concern for his personal legacy. Unlike most of the major founders, he made almost no effort to preserve his papers, or texts of his major speeches. For historians, this lack of attention to the autobiographical record causes peculiar problems. What record we do have for the "Liberty or Death" speech is a version published in 1816 by William Wirt, a Virginia politician who became attorney general under President James Monroe. Wirt corresponded widely with associates of Henry to craft his biography *Sketches of the Life and Character of Patrick Henry* and seems to have depended heavily on the recollections of Virginia judge St. George Tucker for the wording of the speech. The speech's content seems consistent with Henry's style and radical ideology, so we can be confident that the essence of the text came from the original.[14]

"Liberty or Death" relied heavily upon biblical references for its persuasive power. These are easily missed now, but they would have been familiar to the audience at the Virginia Convention, who grew up in the Bible-soaked culture of colonial America. Several phrases came directly from the prophet Jeremiah. For example, Henry warned that British assurances of benevolent intentions would "prove a snare to your feet" (Jeremiah 18:22). He worried that Virginians would become like those "who having eyes, see not, and having ears, hear not" (Jeremiah 5:21). And he warned that "gentlemen may cry, peace, peace—but there is no peace" (Jeremiah 6:14).[15]

Henry also explained his suspicion of the British by referencing his own worldview regarding the natural human tendency to engage in deceptive behavior. He had "but one lamp by which his feet were guided; and that was the lamp of experience." The British had given the colonists no reason to trust them, he declared, other than assurances of goodwill, and he warned that behind those assurances, the British were really like the disciple Judas, who had sold out Jesus to his enemies. "Suffer not yourselves to be betrayed with a kiss," he cautioned.[16]

For Patrick Henry, there could be no compromise, no false peace. At the conclusion of the speech, Henry thundered that the time for war had come. "We must fight! I repeat it, sir, we must fight! An appeal to arms and to the God of hosts, is all that is left us! . . . Is life so dear, or peace so sweet, as to be purchased at the price of chains and slavery? Forbid it, Almighty God!" With this, Henry lifted his arms and cried, "I know not what course others may take; but as for me, give me liberty, or give me death!"[17]

IN THE DIMMED LIGHT cast from two centuries past, we may forget how audacious the "Liberty or Death" speech was. Henry's words shocked some and horrified others. While Edmund Randolph thought the speech "blazed so as to warm the coldest heart," a Virginia Tory grumbled that "you never heard anything more infamously insolent than P. Henry's speech."[18]

For the climactic words of his speech, Henry recalled the play *Cato, A Tragedy* by Joseph Addison. Originally published in London in 1713, Addison's play was one of the most popular and enduring in the colonies, opening in Philadelphia in 1749 in a performance by the first professional American drama company. Cato, one of the heroes of Roman antiquity, was revered by colonists for his opposition to political corruption and the power of Julius Caesar. In the play, Cato declared:

> It is not now a time to talk of ought
> But chains, or conquest; liberty, or death.

Appeals to classical antiquity allowed Patriots like Henry to argue for the historic rectitude of resisting encroaching power and corruption. Cato and Brutus had done it, and so should the Americans.[19]

To Henry, the crisis had become a "question of freedom or slavery." By liberally using biblical rhetoric, Henry drew on his Christian heritage and evangelical style to place the Virginians' struggle in a providential frame. Fighting against Britain required more than pragmatic justifications. Moderation at such a time would be an offense not just to the people of Virginia but also to God.

Henry acknowledged the power of the British armed forces, but he believed that waiting to fight would only weaken the American position as the British continued to concentrate their troops on the colonies' shores. The conspiracy against their liberty would grow more insidious. If they fought, he proclaimed, God would be on their side. "Three millions of people armed in the holy cause of liberty, and in such a country as that which we possess, are invincible by any force which our enemy can send against us. Besides, sir, we shall not fight our battles alone. There is a just God who presides over the destinies of nations, and who will raise up friends to fight our battles for us. . . . Our chains are forged. Their clanking may be heard on the plains of Boston! The war is inevitable—and let it come! I repeat, sir, let it come!"[20]

These words resound with Henry's ultimate expression of Christian republicanism. For founders like him, republican ideology, which trumpeted both the value and fragility of liberty, would have been incomplete if not expressed with Christian zeal. Some elite founders privately held unorthodox beliefs about the Christian God, but patriots like Henry who had more traditional faith used Christian themes to mobilize the people at large. One of Henry's critics lamented that Henry was "so infatuated, that he goes about I am told, praying and preaching amongst the common people." Henry, along with most rank-and-file patriots, entered the war against

Britain with the conviction that God would defend the liberty of the righteous.[21]

Henry also believed, along with most patriots, that God moved in the affairs of nations. The notion that "a just God presides over the destinies of nations" would have resonated at the Virginia Convention and among founders as diverse as Washington, John Adams, and Benjamin Franklin. But to Henry, God did not simply bless America because it was America. God defended the liberty of the *righteous*, while confounding the plans of oppressive nations such as Britain. Henry would have added—and did indeed declare later in the war—that if America lost its virtue, then it risked forgoing the blessing of God. This was a constant refrain among many revolutionaries and a theme that also hearkened back to the warnings of Jeremiah and other biblical prophets.

THE CONVENTION WAS CONVINCED. It adopted Henry's resolutions and made him the chair of a committee entrusted with developing a strategy to arm the colony. Under the committee's plan, the counties would form volunteer militia companies that would respond in case of military emergency. Each militiaman, "clothed in a hunting shirt by way of uniform," would be supplied with a gun, ammunition, and a tomahawk. Patriot soldier Dr. George Gilmer, of the Albemarle County volunteers, vowed "never to bury the tomahawk until liberty shall be fixed on an immoveable basis through the whole Continent." These rustic fighters, with their fearsome appearance, would not have to wait long to see action.[22]

The convention selected the same seven men who served in the first Continental Congress to serve in the second, which would gather in Philadelphia in May. All of them, including Henry, received strong support from the other delegates. Thomas Jefferson was chosen as an alternate. Although moderates like Peyton Randolph continued to exercise great influence, all signs pointed toward the establishment of a separate Virginia government and military to resist the British. Events of the next month would hardly slow the momentum.

On March 28, Governor Dunmore issued a proclamation forbidding, by order of the king, the election of delegates to the Continental Congress—three days after the convention had elected Henry and his colleagues to attend the meeting in Philadelphia. Undeterred, Dunmore insisted that government officials stop the appointment of delegates to a gathering the British deemed the latest in a series of illegitimate acts by an increasingly unreasonable crowd of colonists. The conflict drew its first blood in April 1775 at Lexington, Massachusetts, where the British military commander General Thomas Gage sought to arrest rebel leaders and to seize arms held at Concord. In the early morning of April 19, the Massachusetts militia, warned by Paul Revere's network of spies, faced down the redcoat army on the town green of Lexington. No one knows who shot first, but the "shot heard 'round the world" would begin the armed conflict that became the American Revolution. The British then met a fierce resistance at Concord and were forced to retreat to Boston, suffering almost three hundred casualties. Lord Dunmore knew the Virginia Convention had called for its counties to organize militias like those in Massachusetts (although he seemed not yet to know about the events at Lexington and Concord). He ordered marines on the royal schooner *Magdalen* to take a cache of gunpowder held in Williamsburg and remove it to a ship waiting outside of Norfolk before the colonists could steal it. In the early morning of April 21, a small group of British troops loaded fifteen half-barrels of gunpowder into a wagon the governor provided. Someone raised an alarm, but the soldiers successfully fled Williamsburg with the powder.[23]

A mob began to gather in Williamsburg, threatening to attack the governor's palace. No attack came, as moderate leaders calmed the crowd and the city government prepared a sober address to the governor. In addition to decrying the seizure of the gunpowder and demanding its return, the city's complaint also focused on the possibility of slave uprisings, rumors of which had swept up and down the James River the week before. "We have too much reason to believe," the city leaders wrote, "that some wicked and designing persons have instilled the most diabolical notions into the minds of slaves, and that, therefore, the utmost attention to our internal security is become the more necessary." The Virginians were imagining nightmarish scenarios of the British disarming the colonists just at the moment of a great slave insurrection. Or worse, Lord Dunmore might encourage the slaves to revolt to stop the colonists' resistance. Dunmore was keenly aware of these fears, and immediately after removing the powder, he threatened to fulfill white Virginians' worst dreams by declaring freedom for the slaves.[24]

Many Virginians saw his threat, along with the fighting in Massachusetts, as the final phase of the plot to destroy the colonists' liberties. Some of the volunteer militia companies, only recently called up by Henry's resolutions, began to assemble for a march on Williamsburg. The Albemarle County militia departed from Charlottesville, prepared to "demand satisfaction of Dunmore for the powder, and his threatening to fix his standard and call over the negroes." Moderate leaders, such as Peyton Randolph, began circulating letters forbidding these companies to assault the capital.[25]

One militia company the moderates could not stop was Patrick Henry's, the volunteers of Hanover County. Henry had returned to Hanover from Richmond and helped organize the militia by giving a passionate speech, as one participant recalled, "pointing out the necessity of our having recourse to arms in defense of our rights." Many volunteered for the company. Henry knew the gunpowder episode presented a new opportunity to radicalize the population against the British. He told his cousin George Dabney that Dunmore's action was a "fortunate circumstance, which would rouse the people from North to South. You may in vain mention the duties to them upon tea and these things they will say do not affect them, but tell them of the robbery of the magazine and that the next step will be to disarm them, and they will be then ready to fly to arms to defend themselves." Henry summoned the Hanover volunteers to recapture the gunpowder. Understandably, some moderates criticized his plan as "imprudent and impolitic," but the Hanover County committee approved the plan, and Henry became commander of the company. Perhaps chastened by the mounting pressure against him from fellow Virginians, he decided to seek reimbursement for the gunpowder from royal officials. He extracted a promise of such compensation from Carter Braxton, a moderate patriot who had been dispatched by the governor as a peacemaker.[26]

Henry sent the receipt of payment to Virginia's treasurer, Robert Carter Nicholas, assuring him that if the public treasury needed protection from plundering by Dunmore, the Hanover militia would gladly provide it. Nicholas replied that "he had no apprehension of the necessity or propriety of the proffered service." In taking charge of his own militia to confront Dunmore, Henry had clearly begun to test the limits of the Virginia moderates' tolerance. The Hanover volunteers returned home, awaiting further instructions after Henry's attendance at the second meeting of the Continental Congress.[27]

Responses to Henry's expedition were mixed. Hesitant Virginians agonized that the colonists might not be able to avoid violence and popular unrest in pursuing rights and redress from Britain. "A True Patriot," writing in the *Virginia Gazette*, acknowledged that Dunmore's actions were wrongheaded, but he chastised the volunteers for acting without proper government authority. Unchecked zeal for liberty and wild rumors about British intentions were threatening the rule of law, and Henry's acts might become as "pernicious in their consequences as they were intended to be salutary," the True Patriot worried. From the royal perspective, Henry had become a rebel and a terrorist, and on May 6, Dunmore issued a proclamation denouncing him and his followers: "I have been informed, from undoubted authority, that a certain Patrick Henry, of the County of Hanover, and a number of deluded followers, have taken up arms, chosen their officers, and styling themselves an independent company, have marched out of their county, encamped, and put themselves in a posture of war . . . to the great terror of all his majesty's faithful subjects, and in open defiance of law and government." Dunmore warned Virginians not to give any aid to Henry and his ruffians.[28]

Other Virginians congratulated Henry and the Hanover volunteers, however. From Orange County, a committee chaired by James Madison deplored Dunmore's seizure of the gunpowder. Fifteen years younger than Henry, Madison was the son of an elite tobacco-growing family from northern Virginia. He had graduated from the College of New Jersey at Princeton only in 1771, where he studied political philosophy under the renowned Presbyterian pastor and scholar John Witherspoon. In 1775, the twenty-four-year-old Madison was just emerging as a political leader in Orange County. His committee declared that the fighting in Massachusetts represented an attack on Virginia as well, further justifying Henry's actions. The battles at Lexington and Concord were "sufficient warrant to use violence and reprisal, in all cases where it may be expedient for our security and welfare." To radical patriots, threats of violence like Henry's had become necessary because of the British government's flagrant actions against them.[29]

In the days after Dunmore denounced him, Henry remained unapologetic. He scoffed at Dunmore's claim that the gunpowder belonged to the royal government. "His Majesty can have no right to convert the houses or other conveniences necessary for our defense into repositories for engines of our destruction," Henry wrote. He hoped most Virginians would support him, despite the grumblings of moderates, and even hinted that in light of events in Massachusetts, "greater reprisals" could have been justified but that he had declined to pursue them. With such missives, Henry was positioning himself not only as a resistance leader but as a commander of a rebellion.[30]

By the second week of May, Henry had departed for the Second Continental Congress, accompanied by an armed escort to prevent his arrest. His cheering guards sent him across the Potomac, while "committing him to the gracious and wise disposer of all human events, to guide and protect while contending for a restitution of our dearest rights and liberties." Henry's supporters believed that God had raised up Henry and other patriot leaders to face this crisis, and would protect them accordingly. The controversy in Virginia continued to worsen in Henry's absence, and Dunmore abandoned Williamsburg in June, taking refuge on a British frigate near Yorktown.[31]

We do not have detailed records of Henry's activities at the Second Continental Congress, but the relative silence about his impact there seems to confirm Thomas Jefferson's later assertion that Henry played only a supporting role. Jefferson had joined the Congress (replacing Peyton Randolph, who returned to Virginia to help manage the crisis there), and he found Henry "to be a silent, and almost unmeddling member." Jefferson portrayed Henry as at his best when he was debating fundamental issues of liberty and freedom; he did not shine when it came to deliberating over the policies and elements of the new government the Congress had set itself to institute. Henry was a visionary motivator, not a man of organization. As he participated in planning the independent government, Henry was competent, but easily bored.[32]

Moderates at the Second Continental Congress pushed through one more attempt at reconciliation, the "Olive Branch Petition" that reaffirmed loyalty to the king despite the fighting in Massachusetts, and Dunmore's seizure of Virginia's gunpowder. Henry undoubtedly squirmed in frustration as the Congress passed the last-ditch appeal to the British, but he may have recognized that it was useful to have the colonies on record as favoring reconciliation, if possible.

Even as it offered the possibility of peace, Congress planned for war. The delegates created the Continental army, naming George Washington commander in chief of the American forces. Divisions within the Congress at this point ran along moderate and radical lines, not regional ones, with Washington facing opposition from some Virginia delegates, especially Edmund Pendleton, who believed Washington's appointment would signal eagerness for armed conflict beyond Massachusetts. The Virginia moderates supported Artemas Ward of Massachusetts as the top general, to direct a war they hoped would stay in New England. Samuel and John Adams supported Washington not only because of his experience and dignity, but also to raise up a Southern patriot commander, helping to make this an American war.

With characteristic humility, Washington wrote to his brother that he had "embarked on a wide ocean, boundless in its prospect and from whence, perhaps, no safe harbour is to be found. I have been called upon by the unanimous voice of the colonies to take the command of the Continental Army—an honour I neither sought after, nor desired, as I am thoroughly convinced that it requires greater abilities, and much more experience, than I am master of." Henry enthusiastically supported his colleague Washington out of personal loyalty developed during a decade of legislative service together. The choice also complemented Henry's growing partnership with the Massachusetts radicals.[33]

Henry returned to Virginia in August and found himself summoned to his own military command. Remarkably, despite his lack of military experience, the Virginia Convention named him commander in chief of Virginia's regular forces. Patrick Henry had won immense popularity in Virginia because of his advocacy of war. Now he would lead Virginia into that war against the greatest military power of the eighteenth century.

# 6

## "TO CUT THE KNOT"

## Independence

O N SEPTEMBER 18, 1775, Patrick Henry was commissioned as a colonel and as the leader of Virginia's armed forces. Standing before the Virginia Committee of Safety, convened in Hanover, he solemnly declared, "I, Patrick Henry, do swear that I will be faithful and true to the colony and dominion of Virginia; that I will serve the same to the utmost of my power, in defense of the just rights of America, against all enemies whatsoever." He further promised to lay down arms when instructed by the assembly. "So help me God," he intoned.[1]

Edmund Pendleton, president of the committee, presented Henry with a signed commission on parchment, directing him to "resist and repel all hostile invasions, and quell and suppress any insurrections which may be made or attempted against the peace and safety of this his majesty's colony and dominion." Even in this document of rebellion, the commission still acknowledged Virginia as the dominion of "his majesty," the British king. With George Washington out of the colony, serving with the army in the North, that radical advocate for liberty, Patrick Henry, had become the most powerful man in Virginia. And, some thought, the most dangerous.[2]

OTHERS SAW LORD DUNMORE, the royal governor, as the colony's most dangerous man. On November 7, 1775, Dunmore irredeemably alienated many of the remaining colonists who still supported him or sought to negotiate with him. Ever since Henry's "Liberty or Death" speech in March, Dunmore had been threatening to free Virginia's slaves. Now, in what he called "a most disagreeable but absolutely necessary step," Dunmore declared "all indented servants, negroes, or others, (appertaining to rebels,) free that are able and willing to bear arms, they joining His Majesty's troops as soon as may be." Even though Dunmore (a slave owner himself) offered freedom only to those slaves who took up arms for the king, this was an unprecedented step toward emancipation. White Virginians were horrified. As colonel over Virginia's armed forces, Henry warned county officers that the proclamation was "fatal to the public safety." He called on all masters to monitor their slaves carefully, and advised slave patrols to watch for runaways.[3]

Even though Virginians such as Henry and Thomas Jefferson were fighting for liberty for Anglo-Americans, they could not fathom Dunmore's declaration of liberty for slaves. In the Virginia of fall 1775, there existed no greater catalyst for independence than Dunmore's proclamation; it convinced even reluctant rebels that the British meant to destroy them. The conflict between the colonists' ideals of freedom and the realities of slave-owning and war produced contradictory positions in white Virginians. In the short term, freedom for white southerners meant keeping the slaves under control. At the same time, the patriots' rhetoric of human liberty also forged the argument for the eventual freedom of slaves. Whatever slave-holding patriots, such as Jefferson, meant when they said "all men are created equal," they could not keep their words from implicating slavery. The Revolution, in this ironic sense, set the stage for the Civil War and emancipation.

THE VIRGINIA CONVENTION DID NOT OFFER Henry his colonelship without reservation. Moderates such as Robert W. Carter worried that Henry was too radical. "I really fear trusting him, as he is very popular, and I know his principles," Carter wrote to his father. Henry actually lost the first vote for command of Virginia's First Regiment, but won a majority in a runoff. The convention made it clear to Henry that he was authorized to act only on their orders and that he was forbidden from taking off on any more unauthorized expeditions like the one following Dunmore's seizure of the gunpowder. The convention believed that because of his popularity, Henry was the right choice for the job, and indeed he would find it relatively easy to recruit soldiers for his regiment, encamped near the College of William and Mary. Still, Henry's radical tendencies worried them. To control their new military leader, the convention appointed a Committee of Safety to direct the war effort, with the moderate Edmund Pendleton as its chair. Henry would continuously clash with this committee during his brief tenure in charge of Virginia's military.[4]

Henry's exclusive command quickly came into question. In late October, the Committee of Safety ordered Colonel William Woodford, an officer with experience from the Seven Years' War, to go to Norfolk to head off a British attack they feared would be launched there. They even granted Woodford authority to "give notice" to Henry if Woodford needed more men. Woodford's regiment prevented the British from burning the town of Hampton, but the colonel's action incited controversy over Henry's precise role in the Virginia militia. By early November, a group of Henry's officers complained to the Committee of Safety, a move that elicited a rebuke from Pendleton and the committee, who blamed Henry for his officers' "irregular" meeting, which they viewed as a "mark of [the officers'] suspicion of our judgment and prudence in providing for the safety of this place."[5]

Henry did continue to garner some admirers during his time as Virginia's military commander. Philip Mazzei, an Italian business-man in Virginia who would play an active role in the Revolution, re-called meeting Henry, whom he called "a man who has no superior in eloquence or in patriotism," on the way to Hampton. Henry mov-ingly thanked the volunteers for coming on the expedition, even though they had not yet engaged the British directly. Mazzei and his Italian friends, along with the Virginia troops, were charmed.[6]

By late November 1775, Virginia was descending into chaos. Lord Dunmore's notorious proclamation had heightened fears of vio-lence among Virginians, but some in the colony warned slaves not to be duped by the British. Dunmore had offered slaves freedom only if they did his bidding, noted a writer in the *Virginia Gazette*. This writer—likely addressing white patriots more than slaves— said the Americans were the true friends of freedom, claiming they had long tried to stop the "horrid traffic" in chattel slavery and re-minding readers of failed attempts by the House of Burgesses to ban the importation of slaves. The writer also warned the slaves that Dunmore might only sell them to the West Indies. "Be not then, ye negroes, tempted by this proclamation to ruin yourselves," the *Gazette* cautioned.[7]

Nevertheless, Dunmore's proclamation immediately led hundreds of slaves to join his forces. All told, somewhere between 800 and 1,500 Virginia slaves responded to the governor's call. Aggravating the alarm among Virginians were rumors that the British agents in the backcountry were trying to recruit Native Americans to fight against the patriots, in attacks that would amount to a pincer move-ment with Dunmore's slaves. The threats from slaves and Native

Americans, combined with the presence of Loyalists in the Tidewater region, made the patriots fear what December might bring. Dunmore went on to occupy Norfolk, sending patriots streaming into the colony's interior. The Goochland County Committee promised to take in refugees and called on fellow Virginians to "put their trust and confidence in the Supreme Being, whose arm is mighty to save, and who will, in due time, defend the cause of the oppressed."[8]

The first sign of relief for the patriots came December 9, when, in the first major armed confrontation of the Revolution in Virginia, William Woodford won a critical battle against Dunmore at Great Bridge, near Norfolk. Woodford and Dunmore set up fortifications on opposite sides of the Elizabeth River, north of Norfolk. Fearing impending rebel reinforcements, Dunmore ordered British troops across the bridge, only to have them brutally repulsed. The battle showed Virginians the hellish nature of armed conflict, with one participant writing that he saw "the horrors of war in perfection, worse than can be imagined; 10 and 12 bullets through many; limbs broke in 2 or 3 places; brains turning out. Good God, what a sight!" Woodford tartly boasted that Great Bridge was "a second Bunker's Hill affair, in miniature, with this difference, that we kept our post." Patriots marched captive slaves and Loyalists in chains to the Williamsburg jail. Eager to get the imprisoned slaves out of Virginia, the patriots sold them to traders in the West Indies and reimbursed their Virginia owners—at least those masters who were not Loyalists.[9]

The patriot victory at Great Bridge did not resolve tensions over Henry's position as commander in chief of Virginia's military. If anything, Woodford's success exacerbated the dissension between them. Henry hardly relished hanging back in the capital while Woodford confronted the hated Dunmore. Shortly before the Great Bridge battle, Henry complained to Woodford that he wasn't receiving intelligence about the situation at Norfolk, plaintively telling Woodford that "in case you think any thing could be done to aid and forward the enterprise you have in hand, please to write it." Henry was impatient for battle but could only wait to receive reports from Woodford. He continued to complain to the Committee of Safety, which lightly chastised Woodford two weeks after Great Bridge. They told Woodford that although he had a separate command from Henry's, he ought to communicate promptly with the commander in chief about the status of his regiment and explained that Woodford was subject to Henry's orders "when the Convention or Committee of Safety are not sitting, but that whilst either of these bodies are sitting he ought to receive his orders from one of them."[10]

The Committee of Safety's actions only postponed a resolution of Henry's role. Some officials had begun to question Henry's military skills, suggesting that his meteoric celebrity, not military qualifications, had led him to receive his command, and wondering whether Henry should return to a legislative role. Edmund Pendleton, Henry's antagonist on the Committee of Safety, wrote directly to Woodford and expressed concerns about Henry's competence. Pendleton told Woodford that "the unlucky step of calling that gentleman from our councils where he was useful, into the field in an important station, the duties of which he must in the nature of things, be an entire stranger to, has given me many an anxious and uneasy moment." Even George Washington wrote caustically in February 1776 that "my countrymen made a capitol mistake when they took Henry out of the Senate to place him in the field; and pity it is he does not see this, and remove every difficulty by a voluntary resignation." Henry had not done anything wrong except to make moderates nervous, but officers such as Washington legitimately preferred leaders in the field who had military experience.[11]

Henry's closest friends also suspected his talents were better suited for the civil sphere than for the military. John Adams, one of Henry's firmest patriot allies outside of Virginia, believed Henry would be useful in the army at this point because his oratorical gifts would motivate men for war. But he believed that Henry and Pennsylvania's John Dickinson were "better statesmen than soldiers, though I cannot say they are not very good in the latter character. Henry's principles, and systems, are much more comfortable to mine than the others, however."[12]

The uproar over Henry's position in the army climaxed when the Continental Congress merged regiments of the Virginia military into the Continental army. The Congress retained Henry as colonel over the First Virginia Regiment but took away his position as commander in chief. Moderates in Virginia, especially Edmund Pendleton, undoubtedly played a role in Henry's demotion. When the Committee of Safety offered Henry his commission as colonel, he "declared he could not accept of the same" and abruptly retired from military service.[13]

Henry's demotion and resignation nearly caused mutiny in the First Regiment. Patriot soldiers admired Henry's leadership record and questioned whether they could keep serving leaders who treated their hero this way. When they got the news of his resignation, the troops went into "deep mourning" and told Henry that they applauded his "spirited resentment to the most glaring indignity." Henry tried to reassure them, saying "I leave the service, but I leave my heart with you. May God bless you, and give you success and safety, and make you the glorious instruments of saving our country." The day the news reached his troops, Henry dined with many of the soldiers at the Raleigh Tavern in Williamsburg, where some of the men threatened to resign in protest of Henry's demotion, saying they would not serve under any other commander. To quell this revolt, Henry stayed an extra night in Williamsburg, assuring the soldiers that they could keep serving in good conscience and that he would work for the patriot cause in a legislative capacity. This quieted the surge of unrest, and the *Virginia Gazette* reported that the men were "pretty well reconciled" again to the American cause.[14]

The controversy over Henry's demotion and resignation churned in Virginia newspapers throughout March 1776, only months before the colony would declare independence from Britain. "A Friend to Truth" gave an account of the affair in the *Virginia Gazette* and claimed that the Committee of Safety had not meddled in Congress's decision. It was a matter of military policy, not personal rivalry, that had dictated the change in leadership. In the same issue, "An Honest Farmer" countered that jealous moderates had tried to neutralize Henry by confining him to a meaningless position. No one could keep Henry down, the Honest Farmer asserted, because he was Virginia's "able statesman, the soldier's father, the best of citizens, and liberty's dear friend. Clad with innocence, as in a coat of mail, he is proof against every serpentile whisper."[15]

The squabbling between Henry and the Virginia moderates had almost created a revolt in the army, but by late March, Richard Henry Lee wrote that it gave him "pleasure to find the mutinous spirit of our soldiery so well subdued." As Washington had noted, Henry probably was not suited to military leadership. Ironically, the shabby treatment he received from the Committee of Safety may have produced an outcome in Virginia's best interest: Henry's return to the political stage, where he had belonged all along.[16]

PATRICK HENRY HAD LONG PUSHED Virginians to resist parliamentary authority and to fight for America's liberty. But in 1776, he and his fellow patriots had to confront the most difficult decision they would face in all their years of advocating for the rights and liberties of Americans: declaring independence. It may seem strange that the fighting with the British commenced more than a year before Americans finally declared their commitment to self-rule, but this delay indicated how fearsome the prospect of independence was for most colonists. Independence entailed not only resistance to an unjust government but also an outright rejection of the king himself. It would indisputably cast America's political leaders like Henry as traitors, and require the formation of new alliances with European powers, such as the long-despised French. Even radicals, including Henry, seemed to take a collective breath before venturing into the uncharted landscape of independence.

Lord Dunmore had made independence a more compelling option for most of Virginia's colonists through his offer to emancipate slaves, but the patriots still had to make the case publicly. In Virginia, as elsewhere, the anonymous publication of Tom Paine's provocative pamphlet *Common Sense* in early 1776 electrified the debate over independence. Paine was almost the same age as Henry but had moved to Philadelphia from England only in 1774, leaving behind a ruined marriage and ruinous finances, and the specter of debtor's prison. What he brought with him was a phenomenal talent for rhetoric. Paine's brilliant, passionate writing matched Henry's oratory, and they became the two greatest catalysts of the Revolution.

In February, the *Virginia Gazette* printed a lengthy excerpt from *Common Sense*, ending with Paine's proclamation that the battles of Lexington and Concord in April 1775 had sealed his contempt for King George III: "No man was a warmer wisher for reconciliation than myself, before the fatal 19th of April 1775; but the moment the event of that day was made known I rejected the hardened, sullen-tempered Pharaoh of England forever, and disdain the wretch, that, with the pretended title of father of his people, can unfeelingly hear of their slaughter, and composedly sleep with their blood upon his soul." British sympathizers thought *Common Sense* was deplorable. A cranky Briton in Virginia named Nicholas Creswell, who was desperately trying to find a way to ship out of the colony, wrote in January 1776 that "a pamphlet called 'Commonsense' makes a great noise. One of the vilest things that ever was published to the world. Full of false representations, lies, calumny, and treason, whose principles are to subvert all kingly governments and erect an independent republic. I believe the writer to be some Yankey Presbyterian, member of the Congress." A week later, Creswell harrumphed that "nothing but independence will go down. The Devil is in the people."[17]

Paine and other advocates for independence had their work cut out for them, both in Virginia and in the other colonies. Writing from Cambridge, Massachusetts, in early April, George Washington acknowledged that agreeing to independence would represent a major break with the past for Virginians. "My countrymen I know, from their form of government, and steady attachment heretofore to royalty, will come reluctantly into the idea of independency; but time, and persecution, brings many wonderful things to pass." Washington thought Paine's pamphlet had clinched the argument: "by private letters which I have lately received from Virginia, I find Common Sense is working a powerful change there in the minds of many men."[18]

Although he had always been Britain's chief adversary among Virginia patriots, even Patrick Henry did not quickly decide for independence. His reservations had less to do with moral qualms than with timing. The question that gave him pause was whether Americans should wait to secure alliances with France or Spain before declaring independence. A resolution for independence would be the main topic of debate at the next Virginia Convention, where Henry would again represent the people of Hanover County. Days after his selection as a convention representative, Henry received an urgent letter from Richard Henry Lee, a delegate in the Continental Congress, pleading with Henry to rally Virginia behind immediate American self-determination. "Ages yet unborn, and millions existing at present, must rue or bless that assembly, on which their happiness or misery will so eminently depend," Lee wrote. "Virginia has hitherto taken the lead in great affairs, and many now look to her with anxious expectation." As for the issue of waiting until potential allies came to America's aid, Lee believed the nations of Europe would not align with America until it declared independence.[19]

Dunmore's November proclamation influenced the Congress to call for a day of prayer and fasting in May 1776, to repent for America's sins and to ask God for wisdom about the next step its people should take in light of the "warlike preparations of the British Ministry to subvert our invaluable rights and privileges, and to reduce us, by fire and sword, by the savages of the wilderness, and our own domestics, to the most abject and ignominious bondage." The Congress failed to note the contradiction inherent in their fear that the British incitement of Americans' "domestics" (slaves) would force free whites into bondage. They hoped that "through the merits and mediation of Jesus Christ" they might obtain forgiveness and victory. They further asked for God to "direct them to the most efficacious measures for establishing the rights of America on the most honorable and permanent basis." In other words, they sought God's guidance on whether they should declare independence now. The Virginia Convention happily complied with the request to observe the solemn day, with delegates instructing their chaplain, Thomas Price, to preach at Williamsburg's Anglican church, Bruton Parish, on the occasion.[20]

By the time its people appointed a new convention, many in Virginia had already decided in favor of immediate independence. Freeholders from Charlotte County directed their delegates to support a break with Britain right away. Their instructions railed against the British government's plot to destroy Americans' liberty, declaring that British conspirators against freedom had sought to "enforce their arbitrary mandates by fire and sword, and likewise encouraging, by every means in their power, our savage neighbors, and our more savage domestics, to spill the blood of our wives and children." The residents of Charlotte County believed "nothing is intended for us but the most abject slavery." Fear of attacks from Indians as well as insurrection by slaves, both openly encouraged by the British, pushed these Virginians over the edge; now they would settle for nothing less than severing the connection with Britain.[21]

Henry also wanted independence, but he continued to puzzle over the timing. We gather a sense of his reluctance from an insistent letter sent by General Charles Lee, a veteran of the Seven Years' War whom the Congress named commander of the Southern Department of the unfolding conflict. Like Tom Paine, Lee had only recently moved from Britain to America, acquiring an estate in northwestern Virginia, and he had quickly become convinced that independence was inevitable. Lee was a peculiar person: tall, thin, slovenly, and generally unpleasant. John Adams called him a "queer creature" who took his large pack of dogs with him wherever he went. "You must love his dogs if you love him," Adams wrote, "and forgive a thousand whims for the sake of the soldier." Lee spoke with Henry about the break with Britain on May 6 and followed up with his letter the next day. He was exasperated that Henry thought Americans might need to wait on independence until they could be confident of foreign aid, and told Henry he had received intelligence that France in particular would come to America's side. (Lee was eventually proven correct in this assumption.) Lee also insisted that the popular mood in Virginia, especially among the soldiers, favored American autonomy. "The spirit of the people (except a very few in these lower parts of Virginia whose little blood has been sucked out by mosquitoes) cry out for this declaration, the military in particular." Because of Henry's insight into the hearts of the fighting men, Lee felt sure that he would realize the time for independence was upon them. Any other path would lead to tyranny, he warned.[22]

Henry was finally convinced. An immediate declaration of independence would put America in a stronger diplomatic position. Richard Henry Lee and Charles Lee persuaded him that France and Spain would never consider an alliance with America as long as it considered itself under the authority of Great Britain. Proclaiming independence would communicate America's seriousness about forging ahead on its own, and it would show other European nations that they could make deals with America at Britain's expense. The patriots would try to appease Britain no longer.

The Virginia Convention was almost unanimously behind independence, but the wording of the declaration remained in question. Everyone expected Henry to deliver a final speech on the subject, in the tradition of his Stamp Act and "Liberty or Death" speeches, which would stir the delegates and help define their rhetoric. But Henry hung back, apparently wanting no one to think the convention had agreed to independence merely because of his emotional appeals. The convention considered several versions of resolutions, including one drafted by Henry but introduced by Thomas Nelson Jr., a Tidewater aristocrat and committed patriot. As usual, Henry produced the most radical resolution on the subject, accusing the British of "making every preparation to crush us" and inciting Indians and slaves to attack. It called King George III a tyrant and, in what it declared to be an act of self-preservation, dissolved Virginia's relationship with Great Britain. It also insisted that the Continental Congress move immediately to declare the united colonies independent.[23]

Having introduced this resolution, Henry waited to let consensus build before stepping forward. Finally, as Edmund Randolph put it, Henry "appeared in an element for which he was born. To cut the knot, which calm prudence was puzzled to untie, was worthy of the magnificence of his genius. He entered into no subtlety of reasoning but was roused by the now apparent spirit of the people as a pillar of fire, which notwithstanding the darkness of the prospect would conduct to the promised land." In Randolph's view, Henry led Virginians like Moses, out of the clutches of British enslavement.[24]

A compromise version of the resolution for independence borrowed heavily from Henry's, proclaiming that despite the colonists' best attempts to reconcile with Britain, imperial officials wished to "effect our total destruction," and singling out Lord Dunmore for "carrying on a piratical and savage war against us tempting our slaves by every artifice to resort to him and training and employing them against their masters." The declaration was not as direct as Henry's, but it certainly indicated that the Virginia Convention wanted the Continental Congress to declare independence for the colonies as a whole, which they would do in July. Virginians would take the lead there, too, with Richard Henry Lee introducing the motion for national independence, and Thomas Jefferson penning the declaration itself.[25]

The convention unanimously adopted Virginia's compromise resolution on May 15. Only one cautious delegate, Robert Carter Nicholas, spoke against independence, but even he decided not to register a vote against the resolution. Henry was delighted with the action taken, though not thrilled with the resolution's wording. He wrote to John Adams that he "put up with [the resolution] in the present form, for the sake of unanimity. 'Tis not quite so pointed as I could wish." Henry rarely felt that his colleagues moved fast enough, but in this case he conceded to moderation to preserve unity. A split vote for independence would have communicated the wrong message at this critical moment.[26]

Williamsburg broke out in celebration as the word spread. Residents took a collection to throw a party for local soldiers, who held a parade the day after the resolution passed. A new American union flag was flown from the capitol. Then, on May 17, delegates gathered at Bruton Parish Church for the day of prayer and fasting called earlier by the Continental Congress. The sermon for the day was on

II Chronicles 20:15: "Thus saith the Lord unto you: Be not afraid, nor dismayed, by reason of this great multitude; for the battle is not yours, but God's."[27]

Elsewhere in America, patriots rejoiced at the news of Virginia's independence. John Adams wrote to Henry and exulted that "the decree is gone forth, and it cannot be recalled, that a more equal liberty, than has prevailed in other parts of the earth, must be established in America."[28]

Having called for independence, the Virginia convention set about crafting a Declaration of Rights and a new state constitution. Henry played an important role on the committee delegated to prepare them. John Adams sent him suggestions for the constitution. "Happy Virginia, whose Constitution is to be framed by so masterly a builder," he wrote. Henry would hardly act alone, of course. "The political cooks are busy in preparing the dish," Edmund Pendleton wrote to Jefferson, and the main course of the convention was the Declaration of Rights. The committee drafting the Declaration was formidable, and it was Henry's and young James Madison's first opportunity to work together directly. But George Mason took the lead in writing the Declaration of Rights and the Virginia constitution. Mason, eleven years older than Henry, lived on the Gunston Hall estate on the Potomac River, close to George Washington's Mount Vernon. Like Henry, Mason had little formal schooling, but he had read deeply in the traditions of constitutional law. In the Declaration of Rights, the Virginia Convention had an opportunity to ground the state's political liberties on the inviolable basis of natural rights. What Mason and the convention produced would help shape America's Declaration of Independence and, later, the Bill of Rights.[29]

The first article of the Declaration proclaimed that "all men are by nature equally free and independent, and have certain inherent rights." This wording caused some consternation at the convention, when members such as Robert Carter Nicholas feared that it would fuel more unrest among the slave population. Edmund Randolph recalled that the convention generally felt that when "asserting the general rights of man, we ought not to be too nice and too much restricted in the delineation of them." And planters did not consider slaves as members of political society; the article made clear that only members of that society could claim political rights. Within the month, Thomas Jefferson would modify Mason's language in this article as he crafted the Declaration of Independence.[30]

Edmund Randolph also remembered that Patrick Henry had proposed the fifteenth and sixteenth articles of the Declaration of Rights. Henry did not actually write these articles, which were penned by Mason and James Madison, respectively. But he undoubtedly backed their adoption. The fifteenth article distilled the kind of Christian republicanism Henry always propounded: "That no free government, or the blessings of liberty, can be preserved to any people but by a firm adherence to justice, moderation, temperance, frugality, and virtue and by frequent recurrence to fundamental principles." Liberty would degenerate without virtue, Henry and his fellow founders believed, because true freedom served noble purposes. For a republic to stay on the right path, its leaders had to renew its reliance on the great traditional sources of morality and liberty—the classics of Greek and Roman antiquity, and the Bible—to test the legitimacy of current practices.[31]

Henry played a critical role in crafting the Declaration of Rights' sixteenth article, regarding religious freedom. Henry had long supported religious liberty in Virginia, going back to the ferment of the Great Awakening and to his role in the Parsons' Cause of 1763. Henry had consistently worked in the House of Burgesses to establish legal toleration for dissenters. In an undated fragment probably written in the late 1760s or early 1770s, Henry declared that a society that permitted religious dissent was on the path to virtue and prosperity. No one denomination had an exclusive title to Christian morality, so allowing all to practice their faith freely would allow virtue to flourish, Henry averred. Such freedom would also attract a variety of European immigrants and workers, many of whom were Presbyterian, Lutheran, or other types of non-Anglican Christians, whose presence and hard work would strengthen the society's moral and economic fiber. For Henry, such settlers were much preferable to bound African-Americans, because of slavery's negative effects on whites and blacks. He feared that Virginia was becoming a "gloomy retreat of slaves," and much preferred a diverse society of free European Protestants.[32]

Religious pluralism was already becoming a salient tenet of the era's revolutionaries. Henry and George Washington both supported having a variety of Protestant ministers serve as chaplains in the army. In 1775, Virginia Baptists petitioned the convention to allow their ministers to serve Baptist soldiers. During the May 1776 convention, Henry drafted a resolution allowing the practice. Similarly, Washington always encouraged a range of denominational chaplains in the Continental army; their presence fostered moral behavior, and ministers of different denominations defused religious controversies among the troops. Congress even authorized the employment of a Catholic chaplain to serve regiments from Canada.[33]

Once the Virginia Convention declared independence from Britain, many in the state believed it was time to end the state's support for the Anglican Church. For years, the Baptists had been petitioning the House of Burgesses for relief from the requirements of the Anglican establishment. Within days of independence, Baptists from Prince William County again petitioned the convention, arguing that since Americans were contending for their basic liberties, Virginians should also respect the fundamental religious rights of their fellow citizens. Disestablishing the Anglican Church would prevent internal divisions over religion in Virginia, they maintained, going on to ask that they be allowed to worship God with no state interference and be relieved from religious taxes that supported the Anglican Church. Henry was certainly sympathetic to their argument for religious freedom; he understood that the Anglican patriots should actively court the Baptists to win their support for independence. In a public letter he wrote in August, Henry praised the growing interdenominational spirit in America and declared that "the only contest among us, at this most critical and important period, is, who shall be foremost to preserve our religious and civil liberties." As patriots, Anglicans and Baptists were "brethren who must perish or triumph together."[34]

Mason, Henry, and the other delegates were coming under considerable pressure to make a statement on religious freedom in the Declaration of Rights. After much debate, the committee concluded "that religion, or the duty which we owe to our Creator and the manner of discharging it, can be directed by reason and conviction, not by force or violence; and therefore, all men are equally entitled to the free exercise of religion, according to the dictates of conscience; and that it is the mutual duty of all to practice Christian forbearance, love, and charity towards each other." James Madison, who loathed the persecution of the Baptists, drafted this article. He also had Henry introduce an amendment to the article that seemed to imply disestablishment of the Anglican Church, asserting that "no man or class of men ought on account of religion to be invested with peculiar emoluments or privileges; nor subjected to any penalties or disabilities." When other delegates challenged him, however, Henry denied that this amendment was intended to end state support for the Anglican Church, although that probably was Madison's goal. Henry, unlike Madison, saw no inconsistency between state support for religion and religious freedom.[35]

The convention formally approved the Declaration of Rights on June 12. The document was a momentous articulation of the human rights upon which government should not intrude. Virginia had adopted these articles, Edmund Randolph explained, so that "in all the revolutions of time, of human opinion, and of government, a perpetual standard should be erected, around which the people might rally and by a notorious record be forever admonished to be watchful, firm, and virtuous."[36]

The convention, led by George Mason, also established a new state constitution, in which the lower house of the legislature, now called the House of Delegates, held most of the power. Henry was concerned that the proposed constitution gave too little authority to the governor. The convention apparently feared the dangers of executive power, having just entered a war against one of the world's most powerful monarchs. But Henry believed that war required stronger executive power, and in the debates over the document, he insisted that the governor needed veto power over legislation. Henry declared that under the new constitution, the governor would be a "mere phantom," dependent on the will of the legislators. Henry's position on the governorship is somewhat strange, given that he would oppose the new federal Constitution in 1788 partly based on the expansive executive power it gave the president. But his stance also signaled Henry's fundamental pragmatism: compared with Jefferson, Madison, and John Adams, Henry was always more concerned about responding to current circumstances than maintaining ideological purity.[37]

On June 29, the same day they unanimously adopted the new constitution, the delegates voted for the commonwealth's first governor. Ironically, they chose Henry, the chief critic of the new governor's office. Whatever reluctance he may have felt, Henry accepted the position. Believing that "the lasting happiness or misery of a great proportion of the human species" was at stake in the war, he knew the state needed effective leadership more than ever.[38]

Because Henry remained the most popular politician in Virginia, and a favorite of Virginia's military, his election as governor garnered public support for the new government. Moderates may have also seen his election as a way of controlling Henry. It would not be the last time they would remove him from the legislature by making him governor. When the first legislature convened that fall, they chose Henry's archenemy, Edmund Pendleton, as the first Speaker of the House of Delegates, which arguably was the most powerful position in the government. But legislative power—the ability to control the processes of government—is not the only kind of power. Henry's personality would prove hard to contain, even in the governor's mansion.[39]

# 7

## "OUR WORTHY GOVERNOR"

## Patrick Henry in Wartime

L ANDON CARTER, ONE OF VIRGINIA'S most wealthy and reactionary planters, knew Henry had won the governorship fair and square, so he resolved to mourn the "destructive tendency in secret." But then, on July 13, Carter received exciting news: Patrick Henry had died! Carter deemed this development "particularly favourable by the hand of Providence." Unfortunately for Carter and for Henry's other opponents, it turned out that the governor was only sick, not dead.[1]

Moderate Virginians were hardly thrilled to have Patrick Henry as governor. They saw him as an extremist, and extremism in such a volatile moment was the last thing they thought Virginia needed. Of course, other Virginians were delighted with Henry's election. The soldiers of the First and Second Regiments, among his staunchest supporters, praised him as the ideal governor: "Uninfluenced by private ambition, regardless of sordid interest, you have uniformly pursued the general good of your country," they told him.

Henry wrote back and reminded them that as heavy a burden as the governor's office might be, "to you is assigned the glorious task of saving, by your valour, all that is dear to mankind." He encouraged them to fight on for Virginia's deliverance.[2]

Even as Henry chafed at the constitutional limitations imposed on the governor's office, he became the public face of Virginia during its first three years of independence. The House of Delegates possessed most of the state's legislative authority, but they were in session only part of the year, with Henry administering the war effort year-round, a job he relished because of the close connection he had forged with the military. The British had begun to focus their attention on invading New York City, and the royal governor, Dunmore, having lost control of Virginia, left the state in August 1776. Rumors circulated that Dunmore might return to Virginia at the head of a large British army, but this threat did not materialize.[3]

As indicated by the erroneous reports of his death, Henry struggled badly with his health during the summer and fall of 1776, which distracted him from the daunting challenges he still faced. As the delegates to the Continental Congress drafted, redrafted, and then approved the Declaration of Independence that July in Philadelphia, Patrick Henry was falling seriously ill. He was sworn in as governor on July 6 and quickly left Williamsburg to recuperate at home. Henry's medical troubles would become an issue for the rest of his life. It is often difficult to discern what specifically was wrong with him, medical care and diagnoses being essentially medieval in that era, even for the elite, but the timing of his sickness suggests a malaria-related fever that he might have contracted in Williamsburg. As would become his standard practice during the summer, Henry retreated to Scotchtown, which stood on relatively high ground, away from swampy lowlands and mosquitoes. Bedridden, Henry slowly recovered, and the *Virginia Gazette* reported happily in August that "our worthy governor . . . is so much recovered from his late severe indisposition that he walks out daily." The newspaper hoped he could return to the capital soon, which Henry was indeed able to do.[4]

Arriving in Williamsburg in September, Henry confronted a dire military situation, with little power to respond to the setbacks American forces were experiencing in the northern states. He and Washington exchanged letters shortly after the general's nearly disastrous flight from New York City. The British had abandoned Boston in March 1776 and then attacked New York beginning on August 22. Washington's army staged a defense of Brooklyn Heights, but because Washington had divided his army between Long Island and Manhattan, he was nearly overwhelmed by the British, evacuating his remaining soldiers with no time to spare. Henry reported to Washington some victories against the Cherokees on the western frontier of Virginia, where, despite Henry's amicable statements toward the Indians, troops from the southern states would prosecute a brief, nasty war with them until a preliminary peace was signed in April 1777. Henry also worried that the British might be planning a naval invasion of the state. Lord Dunmore and his British troops had left Virginia for New York, but patriot leaders worried he would eventually return with a much larger force. Henry had heard about Washington's narrow escape from Brooklyn. "I trust every virtuous man will be stimulated by it to fresh exertions," he wrote.[5]

Washington responded with urgency, declaring that he needed a regular army to fight the British—a well-trained and committed national military. He was disgusted with the state militias, "who from an utter disregard of all discipline and restraint among themselves are but too apt to infuse the like spirit into others." In the aftermath of the Battle of Long Island, whole militia regiments had deserted Washington, to his horror. The militiamen might be fit to fight Indians in isolated frontier skirmishes, Washington wrote, but he warned Henry not to depend on them should a British invasion come. In September, the Congress had authorized a recruitment campaign to bolster Washington's Continental army with soldiers who would serve for the duration of the war. Virginia was instructed to deliver fifteen battalions, and Washington urged Henry to do whatever he could to produce the officers and soldiers he needed.[6]

General Washington was desperate. As his army fled through New York and New Jersey in the fall of 1776, the patriots faced their darkest hour. Tom Paine, serving in the Continental army, penned the famous lines "These are the times that try men's souls. The summer soldier and the sunshine patriot will, in this crisis, shrink from the service of his country; but he that stands it NOW, deserves the love and thanks of man and woman."[7]

Alarmed by Washington's letter and frustrated at the constitutional limitations of his office, Henry became convinced that the crisis was so urgent that he needed special wartime powers to raise and supply troops for the national army and for Virginia's own defense in case of an invasion. Recruitment had gone badly earlier in the year, not least because of resentment among the troops and potential soldiers over Henry's treatment by the Committee of Safety. Many Virginians also feared that enlisting would mean serving in the Continental army outside of Virginia, with little guarantee of supplies, payment, or success. In December, the House of Delegates gave Henry the broad authority he sought to make requisitions, pay for supplies, order troop movements, and raise additional battalions. Jealous of its prerogatives, the legislature limited the term of his mandate to only a few months. The delegates warned Henry that "this departure from the constitution of government, being in this instance founded only on the most evident and urgent necessity, ought not hereafter to be drawn into precedent." Virginia was already wrestling with the problems of a weak governor's position in wartime.[8]

Thomas Jefferson was among those unhappy with the legislature's authorization. Five years later, he would assert that Henry and the delegates were trying to create "a dictator, invested with every power legislative, executive, and judiciary, civil and military, of life and death, over our persons and over our properties." By any standard, his claim was an exaggeration. Nevertheless, it is significant to note that Henry did often support strengthening the governorship. He did not abuse his power during the emergency, and his bid made sense given the intense panic among the patriots in December 1776, when it seemed that all could be lost. His brief expansion of executive authority was a pragmatic move, yet it is one that contradicted his later opposition to executive power granted under the U.S. Constitution. Perhaps Henry reasoned that a temporary but robust expansion of power (placed in his own responsible hands, of course) could be justified due to the greater threat to liberty the British army presented.[9]

Even with the governor's expanded command, enlarging the army continued to prove extremely difficult. Beyond the rampant inflation that encouraged speculators to gouge the army with high prices for basic supplies, agents from other states were also recruiting soldiers from Virginia, driving up costs for the bounties that the state paid enlistees and reducing the number of available men. Disease was also ravaging the soldiers who had already enlisted. "The terrors of the smallpox, added to the lies of deserters and want of necessaries, are fatal objections to the continental service," Henry wrote to Richard Henry Lee. Washington agreed with Henry that fear of smallpox was keeping many from enlisting, but instead of turning to short-term volunteers, he suggested that Henry move forward with more aggressive inoculation campaigns. Henry sympathized with these tactics: he himself had received inoculation (the intentional introduction of a mild strain of smallpox, to promote immunity) from Dr. Benjamin Rush while in Philadelphia for the Continental Congress. Washington had already ordered Virginia troops to receive inoculation as soon as they enlisted.[10]

In December 1776, some relief did come for Washington, when his army scored a great symbolic victory at the Battle of Trenton in New Jersey. On Christmas night, the general's weary force crossed the Delaware River in the midst of a blizzard of sleet, surprising and capturing a garrison of 1,500 Hessian troops, mercenaries hired by the British to fight in the war. Washington pulled off another win a week later at Princeton, New Jersey, helping to convince Americans that the war was worth carrying forward.

Trenton and Princeton were valuable victories, but they hardly solved the problems of enlisting soldiers. The difficulty in recruitment created tension between Henry and Washington, who had very different views of how best to fill the ranks of the army. Henry asked Washington in March 1777 to approve a plan that would allow him to return to raising volunteers for six- to eight-month terms. He had recently recruited such volunteers from the western parts of Virginia, in the Shenandoah Valley, and he thought they could supply their own firearms and clothing. He also suggested that these volunteer companies could choose their own captains.[11]

Washington angrily replied to Henry that he needed a professional army that he could train, discipline, and count on to stay long-term. As for Henry's volunteer scheme, Washington wrote, "I can not countenance in the smallest degree, what I know to be pernicious in the extreme. Short enlistments when founded on the best plan, are repugnant to order and subversive of discipline, and men held upon such terms, will never be equal to the important ends of war; but when they are of the *volunteer kind*, they are still more destructive." Henry quickly dropped the idea, saying that he deferred to the general's opinions in military matters. Despite their disagreements, Washington's pleas had gotten Henry's attention. The governor wrote repeatedly to Colonel Charles Lewis of Albemarle County in early 1777 instructing him to take his regiment north to support Washington. He urged Lewis to move as quickly as possible, despite the incompleteness of his regiment, before the Continental army should "receive a wound that may prove mortal."[12]

Even though he was struggling to manage the war in Virginia and support the military campaign of the new United States, Henry was reelected as governor in May 1777. But he would be plagued by the same problems in his new term. In May, the legislature passed a plan for more vigorous recruitment and, if necessary, a compulsory draft. But the new policy resulted in desertions and ever-higher expenses. "Although it seems impossible to enlist continental recruits here," Henry told Washington, "yet the zeal of our countrymen is great and general in the public cause." But revolutionary zeal often could not overcome Virginians' fear of the prospect of deprivation or death when serving as soldiers in the Continental army.[13]

Henry faced a fundamental problem common across a nation barely a year old: many Virginians were motivated to fight for their homes and their state, but not for the new country called "America." When a British fleet entered the Chesapeake Bay in August 1777, Henry called out county militias to defend against invasion and, in a letter to George Wythe, expressed his delight at the response he received: "amid all the discouragements which the backwardness of our countrymen to enlist into the regular service throws us under, I congratulate you, Sir, on the zeal and alacrity with which that demand was generally complied with." As many as 5,000 men were said to have risen up to defend Virginia against the invasion (which never materialized). Given the stark contrast between Virginians' enthusiastic participation in the militias, and their resistance to enlisting in the Continental army, we can understand Henry's sanguine attitude about militias. For these volunteers, Virginia commanded more allegiance than did their new nation. This devotion to one's state was a sentiment many Americans would continue to feel strongly, even after the war's end.[14]

The Continental army continued to struggle in the North. The British launched a massive campaign against Philadelphia in July, resulting in a clash at Brandywine Creek, about thirty miles southwest of Philadelphia, on September 11. There, Washington suffered a humiliating defeat with about 1,100 men dead, wounded, or captured. Two weeks later the British occupied Philadelphia itself. On October 4, Washington tried to surprise a British garrison at Germantown, five miles north of Philadelphia, but his complicated plan of attack was repulsed. The Continental Congress was forced to flee to York, Pennsylvania.

Washington was discovering that America's national government was not designed for the kind of nimble authority needed in wartime. In 1776, the patriots had summoned the Continental Congress to address the crisis with Britain, not to create a national entity that would be sovereign over the states. America's initial political framework was formalized in late 1777 when Congress approved the Articles of Confederation, the first constitution of the United States. Then Congress sent it to the states for ratification, a dilatory process that lasted until 1781. But from 1777 until 1789, the Articles comprised America's government. The novelty of American political union is evident in the very beginning of the document, when Article I states that the "style of this confederacy shall be, 'The United States of America.'" Until then, no one really knew what the independent country would be called.[15]

As its name suggested, the national government under the Articles was a *confederation* of sovereign, independent states. This was no fully integrated nation. The Articles meant only to codify a unified entity authorized to conduct war and diplomacy on behalf of the states. But even the Confederation's power to make war was restricted by the fact that the Congress—the only branch of the new government—lacked the power to tax. Instead, the state legislatures were supposed to tax their respective citizens and deliver funds for the "charges of war" to the Congress. The contributions due from the states would be proportional to the value of the land in each. This sounded good in principle, but in the desperate economic circumstances of war, the states routinely evaded their responsibility to supply requested funds.[16]

Despite its structural defects, the Confederation government was not totally ineffective, as some historians have suggested. It was functional enough, after all, to enable Americans to defeat the British in the American Revolution. But the lack of taxing authority did result in paralyzing inefficiencies that George Washington found exasperating as commander of the Continental army. After the war, Washington and his allies James Madison and Alexander Hamilton would decide the Articles of Confederation did not afford the nation nearly enough power—a decision that Patrick Henry would ultimately denounce, in the debate over ratifying the Constitution.

Washington's humiliation in Philadelphia threatened to arouse the same desperation Americans had felt after the defeats of the previous fall. New movements by British forces sought to drive a wedge between New England and the rest of the colonies. In fall 1777, General John Burgoyne hoped to move his lumbering force of 9,000 men to the south along Lake Champlain to the Hudson River and Albany. But repeated battles with Continentals and American militia wore his army down, and ultimately Burgoyne surrendered his army at Saratoga, New York, on October 17.

News of the great victory arrived in Virginia within two weeks, and Williamsburg held a military parade to celebrate. Cannon discharges and three volleys of musket fire were followed by "3 huzzas from all present; joy and satisfaction, upon the occasion, was evident in the countenance of every one; and the evening was celebrated with ringing of bells, illuminations, and etc." Governor Henry enhanced the festivities by ordering a "gill of rum" for each soldier.[17]

Henry knew the victory at Saratoga warranted more than merriment. He proclaimed a day of public thanksgiving, with the hope that Virginians might not, "through a vain and presumptuous confidence in our own strength, be led away to forget the hand of Heaven, whose assistance we have so often in times of distress implored, and which, as frequently before, so more especially now, we have experienced in this signal success of the arms of the United States, whereby the divine sanction of the righteousness of our cause is most illustriously displayed." According to Henry and other Christian patriots, proper dependence on God began with their acknowledgment of divine blessings, of which Saratoga was an obvious example. Henry worried that Americans might turn away from God, ironically, at those moments of military success for which they had prayed. Victory might tempt them to become ungrateful, arrogant, or lazy. He closed the proclamation with the prayer "God save the United States," replacing the familiar pre-Revolutionary prayer of "God save the king."[18]

AMID THE ANXIETIES OF WAR, Patrick Henry found some personal happiness. In October 1777, two and a half years after Sarah's untimely death, he married Dorothea Dandridge. Dorothea, in her early twenties, was much younger than Henry, who was forty-one. Coming from a prestigious family—she was the daughter of Nathaniel West Dandridge, Henry's family friend and law client—she helped Henry grow even more connected to wealthy Virginia elites. She and Patrick would eventually have eleven children together—in addition to his six children from his marriage with Sarah—although two of them died very young. Dorothea brought twelve slaves into the marriage, upping Henry's total number of bound workers to forty-two. He sold his Scotchtown plantation and moved his family onto a new one, Leatherwood, situated on 10,000 acres in Henry County, a new jurisdiction in southern Virginia recently named for him. Such new land acquisitions appealed to Henry and other Virginians of means, even in wartime. Many, including Henry, wanted the state to expand its power into the western territories, especially Kentucky, to develop more land. But with this push, Virginians also wanted to eliminate the western territories as a base for British operations and to secure settlers against disgruntled Native Americans, who were inclined to side with the British in the Revolution.[19]

George Rogers Clark, a young surveyor and soldier in Kentucky, became Virginia's leading fighter against the British and Native Americans in the West. (Clark was the older brother of William, who would become famous thanks to the Lewis and Clark expedition, which occurred during Thomas Jefferson's presidency.) Clark not only clamored for a vigorous defense of Kentucky, which had recently been organized as a large county of Virginia, but he also proposed attacks against small British outposts in the distant Illinois country. Ultimately he hoped to lead an army against the British fort at Detroit, where a victory could end all western threats against Virginia.

To begin his campaign, Clark appealed to Henry for permission to attack the small British and French settlement at Kaskaskia in southern Illinois. He claimed, dubiously, that Kaskaskia was a key staging area for British and Native American attacks against Kentucky. Nevertheless, in December 1777, Henry and the Virginia government agreed to sponsor the expedition. The governor issued two sets of instructions to keep Clark's real mission a secret. Publicly, Clark was authorized simply to raise a militia and proceed to Kentucky. The secret orders directed Clark's militia to push ahead and attack Kaskaskia. Henry advised Clark to treat mercifully any British residents of Illinois who professed allegiance to Virginia. But those who remained loyal to the empire "must feel the miseries of war," the governor insisted. Jefferson, George Mason, and George Wythe also supported Clark's expedition, hoping it would score revenge for the area's recent Indian attacks, which they viewed as cruel and unprovoked. They assured Clark that his militiamen could count on a reward of three hundred acres each, derived from lands taken from Native Americans.[20]

The promise of the expedition immediately clashed with the realities of wartime Virginia. The state had few excess men or resources to draw on for a grand campaign into the West. Within three weeks of giving his approval, Henry was scolding Clark for trying to recruit volunteers from south-central Virginia. Any available men from those counties were needed for the Continental army, and Henry understood that Clark had agreed to seek recruits primarily from Kentucky and the western counties. Clark struggled badly to raise his militia; soon he also had to combat rumors spreading among his small army that the expedition against Illinois was only a pretext for a land grab by Clark, Henry, and others in the Virginia gentry, which led to a rash of desertions. Nevertheless, Clark and his troops easily seized Kaskaskia and Vincennes in July 1778, a success that Henry said "equaled the most sanguine expectations." One of Henry's letters to Clark during this period revealed a somewhat surprising glimpse of vanity in the governor, when Henry pressed Clark to secure him "two of the best stallions that [can] possibly be found at the Illinois." The expense of the horses and their transport to Virginia was no object, Henry wrote, because he simply wanted the best pureblood Spanish horses available. Letters like this, as well as Henry's preoccupation with land acquisitions, show that despite Henry's emphasis on virtue, he too wrestled occasionally with the temptations of luxury.[21]

Clark's claims of victory, and Henry's subsequent trumpeting of them, minimized the difficulty and qualified success of this western campaign. Clark's venture would not turn out quite as well as expected; Vincennes was soon retaken by British and Indian forces from Detroit. Clark unexpectedly decided to attack Vincennes again during the winter, marching through flooded, icy rivers to lay siege to the lightly defended fort in February 1779. After managing to capture a small detachment of British-allied French and Indian scouts, Clark's men tomahawked three of the Indian prisoners. Then, on Clark's orders, they proceeded to partially scalp one of the French Canadian soldiers within sight of the fort. This brutal measure had its intended effect, and the British promptly surrendered Vincennes back to Clark. Again, Henry reported that the campaign had "succeeded to our utmost wishes."[22]

Despite Clark's early success, Henry and Clark never cooperated well. By the time of Clark's second Vincennes campaign, serious problems began to divide them. Clark grew angry that Henry and his government failed to communicate regularly with the western frontier. He wrote in February 1779 that he had not received any intelligence from Henry for almost a year, at a time when he desperately wanted reinforcements. Clark still appealed to Henry to help him to secure frontier lands, but knew that his hope for wealth and acreage was becoming illusory. The western front was only of secondary concern to Henry, and inefficient means of communication continually degraded his relationship with Clark.[23]

After Henry left the governor's office in 1779, his successor, Thomas Jefferson, would continue to take a hopeful view of Clark's foray into the Illinois country. Other Virginia officials, including Henry, began to think Clark was squandering Virginia's opportunities there by draining resources in roguish expeditions and failing to secure the state's control of the region. Rumors suggested that Clark was a drunk. Back in the Virginia legislature, Henry became one of Clark's chief enemies and opposed any further plans for an attack on Detroit by Clark's militia.

Henry's and Jefferson's developing animosity—which would boil over in 1781, when Henry proposed an investigation of Jefferson's conduct as governor—may have hurt Clark, too. Jefferson sympathetically wrote to Clark in 1782 and commented obliquely that he was surprised "to find one person hostile to you as far as he has personal courage to show hostility to any man. Who he is you will probably have heard." Jefferson left little doubt about this enemy's identity when he noted that he considered the man as "all tongue without either head or heart" and consumed with "crooked schemes." Many of Henry's antagonists would have agreed with that description. In their view, Henry was a gifted orator who did not act on his own fine words, and who exhibited less than virtuous behavior in land grabs and ill-conceived ventures in the West, including Clark's. Henry was not Clark's only enemy, however. Benjamin Harrison, who became Virginia governor after Jefferson, excoriated Clark for failing to build forts in the West that the Virginia government had ordered. When Clark arrived in Richmond in 1783, hoping to plan a new war against the western Indians, Harrison removed him from his command.[24]

Henry's involvement with the sometimes sordid exploits of George Rogers Clark reminds us that Henry and the Virginians were interested in controlling the West for various reasons: security, expansion, and personal wealth. As noble as Henry's patriotic ideals may have been, he was not averse to profiting from the removal of the British.

DESPITE THE ATTENTION Clark's expedition garnered, in the winter of 1777–78, Henry and his fellow patriots were chiefly concerned with the survival of the Continental army. Although the victory at Saratoga had lifted Americans' spirits, the fact remained that Washington's branch of the army had been humiliated in the battles around Philadelphia. Washington settled into winter quarters at Valley Forge, where a disaster slowly unfolded: poor supplies and disease would eventually lead to the loss of nearly a quarter of the Continental troops at the camp. Although it is hard to imagine in retrospect, this winter of discontent easily could have led to Washington's ouster as general. Some of the general's commanders, including Saratoga hero Horatio Gates, had begun a whispering campaign to have Washington replaced. Henry had his share of disagreements with Washington about military affairs, and in early 1778 his loyalty to the general would face a severe test.

News of the conspiracy to oust Washington reached Henry by mid-February, when he received a shocking letter from a correspondent who claimed to know him but identified himself only as a "Philadelphia friend." The letter began by flattering Henry, recalling how he "taught us to shake off our idolatrous attachment to royalty, and to oppose its encroachment upon our liberties with our very lives. By these means you saved us from ruin." The writer went on to lament the troubles Americans had brought on themselves in the past year. He particularly worried about Washington's army, which he considered an undisciplined mob. But the correspondent thought the patriot cause could be revitalized if Gates or another general from the northern branch of the Continentals replaced Washington.[25]

The anonymous writer seemed to have assumed that Henry would recognize his identity; he implored Henry not to tell anyone about the letter or its author, even asking Henry to destroy it. Would Henry, he asked, spread the word that it was time to remove the general? In an admirable display of integrity, Henry did not. To the contrary, he immediately packaged the letter with one of his own and sent them off to Washington.

Henry wrote to the general that "you will no doubt be surprised at seeing the enclosed letter, in which the encomiums bestowed on me are as undeserved, as the censures aimed at you are unjust. I am sorry there should be one man who counts himself my friend, who is not yours." He assured Washington that the conspiracy would get no assistance from him. "Believe me Sir, I have too high a sense of the obligations America has to you to abet or countenance so unworthy a proceeding. The most exalted merit hath ever been found to attract envy. But I please myself with the hope, that the same fortitude and greatness of mind which have hitherto braved all the difficulties and dangers inseparable from your station, will rise superior to every attempt of the envious partisan." Washington's reply was delayed, so Henry wrote him again in two weeks to confirm that he had received the secret letter. Those who conspired against him risked fighting against God's providence, Henry said. "While you face the armed enemies of our liberty in the field, and by the favor of God have been kept unhurt, I trust your country will never harbor in her bosom the miscreant who would ruin her best supporter."[26]

Washington finally replied, the delivery of the original letters having taken about a month. Even though the general already knew of attempts to have him removed from command, he was understandably grateful to Henry for forwarding the anonymous letter to him. He appreciated even more Henry's continued support, the loss of which would have been devastating to Washington, who had few military successes to show for himself in the early years of the war. "Your friendship, Sir, in transmitting me the anonymous letter you had received, lays me under the most grateful obligations," the general said. The next day Washington wrote to Henry again, having received the second letter on the subject. Again he profusely thanked Henry and then revealed the person he believed to have written the anonymous letter: Dr. Benjamin Rush, the Philadelphia patriot and physician who had inoculated Henry, and who was serving as medical director for the middle department of the Continental army. While Rush would only later admit to writing the letter, Washington immediately discerned that Rush was the author because of a "similitude of hands" between this new letter and earlier ones he had received from the doctor. The general was disgusted with Rush's hypocrisy, for he recalled that Rush had spoken very kindly to him, even since the time he would have sent his secret letter to Henry. Rush was understandably concerned about the deplorable conditions of the troops, but his participation in a subversive campaign against Washington has detracted from his historical reputation. Washington, having information like Rush's letter in hand, began to make the conspiracy against him publicly known, which immediately deflated the prospect that he would be removed.[27]

Rush obviously believed that if a prominent patriot such as Henry could be turned against Washington, then the conspiracy might have gained traction. But Rush had badly judged Henry's disposition. Despite his temporary squabbles with Washington, the loyalty of Virginia's governor to the Continental army commander was unshakeable. Henry had acted boldly and riskily in forwarding the letter to Washington. What if the conspiracy had worked, and the general had been removed? Henry surely would have suffered as well. Washington always remembered Henry's loyalty to him. Sixteen years later, as president, Washington wrote, "I have conceived myself under obligations to [Henry] for the friendly manner in which he transmitted to me some insidious anonymous writings that were sent to him in the close of the year 1777, with a view to embark him in the opposition that was forming against me at that time." Who knows what might have happened if Henry had lent his powers of persuasion to the effort to remove Washington?[28]

Henry's support for Washington helped ease the tensions between the two men. Henry struggled to raise Virginia militiamen in 1778 to face threats from western Indians and gangs of outlaws within the state. He came to believe the patriots were losing momentum and the state might descend into lawlessness, so he pushed for harsher punishments against militia deserters and marauding criminals, writing Benjamin Harrison in May 1778 that "no effort to crush these desperadoes should be spared." He sought more authority from the legislature to coerce Virginians into military service but got little response. Despite these problems, Henry was chosen for a third yearlong term as governor that May.[29]

By June, Henry had grown almost disconsolate about the war. The recent good news of the French alliance with America—secured following the triumph at Saratoga—cheered him. But within Virginia, the mood was gloomy. "Public spirit seems to have taken its flight from Virginia," he wrote Richard Henry Lee. The state was below half its quota of troops, and the "great bounties" in cash and real estate offered by Virginia for enlistment would only put Virginia in a worse light, he feared. "Let not Congress rely on Virginia for soldiers," for almost nothing could convince men to serve, Henry lamented.[30]

The war's cruel grinding-on even brought some Virginians to the edge of revolt against the state government. One of Henry's military correspondents warned him in November that far-western Montgomery County, Virginia, was at serious risk of a "general mutiny." Young men were chafing under the relentless demands for military service, which would take them away from home for many months and expose their families to "ruin and beggary, which many of them are on the brink of already," owing to the disruptions of war and longtime hostilities with local Native Americans. Henry desperately tried to find the right balance: How could he request reasonable sacrifices without pushing Virginians into utter destitution? Many citizens found that the war just required too much of them, so they balked at every request from the governor.[31]

MILITARY RELIEF CAME from an ironic source: France. The French might well have chosen to stay out of the war in America, given their old rivalry with the American colonists from the wars of empire earlier in the century, and the continuing anti-Catholicism that pervaded British American culture. But the victory at Saratoga convinced the French that the Americans could win independence, and an American alliance gave them another opportunity to harm their inveterate enemies, the British. Benjamin Franklin had been working on a Franco-American alliance since the nation first declared its independence, but only news of a major military victory could convince the wary French. Henry viewed the alliance as a providential blessing: "I look at the past condition of America, as at a dreadful precipice, from which we have escaped, by means of the generous French. . . . Salvation to America depends upon our holding fast our attachment to them." Henry knew that the chastened British had evacuated Philadelphia following the French alliance and had begun to suggest that they might offer peace to the Americans, if the patriots forsook independence. He railed against such a possibility but feared that some lagging Virginians might consider the offer. For him, the prospect of peace with Britain was like the desire of ancient Israelites to return to slavery: "The flesh pots of Egypt are still savory to degenerate palates." Henry had not lost his radical edge in pursuit of independence, and he fumed at many Virginians' lack of commitment to that goal.[32]

Through 1778, Henry struggled to discern the intentions of the British, who were beginning to shift their focus to the southern theater of the war. Would they stage a direct attack on the Chesapeake states? Fear of British invasion made Henry and the Virginia assembly reluctant to respond to Congress's periodic requests to deliver assistance to Georgia or South Carolina, where the British threat seemed more significant. In November, Henry explained to Henry Laurens, president of the Congress, that the assembly would agree to send Virginia troops out of state only when an invasion was imminent elsewhere. Recurrent rumors suggested that the British might come ashore in Virginia, but their first major strike in the South was actually against Savannah, Georgia, which they captured in December 1778.[33]

The bleak mood following Savannah's defeat led Congress to issue another call for a day of prayer and fasting, one that Henry implored Virginians to observe. The Congress summoned Americans to pray that they would learn the lessons behind God's chastisements, including Savannah's fall, and that God would "extend the influence of true religion, and give us that peace of mind which the world cannot give. That he will be our shield in the day of battle, our comforter in the hour of death, and our kind parent and merciful judge."[34]

Shortly after the day of prayer, the attack on Virginia finally came. On May 8, 1779, a fleet of about thirty ships entered the Chesapeake Bay and unloaded a couple thousand British troops, who attacked Portsmouth and Suffolk, seizing and destroying supplies valued in the millions of pounds sterling. For the first time in three years, as many as 1,500 slaves fled to the British. A week after the invasion began, Henry issued a proclamation calling for county lieutenants to raise militias and proceed to the eastern counties to counter the attack. He lamented how the British had committed "horrid ravages and depredations, such as plundering and burning houses, killing and carrying away stock of all sorts, and exercising other abominable cruelties and barbarities," warning that they were likely to devastate the rest of Virginia with this kind of violence. The assembly also sent out calls for help to Congress and neighboring states, a move Henry did not like. "Will it not disgrace our country thus to cry out for aid against this band of robbers?" he asked Richard Henry Lee. "However, the assembly have done it and I must submit." The British seemed to have choked off Virginia's seafaring connection to the rest of the colonies, but the attack was a raid, not an invasion, and the British departed on May 24, before Virginians could mount a serious resistance. The British naval commander, George Collier, wanted to remain in Portsmouth and perhaps launch an invasion of Virginia, but commander in chief Henry Clinton overruled him and ordered the withdrawal, concerned that the Continentals might be planning an attack on New York.

The British withdrawal was particularly well-timed, for Henry had come to the end of his third term as governor and was constitutionally required to step down. Some Virginians criticized Henry's performance as the state's chief executive. St. George Tucker wrote that if the new governor, Thomas Jefferson, "should tread in the steps of his predecessor, there is not much to be expected from the brightest talents. Did the enemy know how very defenseless we are at present, a very small addition to their late force would be sufficient to commit the greatest ravages throughout the country." Tucker may have been right about Virginia's military weakness, but Henry was not constitutionally empowered to fix the problems of recruitment and supplies. The governor himself would have insisted that Virginia's fate depended less on soldiers than on the virtue and public spirit of the people, which lagged as the war ground on. Henry never placed unconditional confidence in the people; he believed that the welfare of the state—and of the nation—was contingent on their moral courage.[35]

Some Virginians wanted Henry to continue as governor, but he felt it was better to observe the three-term constitutional restriction and retire. He was worn out and had suffered from poor health most of the spring of 1779. The assembly thanked their governor "for his faithful discharge of that important trust, and his uniform endeavors to promote the true interests of this state and of all America." Henry, Dorothea, their family, and their slaves soon left for his new Leather-wood plantation, near the North Carolina border, a few miles east of present-day Martinsville. He had done his best to fulfill the promise of American independence in wartime, but as he left Williamsburg, the fate of Virginia and America remained highly uncertain.[36]

# 8

## "VIRTUE HAS TAKEN ITS DEPARTURE"

## The War's End and a New Virginia

HENRY'S RETIREMENT TO HIS LEATHERWOOD FARM did not brighten his outlook on the war. He wrote to Governor Thomas Jefferson in February 1780 lamenting the state's fierce inflation and its indulgence of Loyalist actions subverting the war effort. "Tell me," he implored Jefferson, "do you remember any instance where tyranny was destroyed and freedom established on its ruins, among a people possessing so small a share of virtue and public spirit? I recollect none." How could Virginians hope to win this war, when so many seemed greedy, selfish, and irresolute?

The worries Henry expressed plagued all of Virginia's leaders in the last years of the war. The difficulties in recruitment, combined with soaring prices, rampant fraud and price gouging, persistent outbreaks of Loyalist resistance, and bickering in Congress all seemed to evidence a deep crisis of virtue. The rapid pace of inflation led panicky merchants to raise prices in anticipation of even more inflation, making everything ridiculously expensive and debilitating the state's capacity to supply its militia or the Continental army. Henry's anxieties were "principally occasioned by the depreciation of our money," he told Jefferson. The legislature could respond only by printing more money, which in the long run just made things worse.[1]

Commitment to the war effort had faltered. Some people seemed more interested in frittering away their time gambling and making a quick profit than defeating the British. Washington's stepson John Parke Custis told the general that even with jacked-up bounties to entice recruits, he doubted the army could meet its quotas. "Our money is so depreciated, and the minds of the people are so depraved, by gaming and every other species of vice, that virtue seems to have taken his departure from Virginia, in general; and, it is with much real concern and shame that I confess there are but very few of my countrymen who deserve the glorious appellation of virtuous."[2]

The weary Washington agreed, disgusted at the unscrupulous merchants who tried to profit from the desperation of the Continental army: "There is such a thirst for gain, and such infamous advantages taken to forestall, & engross those articles which the army cannot do without, thereby enhancing the cost of them to the public fifty or a hundred percent, that it is enough to make one curse their own species, for possessing so little virtue and patriotism."[3]

Despite the grim circumstances facing the state, Henry feared that his own failing health would prevent him from serving Virginia much longer. Indeed, he speculated to Jefferson that he might die— perhaps from another bout with malarial symptoms—before the next meeting of the legislature in May 1780. He wished his old colleague health and prosperity, and signed his 1780 letter "your affectionate friend and obedient servant"—but soon their friendship would enter a season of bitter frost, just when Virginians faced the most dangerous phase of the war.[4]

Henry still did not view himself as a professional politician, and he had resolved to step away from government, at least for a time. "A long and painful attention to public matters obliges me to go for awhile into retirement which is equally necessary to my health, finances, and domestic affairs," he wrote shortly after leaving the governor's mansion. Six years of unrelenting service as a legislator, colonel, and governor had taken their toll on Henry and his assets. It is likely that his time in the governor's office—as well as the rapidly rising prices in the state—had sent Henry into debt again, a condition he loathed. The legislature soon chose him as a representative to the Confederation Congress, but he refused to serve, intent upon recovering his health and personal prosperity. The national political stage held little appeal for him. He always seemed to fight against indebtedness, and his land speculations rarely produced the kind of profit he hoped. Dorothea was pregnant with their second child. Henry's desire to make his family financially secure in this time of economic instability would undercut his ability to serve his state, distracting him when Virginia badly needed him to step forward once more.[5]

Yet Henry found it difficult to remove himself from Virginia politics. He served in the state legislature again during the 1780 session, speaking in opposition to a congressional plan designed to revalue Continental currency and implement new state taxes. Henry and many leading southern politicians opposed the plan, claiming it would boost the northern states' economies at the expense of the southern states, and Henry's oratory clinched the assembly's vote against it. But when Henry left the legislature early in June, apparently returning to Leatherwood to continue his convalescence, supporters of the plan managed to get the assembly to adopt the congressional scheme. It would not be the last time Henry would prematurely assume legislative victory.[6]

The depredations of war loomed over Virginia, even as legislators futilely tried to stabilize the economy. The British, having been stymied in the North, decided to try their fortune in the South, where the population was thought to be friendlier to the empire. In early April 1780, they laid siege to Charleston, a city that lay on a narrow neck of land between the Ashley and Cooper Rivers, trapping American troops, including Virginians who had just arrived as reinforcements. After a month of bombardment, the great southern port was reduced to a smoldering ruin, and its residents faced squalor and starvation. Charleston finally surrendered on May 12. About 1,400 Virginians were among the 5,500 American troops captured there. In terms of dead and captured soldiers, it would be America's worst defeat of the war.[7]

The loss of Charleston was followed in August by the humiliating defeat of Horatio Gates, the hero of Saratoga, at Camden, South Carolina. When he engaged British General Lord Cornwallis's army, the typically unreliable state militias serving under Gates collapsed. Gates himself abandoned the field almost as quickly as the militiamen; mounting a swift horse, he made it sixty miles north to Charlotte, North Carolina, by nightfall. Gates was blamed for the defeat and replaced soon thereafter. Until patriot victories at Kings Mountain and Cowpens stopped his progress through South Carolina, Cornwallis seemed well on his way to securing the lower South.

Virginians feared being caught in a pincer movement between Cornwallis and the notorious Benedict Arnold, who had been a patriot hero at the Battle of Saratoga but in 1779—enticed by bribes and the promise of more respectful treatment—had secretly defected to the British. Earlier in 1780, he had almost succeeded in betraying West Point, New York, his last post as a Continental officer, to the British. Now working openly as a redcoat officer, Arnold invaded Tidewater Virginia in late December 1780 and moved unopposed up the James River, reaching the new capital at Richmond—which had been presumed safer from enemy attack than Williamsburg—on January 5, 1781. As governor, Thomas Jefferson had done little to prepare Richmond for the attack. Indeed, in the weeks leading up to the invasion, Jefferson was more consumed with the prospect of a British and Native American attack from the west, and he offered to send General George Rogers Clark extra supplies and upward of 1,000 Virginia militiamen. But the western attack did not materialize, even as Arnold's force cruised south from New York.[8]

Arnold was under orders only to capture the key town of Portsmouth, Virginia, but as was his tendency, he went against commands and sought to capture the state's patriot government. Jefferson received reports of a fleet in Chesapeake Bay on New Year's Day 1781, but he was not sure of the fleet's origins (was it French or British?). For the next couple of days, Jefferson attended to personal business and serenely sought advice and intelligence on the appearance of the navy ships. The delay worsened the unfolding disaster, and when Jefferson finally called up the militia after two days, they were no match for Arnold's 1,000 well-trained soldiers.[9]

When Arnold began the invasion, Richmond had been the state capital for only nine months, and the town remained little more than a frontier village, with about six hundred residents, about half of them slaves. Jefferson and his family, including a sickly five-week-old daughter, fled the city and went to Charlottesville as Arnold's army captured Richmond. Although Arnold soon withdrew to Portsmouth, Virginians were horrified that the British could so easily penetrate the heart of the state.[10]

IN FEBRUARY, WHEN LORD CORNWALLIS also began advancing toward the North Carolina border with Virginia, Continental General Nathanael Greene (Horatio Gates's replacement) looked to Patrick Henry to recruit volunteers for the state's defense. Henry and others still found it difficult to summon new soldiers, but at the battle of Guilford Courthouse, North Carolina, in March, the majority of

Greene's troops were Virginians. Inspired by successful tactics used at the Battle of Cowpens in South Carolina, Greene had placed the North Carolina militia on his front line, but when Cornwallis's redcoats began their assault, many of the militia ran. They fled, according to one of their officers, like "a flock of sheep frightened by dogs." Others stayed to fire at close range, but soon the fighting bogged down on the forested battlefield. Cornwallis, recognizing that this battle would decide the fate of his army, coldly ordered an artillery assault on the confused field. The British mowed down both redcoats and patriots in the bloody chaos. This strategy succeeded, but it was costly; the British lost twice the number of troops as the Americans. Cornwallis's Pyrrhic victory at Guilford Courthouse convinced him to move into Virginia and unite with the branch of British army that had successfully invaded that state. His men were exhausted, and Cornwallis was "tired of marching about the country in quest of adventures." In May, he arrived in Petersburg, south of Richmond.[11]

Angered by the surging strength of the British and ever-faltering recruitment efforts in Virginia, Henry thought Congress and the northern states had forgotten about the South once the war turned in that direction. In the assembly in March, Henry served on a committee that drafted a furious remonstrance to Congress. It was not adopted because news unexpectedly arrived that part of the Continental army would soon make its way to Virginia, but the document nevertheless revealed Henry's mood in these anxious months: "Virginia, then, impoverished by defending the Northern department, exhausted by the Southern war, now finds the whole weight of it on her shoulders. . . . Straining every nerve in present defense, pressed with a great hostile army, and threatened with a greater— beset with enemies both savage and disciplined—the Assembly of Virginia do, in behalf of their State and in behalf of the common cause, in the most solemn manner summon the other States to their assistance. . . . If they are denied, the consequences be on the heads of those who refuse them." Frustrated as he was, Henry would become even more disturbed over Congress's reluctance to aid Virginia in the coming years.[12]

If Henry was angry about Virginia's perilous state, Thomas Jefferson had become truly desperate, so much so that in late May, he plaintively wrote to George Washington, asking him to return with his army to deliver his fellow Virginians. "Your appearance among them I say would restore full confidence of salvation, and would render them equal to whatever is not impossible." Jefferson knew his own reticent personality had no such power to rally Virginia's citizens, and he dreaded the consequences if the British were allowed to rampage through the state.[13]

For the time being, Washington remained in the North, hoping to recapture New York. The British moved through Virginia almost unopposed. Days after Jefferson's letter to Washington, the infamous British Colonel Banastre Tarleton rode his cavalry into Charlottesville, where the assembly had fled the advancing redcoats. A year earlier, Tarleton had earned his nickname, "Bloody Ban," for refusing to give quarter to captured Virginia Continentals at the Battle of Waxhaws in South Carolina, and many of Tarleton's patriot prisoners were hacked to death with sabers. Now Tarleton galloped into Charlottesville, nearly capturing Jefferson, Henry, and the rest of the state's leadership. Only the quick actions of a patriot scout who raised the alarm avoided total calamity for the governor and legislators.

The assemblymen fled farther westward, to Staunton in the Shenandoah Valley, while Jefferson narrowly escaped from his Monticello home at Charlottesville. With his term about to expire, Jefferson informed legislators that he would no longer serve as governor and that they should appoint a replacement for him. Then he took off for the safety of his isolated Poplar Forest plantation, far to the south, in the wooded hills near present-day Lynchburg. Thanks to Jefferson's unexpected departure, for about a week Virginia essentially had no leader. On paper, his time of service was over, but abandoning his post at this critical juncture was nothing short of cowardly.[14]

Faced with a dire emergency and the flight of its elected leader, the assembly met in Staunton and considered appointing a replacement governor with extraordinary powers similar to those they allowed Henry in late 1776. According to an account written many years later, Henry was one of the principal advocates of this action, seconding the motion for it and asserting in the debate that "it was immaterial with him whether the officer proposed was called a dictator, or governor with enlarged powers, or by any other name, yet surely an officer armed with such powers was necessary to restrain the unbridled fury of a licentious enemy." No doubt Henry and his supporters were reacting to Jefferson's untimely exodus, seeking to reassert the authority of executive leadership, but ultimately the move for a governor with dictatorial powers was defeated. In *Notes on the State of Virginia*, Jefferson would criticize the assembly's debate over installing a wartime commander, failing to recognize that his own lack of leadership had brought Henry and the assembly to a point of utter panic. Moreover, it is hard to imagine what kind of role Jefferson imagined for Washington when he had recently asked him to return, if not as some kind of military dictator. A few weeks later, in mid-June, Richard Henry Lee explicitly asked Congress to give Washington these kind of "dictatorial powers" in Virginia, acidly noting that Jefferson's resignation had left his own state "in the moment of its greatest danger without government, abandoned to the arts and the arms of the enemy." Jefferson himself clearly favored Lee's proposal, but by the time he published *Notes*, he had changed his tune about the virtue of empowering an executive to save Virginia.[15]

Although the assembly did not name a dictator, it did grant the new governor, Thomas Nelson, broad powers like the ones given to Henry in 1776. Nelson had been serving as a militia commander, and the legislature gave him authority to call out the militia at will, seize supplies, and detain suspected Loyalists. They also resolved that no further aid be sent out of state to help the Continental army while Virginia remained under direct assault. Excoriating Congress for its neglect of Virginia, the assembly adopted a complaint it had commissioned Henry to write. Despite his private doubts about Virginians' moral courage, he painted the citizens of his home state as heroic and beleaguered: "the sufferings of a virtuous people, who now feel everything that a cruel, vindictive, and enraged enemy can inflict, compel us to make the demand [for aid], and justice ensures a compliance with it on the part of Congress."[16]

Henry also struck out against Jefferson for his conduct as governor. At Henry's instigation, George Nicholas made a motion that the House of Delegates inquire into Jefferson's service as governor to determine what misdeeds, if any, had occurred. At its December meeting, at a time when military victory had turned the state's mood from vindictive to celebratory, the assembly thought better of trying to humiliate Jefferson, clearing him of charges of cowardice and thanking him for his devoted service. Nevertheless, Jefferson seethed with anger toward Henry. Nicholas was not to blame for this outrageous investigation, Jefferson wrote to another legislator. "The trifling body [Nicholas] who moved this matter was below contempt; he was more an object of pity. His natural ill-temper was the tool worked by another hand. He was like the minnows which go in and out of the fundament of the whale. But the whale himself was discoverable enough by the turbulence of the water under which he moved."[17]

Stung by the very suggestion that he might have behaved dishonorably, Jefferson wrote a lugubrious letter to James Monroe, likely intended for circulation among Virginia politicians, suggesting that since the assembly had hurt him so badly, he would take his political talents away forever to his mountain retreat at Monticello. The investigation "inflicted a wound on my spirit which will only be cured by the all-healing grave." Jefferson's loathing of Henry would fester for decades, only moderating long after Henry's death.[18]

Henry seems to have spent most of the second half of 1781 at Leatherwood. His criticism of Jefferson's flight from Charlottesville notwithstanding, he was not particularly engaged in political affairs in these months. Once again, we are left to wish for more of Henry's thoughts, for we know almost nothing of his reaction when a surprising shift in the winds of war produced the final battle in Virginia, and of the Revolution.

Continental troops reinforced their numbers in Virginia in early June, and in late July, Cornwallis received orders from British commander in chief Henry Clinton to hold the Tidewater region. Cornwallis decided to entrench at Yorktown. Washington and his army left New York to meet a French fleet headed for the Chesapeake Bay, and at the end of September a large combined force of French and American troops laid siege to Yorktown. Short supplies and epidemic disease ravaged Cornwallis's camp, with escaped Virginia slaves who had hoped to fight for the British enduring the brunt of the horrors. Cornwallis began expelling blacks infected with smallpox, leaving them to be captured by the Americans, or simply collapse and die in the woods around Yorktown. After the siege, one Pennsylvania soldier observed, "Negroes lie about, sick and dying, in every stage of the small pox. Never was in so filthy a place." The hopes and lives of runaway African-Americans became casualties of the war.[19]

The Americans and French bombarded the British position at Yorktown, sending Cornwallis and his officers running for cover along the York River's edge. Finally, on October 14, Washington's twenty-six-year-old chief of staff, Alexander Hamilton, led a bold assault on the British line, and the humiliated Cornwallis surrendered on October 19, 1781. The struggle for independence, which had begun with Patrick Henry's Stamp Act speech in Williamsburg in 1765, had been won sixteen years later, only a few miles to the east of the site of that famous oration, in the riverine lands of the Tidewater.

PATRICK HENRY FOUGHT CONTINUING ILLNESS as he recuperated from his long service as governor and Revolutionary leader, receiving a leave of absence from the legislature in November 1781. Surely he was delighted at Cornwallis's surrender. The mood among his victorious friends was captured in a letter he received in May 1782 from General Horatio Gates, who congratulated Henry for his part in America's peace and independence. "Now the glorious opportunity approaches," Gates wrote, "when upon the broad basis of civil liberty, may be established, the happiness of the present generation and their posterity." Henry would soon be far less sanguine than Gates that the new nation had the virtue it needed to meet that opportunity.[20]

Gates also expressed hope for "equal liberty" to spread throughout the land, and Virginia took a halting step in that direction in 1782 when the legislature passed a law permitting private manumissions of slaves. Previously, any masters wishing to free their slaves would have to appeal to the state. It had become embarrassingly obvious during the war that the British offered slaves better prospects for freedom than the Americans did. Newer evangelical churches, such as those of the Methodists and the Baptists, often put pressure on members to free their enslaved workers. Some masters in Virginia wished to set their slaves free in their wills, or by some gradual process. Now owners could free their slaves by submitting a legal request to a county court.

Although journal records do not exist for this assembly session, biographers have assumed Patrick Henry supported the bill. Many white Virginians did not; the assembly received more than 1,000 anti-manumission petitions claiming that the new law would encourage unrest. About 10,000 slaves would be manumitted under this law before it was amended in 1806, but its effects were less than revolutionary: many masters used the law only to free a favorite slave, not to free their slaves en masse. Those Virginia slaves manumitted during these twenty-four years represented about only 3 percent of the state's total slave population, which in 1790 was just under 300,000. With legislators worried about the burgeoning free black population, the 1806 amendment required that any freed slaves leave the state, which functionally ended the state's more progressive policy.[21]

In 1782, as the nation settled into an uneasy peacetime, Henry reentered public life, seeking to use his position in the legislature to put Virginia on solid ground economically—and morally. Sometimes his economic and moral imperatives clashed, as they did around the thorny issue of repaying debts to British creditors. The 1783 Treaty of Paris that officially concluded the war stipulated that lawfully contracted debts be paid back to creditors on both sides of the Atlantic, but Henry resisted, countering James Madison's arguments by protesting that the British had not yet vacated their military posts in the Great Lakes region. Only when the British withdrew from their American forts should Virginians and other Americans pay their debts, Henry maintained. The issue would fester until the War of 1812.[22]

Taking priority in Henry's view was debt relief for the struggling people of post-Revolutionary Virginia, including planters large and small. Thanks to the vagaries of their agricultural economy, Southside Virginians—residents of the state's south-central region, where Henry now lived—carried a disproportionate individual debt burden, an encumbrance Henry knew well from enduring the bankruptcies of his youth and watching his dissolute half-brother John Syme struggle financially. But Henry hated the thought that his supporters would be forced to repay the British, no matter if their debts arose from legitimate transactions or even undisciplined consumption of luxury goods.

This issue did not inspire Henry's finest hour. Avoiding the payment of legitimate debts was not consistent with his career-long emphasis on virtue. Even friends such as George Mason challenged the ethics of Henry's position. Writing to Henry in May 1783, Mason implored him to use the opportunity of independence to establish moral foundations for the republic. "Whether our independence shall prove a blessing or a curse, must depend upon our own wisdom or folly, virtue or wickedness," Mason cautioned. Based on Virginians' performance during the war, Mason himself was not particularly hopeful about the future. He knew that some Virginians wondered why they had fought the war if they still had to pay their debts to the enemy they had vanquished. In Mason's view, Virginians had served in the Revolution "not to avoid our just debts, or cheat our creditors; but to rescue our country from the oppression and tyranny of the British government, and to secure the rights and liberty of ourselves, and our posterity." Mason was surprised to find Henry on the other side of the issue. Henry's lifelong championing of virtue was sincere, but as a planter preoccupied with maintaining his own prosperity, he also factored financial considerations into his policymaking and his worldview.[23]

Despite his position against debt repayment, Henry took more pro-British positions in promoting the resumption of British imports to Virginia and encouraging Loyalists to return to the state. Sponsoring a bill renewing commerce with Britain, Henry had to overcome the opposition of many fellow assemblymen, including John Tyler Sr. (father of the future president). Tyler recalled that

Henry unleashed his rhetoric in defense of thriving business: "'Why,' said he, 'should we fetter commerce? If a man is in chains, he droops and bows to the earth, for his spirits are broken, (looking sorrowfully at his feet:) but let him twist the fetters from his legs, and he will stand erect,' straightening himself, and assuming a look of proud defiance.—'Fetter not commerce, sir—let her be as free as air—she will range the whole creation, and return on the wings of the four winds of heaven, to bless the land with plenty.'"[24]

Henry saw no point in holding a grudge against the Loyalists; in his view, Virginia needed as many industrious settlers as it could get. For Henry, the end of the war offered America a chance to become the "asylum for liberty" that Tom Paine's *Common Sense* had envisioned. Asserting that if America opened her doors, the free peoples of Europe would flow in, Henry declaimed, "They see here a land blessed with natural and political advantages, which are not equaled by those of any other country upon earth—a land on which a gracious Providence has emptied the horn of abundance. . . . They see a land in which liberty hath taken up her abode—that liberty, whom they had considered as a fabled goddess, existing only in the fancies of poets—they see her here a real divinity—her altars rising on every hand throughout these happy states—her glories chanted by three millions of tongues—and the whole region smiling under her blessed influence." There was no need to fear British Loyalists, Henry assured the legislators. "Shall we, who have laid the proud British lion at our feet, now be afraid of his whelps?" But even Henry's oratory could not persuade the legislature. It passed a bill prohibiting the Tories' return.[25]

With the end of the war, Henry and his fellow political leaders also had to address an emerging issue that would beset the new nation from its beginnings into its maturity: the balance between a stronger national government and the power of the states. The Articles of Confederation—which had structured America's government since the beginning of the war—provided no power to tax, a constraint that made sense given that the country's controversy with Britain had centered on taxation. Why substitute American taxes for British ones? But Henry had witnessed, and indeed had been engaged in, Washington's struggle to supply his army because of the Congress's inability to raise funds directly. In the late stages of the Revolution, some policymakers had proposed an impost on imported goods. All the states would have to give their assent to such a plan for it to go into effect. Now, as the thirteen states struggled to define themselves as a single entity, the issue of national taxation gripped the Virginia legislature. Henry wavered in his opinion of the impost. He understood that the national government needed to generate more revenue, but he was concerned that the government would abuse its power to tax.

Jefferson thought that Henry instinctively opposed expanding the power of Congress, but he would later suggest that Henry was inclined to support the impost because of a developing rivalry with Richard Henry Lee, who opposed the plan. The friendship between the two men would grow strained because of the dispute over the impost, with Lee preferring that Virginia strictly comply with congressional requisitions rather than submit to the impost, and Henry originally disagreeing. Their debate fueled a larger rivalry between Lee and Henry's ally, John Tyler Sr., over the position of the Speaker of the House of Delegates. Lee won the Speaker's chair in 1780, only to lose it the next year to Tyler, who presided from 1781 to 1784. But the dynamic between the two men changed when a compromise was reached on a modified, broadly acceptable impost, and Lee was reelected to Congress in 1784, which led Lee to write Henry in frank but welcoming terms about their friendship in late 1784. "We are placed now," he said, "pretty nearly in the same political relation under which our former correspondence was conducted; if it shall prove as agreeable to you to revive it, as you were then pleased to say it was to continue it, I shall be happy in contributing my part." They did indeed revive their friendship, setting the stage for their work together as anti-federalist opponents of the Constitution.[26]

Jefferson scoffed at Henry's indecision on the impost, writing to Madison that "Henry as usual is involved in mystery: should the popular tide run strongly in either direction, he will fall in with it." We might give Henry a bit more credit than Jefferson did. Henry knew Congress needed more revenue to support legitimate national projects, but he also feared that giving it any power to tax might lead the national government to disregard the prerogatives of the states and ruin the economy. Henry's initial enthusiasm for the impost waned as he began to suspect that Madison and Alexander Hamilton had more in mind than a modest tax. Hamilton had risen to prominence as Washington's senior aide-de-camp during the war, and he was emerging as a leading politician in New York and a promoter of national power. To counter Hamilton's suggestion in early 1783 that federal tax authority was his ultimate goal, Henry proposed a complex system ensuring that Virginia would not have to pay more than its fair share of the impost duties. Consideration of the impost, both in Virginia and elsewhere, soon became paralyzed in debate.[27]

Henry still wished to make the Confederation government more stable without destroying the independence of the states. Madison, Henry, and others met in Richmond in May 1784 and agreed that Madison would draw up a "plan for giving greater power to the federal government and that Mr. Henry should support it on the floor." For his part, Henry reportedly "saw ruin inevitable unless something was done" to bolster the national government's authority. Nothing came of this meeting, however.[28]

Madison never shared Jefferson's bitterness toward Henry. He was, in general, better able than Jefferson to distinguish political issues from the personal. The two men never had the kind of falling-out that Henry did with Jefferson. But as time went on, it became increasingly difficult for Madison and Henry to compromise on national authority over the states. Henry's fight against Britain taught him that the dangers of consolidated national power outweighed its benefits, a belief corroborated for him by seeing how little Virginia ever benefited from the national government, even in the state's darkest hours. Madison shared with Hamilton a belief that America was destined to become a great nation. It could never embrace that destiny, however, without a nimble national government. The contradictory visions of these two Virginians were bound to clash.

BEYOND HIS CONCERNS WITH THE ECONOMY, Henry remained committed to promoting virtue in Virginia. Independence would be worth nothing if Virginia degenerated into immorality, selfishness, and vice. To Henry, only one institution could adequately support virtue, and that was the church.

At the beginning of the Revolution, Virginia stopped providing financial support to the Anglican Church, and its parishes suffered badly during the war, the financial privation exacerbated by the church's traditional association with Britain. Other churches struggled, too. The militant Methodists had been hurt by their association with Loyalism; their English founder, John Wesley, had opposed the patriot cause. The Baptists were surging toward a massive outbreak of revivals in 1785, but as of 1783, they were not that publicly influential. The outlook for religion in Virginia was bleak.

Henry believed the state should resume public funding for religion, but he knew Virginia would never go back to one exclusive, established church. Instead, he became the champion of a so-called general assessment for religion. Under this system, people would have to pay taxes to support a church of their choice. For Henry and the assessment's many supporters, this arrangement honored both the public importance of religion and the realities of Christian pluralism in the state. He introduced a bill declaring that "the general diffusion of Christian knowledge hath a natural tendency to correct the morals of men, restrain their vices, and preserve the peace of society; which cannot be effected without a competent provision for learned [pastors], . . . and it is judged that such provision may be made by the legislature, without counteracting the liberal principle heretofore adopted and intended to be preserved by abolishing all distinctions of pre-eminence amongst the different societies or communities of Christians."[29]

The general assessment plan is one of the main reasons Henry is not more widely esteemed as a Founder, for in this debate, he seems to have diverted from the progressive flow of history. Jefferson and Madison's campaign for disestablishment and religious freedom— leading ultimately to Virginia's Bill for Establishing Religious Freedom and the First Amendment's religion clauses—pioneered the church-state system that most Americans have embraced. Yet Henry was as much an activist for religious *liberty* as were Madison and Jefferson. He had opposed the clerics' claims for lost salary in the Parsons' Cause, supported the rights of Baptists and other dissenters, and championed the religion article of the Virginia Declaration of Rights. Henry had consistently sought to bolster the rights of religious dissenters and enshrine religious pluralism in law. His general assessment plan would have transitioned Virginia from having a single state church to offering multiple options, ensuring not a strict separation of church and state, but robust religious diversity.[30]

Henry was not alone in his advocacy for a general assessment. Other prominent Virginia leaders, such as George Washington and Richard Henry Lee, backed it as well. Lee wrote to Madison in 1784 cautioning him that "refiners may weave as fine a web of reason as they please, but the experience of all times shows religion to be the guardian of morals—and he must be a very inattentive observer in our country, who does not see that avarice is accomplishing the destruction of religion, for want of a legal obligation to contribute something to its support." Washington thought Christians should be made to support what they professed to believe. Most defenders of the assessment also agreed that tax exemptions could be given for non-Christians.[31]

Strict separation of church and state, which today often means the government should have no connections with religious institutions, was uncommon in the founding period. Jefferson took a strong view of church-state separation, but as president even he felt comfortable permitting and attending church services in government buildings. The notion that government agencies could totally disengage from religion simply did not occur to most Revolutionary-era Americans. Churches were seen as the moral bulwark of the republic. Henry and most of his Revolutionary colleagues on either side of the establishment debate also would not have supported strict separation because they believed that government should promote morality. Two primary ways to do this were punishing immorality under the law, and encouraging morality through churches and schools. The real point of contention concerning the general assessment was whether, as a matter of conscience, people should be required to support a church at all. Jefferson and Madison cooperated with many evangelical dissenters, especially Baptists, in arguing that religion would survive, and even thrive, on a purely voluntary basis. The Baptists also had plenty of experience with state-sponsored persecution in Virginia; as recently as the early 1770s, Baptist preachers were still being sent to jail for illegal preaching. Government support inevitably led to persecution of dissenters and corruption of the official churches, they said.

In mid-1784, the Church of England in Virginia proposed an act of incorporation that would put it on more stable legal footing. This would have given the clergy of what was now the renamed Protestant Episcopal Church both greater independence from state oversight and increased legal protection for church property, which it held as the established church. Henry introduced the measure, but it struggled to gain support in the legislature and was postponed until the next session. Madison thought the bill was outrageous, because it tried to reverse the state's obvious movement toward full religious liberty. He told Jefferson that "extraordinary as such a project was, it was preserved from a dishonorable death by the talents of Mr. Henry."[32]

Later that year, Henry again introduced both the incorporation bill and the general assessment plan. Many Virginians sent petitions to the legislature endorsing the assessment, including the influential Hanover Presbytery (founded by Samuel Davies). As non-Anglicans, the Presbyterians had suffered under the religious establishment of the colonial period, but they still desired a plural system of establishment. James Madison spoke out against the assessment, but the tide seemed to be turning in its favor.

The momentum for the assessment bill abruptly changed when the legislature again elected Henry governor on November 17. Neither the assessment nor the incorporation bill had come up for a final vote, but Henry may have thought he could safely leave the House of Delegates before their approval. He was wrong. Madison was quite pleased to see Henry go to the governor's mansion, and anticipated that the change of offices would prove "inauspicious to [Henry's] offspring." He would be right. Henry was a great communicator, but he would prove no match for Madison's political maneuvering. Henry remained a hero in Virginia; legislators remembered his solid performance as governor in the difficult early years of the Revolution and they were glad to choose him again as governor. Henry was happy to take on the post. After some years of relative ease at his Leatherwood plantation, he felt renewed attraction for the governor's mansion. Madison believed that Henry accepted the governorship for family reasons, and undoubtedly

Dorothea Henry and the couple's growing children relished the prospect of living full-time in Richmond, rather than in the remote southwest of Leatherwood. Having chosen—or having been lured into accepting—the relatively weak governorship, he would not be able to save the general assessment plan.[33]

Although the incorporation bill passed the House, Madison got the vote on the general assessment delayed until 1785. In his *Memorial and Remonstrance*, he crisply stated the reasons many Virginians, including many evangelical Christians, opposed the plan. Religion, he argued, "must be left to the conviction and conscience of every man; and it is the right of every man to exercise it as these may dictate. This right is in its nature an unalienable right." To Madison and his Baptist allies, religious freedom required that the government give no support to churches. Any action government took on behalf of a particular denomination was inherently discriminatory toward people of other faiths or opinions. Ultimately, the legislature set the assessment bill aside due to lack of popular support (the incorporation bill would later pass the Senate). Baptists across the state celebrated. As one minister put it, "this formidable imp was destroyed at the time of his formation, and never suffered to draw breath nor perform one action in this happy land of freedom."[34]

The demise of the general assessment gave new life to the Bill for Establishing Religious Freedom. Jefferson had drafted this bill in 1777, but it lacked support until the controversy over the general assessment focused Virginians' attention on the question of their church-state relationship. In early 1786, Madison won final approval for the statute, which proclaimed that "no man shall be compelled to frequent or support any religious worship, place, or ministry whatsoever, nor shall be enforced, restrained, molested, or burdened in his body or goods, nor shall otherwise suffer, on account of his religious opinions or belief; but that all men shall be free to profess, and by argument to maintain, their opinions in matters of religion, and that the same shall in no wise diminish, enlarge, or affect their civil capacities."[35]

Henry's effort to promote religious liberty by the plural establishment of churches had generated a backlash, resulting in Virginia's remarkably modern position on religion and government. The state no longer could use tax money to help the churches do their business. The Virginia model heavily influenced the First Amendment's encouragement of the "free exercise of religion" and its ban on a national established church. As it turned out, the legal and constitutional endorsement of religious voluntarism would put Christianity on a much stronger basis in Virginia and America generally, with evangelical churches growing exponentially in the next seventy-five years, prior to the Civil War.

The battle over the general assessment accelerated the downward spiral in Henry's relationship with Madison and Jefferson. Although Jefferson was in Paris during this time, serving as ambassador to France, his personal animosity toward Henry grew steadily even in absentia. Jefferson came to see Henry as the opponent of every worthy political goal he endorsed. For example, Jefferson and Madison had dreamed of holding a convention that would revise the state's 1776 Constitution. Jefferson sent Madison a draft constitution in 1783 that would have rearranged the political branches of state government, giving more power to the governor and courts. There was little popular support for such a plan, and Jefferson blamed Henry for it. In his most bitter invective toward Henry, Jefferson told Madison that as long as Henry lived, there was no chance for constitutional reform. "What we have to do I think," Jefferson wrote, "is devoutly to pray for his death." Though Jefferson probably meant this comment sarcastically, he also wrote it in one of his encrypted codes so no one else would see his malevolent wishes for Henry.[36]

DESPITE THE FAILURE OF THE GENERAL ASSESSMENT, Henry remained committed as governor to the public support of religion. He responded enthusiastically to a proposal for Christianizing Native Americans presented to him by England's Selina Hastings, the Countess of Huntingdon. The countess was a key evangelical Methodist leader who corresponded with a number of American religious and political figures, including her distant relative George Washington. George and Martha Washington were so enamored with the countess that they placed an engraving of her on their bedroom wall at Mount Vernon.[37]

Sir James Jay, a prominent physician and brother of New York's John Jay, provided Governor Henry an outline of the countess's plan, including a letter from the countess to Henry. The American Revolution had opened a door for the evangelization of the Indians, she told him, and her plan sought to "introduce the benevolent religion of our blessed Redeemer among heathen and savage nations." The countess wanted the legislatures of Virginia and other states with substantial frontier areas to grant lands for Christian settlers to establish new towns near the Indian tribes. There they would set up schools and churches, attracting Indians with the prospect of education and refinement. The countess would administer the licensing of Christian settlers from Europe. All she needed, she said, was for the legislatures to provide the land and tax incentives toward settlement.

Henry saw the plan as an antidote to the continuing turmoil on the frontier, which he attributed partly to Indian resistance to Christianity and what he saw as their lack of civilization. He longed to introduce more white Christian settlers who would reduce Virginia's overall dependence on slave labor. The plan would ultimately bolster public virtue, which Henry believed had woefully languished during the war. Henry advocated for the countess's plan with the state legislature, but because most of Virginia's vacant land had been deeded to Congress, he directed his appeals there, writing to Virginia's congressional delegates in 1785 and telling them that the twin goals of attracting Christian settlers and evangelizing Native Americans demanded immediate action. Similarly, Henry wrote to Joseph Martin, his prominent neighbor near Leatherwood, expressing his zeal for the plan. "She hopes to do [this] at her own expense chiefly," he said, "and to import large number of people from Great Britain and Ireland that are good whigs and strictly religious."[38]

But concerns over the settlers' political allegiances, and the means of doling out land, derailed the countess's proposal. As Richard Henry Lee told George Washington, who had also strongly recommended the plan, Congress feared the settlers might prove to be British sympathizers, and moreover, all available land was committed for sale to pay off public debts.[39]

Henry continued to promote the plan in the Virginia legislature, but the countess's scheme was doomed, an unsuccessful instance of Henry and Washington's continuing interest in using state power to support religion, virtue, and even missionary work. Lest we think that such ideas were peculiar to Henry and Washington or that they faded after the Constitution and Bill of Rights were adopted, President Thomas Jefferson himself would approve federal funding for a missionary and church in Illinois. Even the great champion of total disestablishment believed that the government could employ religious workers to accomplish public goods, in this case the education and "civilization" of Native Americans. To Revolutionary-era Americans such as Henry and Jefferson, that civilizing project by definition meant instructing them in Christianity.[40]

THE FAILURE OF THE PLAN TO evangelize Native Americans was only one example of Henry's struggles as governor and the lack of assistance he received from Congress. Other problems lingered after the war, such as the difficulty of aligning the state militias with national defense goals. George Washington sought to have militias led by Continental army veterans because he had found the militia units so difficult to control during the war. In the absence of a national wartime army, the militias would need to be ready in case of a new war with Britain or Native Americans.

At times, such conflicts seemed imminent. A series of dubious treaties earlier in the decade, regarding the status of lands north of the Ohio River, angered local Native Americans. Continued intrusions by white settlers and local fighting threatened to incite full-fledged war between Virginia and its Indian neighbors. Henry spent much of 1785 trying to keep Virginians from fighting with the Cherokees of western North Carolina. He also wrote urgently to officials in Greenbrier County (in present-day West Virginia) in June 1785, telling them to prepare their militia for hostilities with Native Americans in that area. He tried to prevent white settlers from crossing the Ohio River into disputed territory, but thousands went anyway, risking their lives to obtain fertile farmland. Indians along the Ohio River in the mid-1780s killed several hundred Americans. Probably even more Indians were killed by Americans.

In July, word came that a party of Virginians on their way to a peace conference with Indians had been murdered north of the Ohio. Daniel Boone, the militia commander and famous frontiersman, wrote to Henry, telling him of the churning violence. In his rough dialect, he said "an Inden Warr is Expected" and that the local militias would not be able to stop an invasion by the Wabash Confederacy. As frontier settlers clamored for retaliation, Henry admonished them to stop advancing into Indian lands; the prospect of Indian war was a "fatal evil" that would unleash new depths of suffering and undermine Virginia's faltering finances. Though Henry was no pioneer of peaceful relations with Native Americans, neither did he seek war with them. Virginia could not afford it.[41]

Virginia's Militia Act of 1784 attempted to address Washington's wishes for a stronger militia by releasing all county lieutenants and field officers from duty by April 1785, with Henry to appoint their replacements. The act was a disaster. The governor received numerous protests against the system of replacements, with some complainants accusing Henry of insulting the existing officers in an undemocratic power grab. The prominent lawyer and militia officer St. George Tucker resigned his newly appointed post, telling Henry that he did not realize the act would be "rendered abortive by the dissenting voice of the people." Henry became convinced that the Militia Act was unenforceable and asked the legislature to amend it, telling the Speaker of the House of Delegates that the "execution of the Militia Law has caused much embarrassment to the executive"—meaning himself. Henry blamed a lack of adequate information for the debacle, but the failure of the reorganization showed heightened expectations among the militia for choosing their own officers, as well as the difficulty of getting Virginians to accept direction in military affairs. The amended act simply restored the positions to the old officers. A chastened Henry even had to write to the counties asking them to provide him complete lists of the officers he was to reinstate.[42]

Also fueling Henry's unease were strange rumors that agents of the Barbary states were in Richmond. The Barbary pirates, based along the North African coast, had harassed and captured European and American ships for decades. When the pirates sensed the weakness of the fledgling American navy, major hostilities between America and the Barbary states erupted in 1785, with Algerians seizing two American ships that year. In November, Henry wrote a peculiar yet ominous letter to the House of Delegates, telling them that "certain persons from the coast of Barbary are now in this city." He sought to ascertain whether he had authority "to arrest dangerous characters coming from abroad." Three suspected Barbary spies were indeed detained and interrogated by Virginia officials. The suspects claimed not to be Algerians but Moors, or Spaniards of North African descent. Their interrogators remained suspicious that they might have subversive intentions, but found no evidence to support that notion. Governor Henry's apprehension at the prospect of Barbary espionage revealed fresh concern for Virginia's security.[43]

CONFRONTING SO MANY TROUBLES on such different fronts, Henry conceivably could have become a defender of the increased national power that the new Constitution would provide in three years' time. Perhaps if things had developed differently in the mid-1780s, he would have. As late as the end of 1786, James Madison still hoped that Henry might join him in the fight for a more energetic national government.

Madison would be sorely disappointed, because Henry would soon emerge as Virginia's leading opponent of the move for a new Constitution. His concern for Virginia's security did not lead him to support a more centralized government, because he viewed Congress as interest-driven and inept. His negative view of the Confederation government crystallized in 1785 and 1786 because of two related issues: Congress's lack of protection for frontier settlers, and a proposed treaty that would have surrendered America's navigation rights on the Mississippi River to the Spanish.

By 1785, Henry had begun to fear that a broader war with Indians was about to erupt. He suspected that Native Americans in the trans-Mississippi West might align with the Spanish, threatening Virginia and other states that had substantial western frontiers. Henry longed to open Kentucky (which was still part of Virginia) and the greater West to settlement, but he knew that Indian and Spanish aggression could pin Americans along the Atlantic coast. Richard Henry Lee warned him in February that Spain's new minister to America, Don Diego Maria de Gardoqui, would claim an exclusive Spanish right to commerce on the Mississippi. "Spain is proud," Lee wrote, "and extremely jealous of our approximation to her South American territory, and fearing the example of our ascendancy on that country, is grasping forever at more territory."[44]

Henry became increasingly exasperated with Congress's failure to protect Virginia settlers in the Ohio River Valley, who continued to suffer periodic attacks from Shawnees and other Native Americans, despite Henry's efforts to limit their settlement to areas safely south of the Ohio River. George Rogers Clark told Henry that war with the Wabash Confederacy was certain and that Kentucky's prospects were bleak, with "so formidable and bloody an enemy to encounter [and] much irregularity in the country."[45]

Henry bluntly appealed to Congress for help in 1786. The management of Indian affairs was one of the few things he needed the national government to do well, but it had failed miserably. Henry, always sensitive to the essential purposes of government, saw Congress's abandonment of settlers in western Virginia as neglect of "the most valuable article of the social compact." To receive the government's protection of their most essential rights—including the rights, as English philosopher John Locke had famously argued, to life, liberty, and property—Americans paid taxes and gave up a measure of their freedom to the national and state governments. If the national Congress would not protect its vulnerable citizens from Indian attacks, then what good was the government?[46]

When Virginia's congressional delegation reported back to Henry regarding his plea for assistance, the news was not good. The northern states without large frontier areas were unwilling to help. "They with reluctance assent to relieving us from difficulties to which they are not themselves likely to be exposed to," they wrote. Henry was "mortified" at this news. "I cannot be persuaded," he told the delegation, "to think it necessary for me to endeavor to excite sympathy for that part of the union whose extermination seems to be attempted by an enemy thirsting for blood." Did Congress intend to protect frontier settlers or not? Their dreadful disregard of the frontier had started rumors of secession from the Confederation government by the western settlers. Henry began to wonder whether he would eventually have to choose between the national Confederation government and Virginians in the West. With sectional issues already hampering Congress's ability to act on Virginia's behalf, what would an even stronger national government mean for Virginia, if the same northeastern interests retained their dominant power?[47]

In August 1786, Henry's consternation regarding the national government reached new heights. John Jay, the secretary of foreign affairs, recommended that the United States give up the use of the Mississippi to Spain for twenty-five or thirty years, in exchange for trade privileges that would primarily profit the northern states. Jay, a wealthy New Yorker nine years younger than Henry, would soon become, along with Alexander Hamilton, one of his state's key advocates for the new Constitution and, in 1789, the first chief justice of the United States. According to Jay, the Mississippi deal would confer short-term commercial benefits on the country, while allowing the possibility that American control of the river could be reestablished after several decades of Spanish control. Virginia's delegates in Congress countered with a motion calling for perpetual American access to the Mississippi, but northern members defeated it. A northern majority gave Jay authority to negotiate away America's access to the great river.[48]

Southerners were outraged. Virginia congressman James Monroe, an army veteran and lawyer who was becoming one of Henry's chief allies, wrote the governor to say he felt Jay's actions were not just misguided but dishonest. Congress had earlier instructed Jay not to put navigation rights up for negotiation, but Jay did so anyway and then convinced northern delegates to rescind the instructions forbidding such a deal. Monroe saw the affair as a plot against southern interests "pursued by a set of men so flagitious, unprincipled, and determined in their pursuits, as to satisfy me beyond a doubt they have extended their views to the dismemberment of the government." Monroe believed that changes in the Confederation would be necessary to preserve the Union, but he doubted whether northern delegates possessed the requisite virtue and common sense to make those modifications.[49]

Convinced that giving up the Mississippi would be a disaster, Henry worked to generate resistance to Jay's plan in Virginia and Kentucky. He wrote to his sister Anne, who lived in Kentucky; her husband, William Christian, had died in the Illinois country in a fight with Wabash Indians, which gave Henry's fears about the turmoil in the West deep personal significance. "Congress are about to agree to give up the navigation of the Mississippi," Henry told her. "I've exerted myself to prevent it." He asked her to encourage their contacts in Kentucky to petition Congress against the treaty. Southern opposition finally did derail the treaty in the Confederation Congress, where a two-thirds majority was required to approve such agreements.[50]

Although Jay failed to negotiate away the Mississippi, he did major damage to the credibility of the Confederation government. In fact, the Mississippi controversy was one of the chief precipitants of the Constitutional Convention of 1787, with many Americans fearing that the Articles had to be reformed lest disunion result. By 1786, almost everyone realized that change was needed, but southerners were divided as to whether the conflict over Jay's Mississippi treaty indicated a need for stronger national government or more power for the states.

James Madison wanted a stronger government but he feared that the Mississippi fracas could jeopardize that effort, particularly because of its effect on Henry and other southerners. Madison wrote to

George Washington in December 1786, telling him, "I am entirely convinced from what I observe here, that unless the project of Congress can be reversed, the hopes of carrying this state into a proper federal system will be demolished. Many of our most federal leading men are extremely soured with what has already passed. Mr. Henry, who has been hitherto the champion of the federal cause, has become a cold advocate, and in the event of an actual sacrifice of the Mississippi by Congress, will unquestionably go over to the opposite side."[51]

The Mississippi treaty turned Henry against the idea of a more formidable national government. He was always a defender of Virginia's interests first, and his Christian republican assumptions also convinced him that large-scale consolidated power could not be trusted. He doubted that politicians from other sections of the country would act on behalf of the nation's interests as a whole—a concern confirmed by Jay's actions.

Before Henry's opposition to the new Constitution became publicly known, he retired again from the governor's office, explaining to his sister Anne that he and Dorothea were "heartily tired of the bustle we live in" at Richmond. The pressures of the governor's office continued to clash with his financial and domestic imperatives. Dorothea had given birth to five children between 1778 and 1785, and Patrick needed to devote more time to his own business to support the family. Two of Henry's older daughters, Anne and Elizabeth, got married in the fall of 1786, shortly before he stepped down as governor. He had to provide a dowry to each, in addition to the costs associated with the weddings. (His beloved Elizabeth, or Betsey, was married in October at St. John's Church in Richmond, where Henry had delivered the "Liberty or Death" speech eleven years earlier.) The dread of financial debility tormented Henry. Nor did he take pleasure in the thought of a sixth term, as he found himself routinely fighting with a national government that seemed either indifferent or hostile to Virginia's interests.[52]

Henry relocated his family to a new home in Prince Edward County, which was closer than his Leatherwood plantation, only eighty miles southwest of Richmond. There they would live in a modest wooden house for the next six years, while he tried to revive his legal practice and ventures in land speculation. The location put Henry at some distance from political affairs, but the separation was intentional. He needed some space away from the demands of government. Politics, he reminded himself, could never become his exclusive work.

Mail delivery was sometimes slow in remote Prince Edward County. When the new governor, Edmund Randolph, wrote Henry in December 1786 asking him to serve as a delegate to a recently summoned Constitutional Convention in 1787, Henry did not receive the letter for about two months. By that time, he had decided that he wanted nothing to do with James Madison's scheme to transform the nation's government.[53]

# 9

## "I SMELT A RAT"

## Defending the Revolution by Opposing the Constitution

MAJOR NORTHERN NEWSPAPERS published the news of Patrick Henry's selection as a delegate to the Constitutional Convention even before he had received the request to serve. But when Henry finally got Edmund Randolph's letter of invitation in February 1787, he politely declined the offer. Not only would attending the convention distract from his private affairs—the condition of which had driven him to leave the governor's office—but he had also turned against the idea of substantially changing the form of the national government. One anecdote holds that when a pro-Constitution opponent demanded to know why Henry had not attended the convention, he replied, "I smell a rat."[1]

Henry scented that decaying rodent in the notion that the states should surrender more power to a new national government. John Marshall, the future chief justice of the Supreme Court, also believed that Henry would rather see the dissolution of the Confederation than surrender America's right to the Mississippi as John Jay had attempted to do. Madison told Jefferson that Henry's revulsion against the Mississippi treaty augured ill for any governmental change. "Mr. Henry's disgust [regarding the Jay Treaty] exceeded all measure and I am not singular in ascribing his refusal to attend the convention to the policy of keeping himself free to combat or espouse the result of it according to the result of the Mississippi business." Madison feared (correctly) that he and Henry were heading for a confrontation over the Constitution. Henry's snub of the convention allowed him to subsequently position himself to oppose the constitutional changes. Madison told Washington that Henry's action "proceeded from a wish to leave his conduct unfettered on another theatre where the result of the convention will receive its destiny from his omnipotence." But Henry, like most Americans, also may not have seen how fundamentally Madison and Hamilton intended to change the Articles. They meant to abandon the Articles altogether.[2]

A MOVEMENT TO REVISE the Articles of Confederation had been growing ever since the government had struggled to provide for the Continental army during the war. Many Americans also were arguing that the national government needed power to regulate interstate and foreign commerce. Some of the new nation's worst economic problems were the result of European trade barriers to American goods. Without a central authority to negotiate tariffs and other commercial policies, the states could only muddle along, futilely trying to get European countries to accept their exports on an equitable basis.

A major problem blocking the revision of the Articles lay within the document itself: it required unanimous approval by the states for amendments. One or two states had often stymied reforms that seemed sensible to the rest. In the mid-1780s, frustration over the Articles led younger political leaders such as James Madison and Alexander Hamilton to wonder whether more drastic action was required than simply proposing new laws and amendments that would be debated, diluted, and ultimately dismissed.

At Virginia's behest, a multistate conference met in Annapolis in September 1786 to consider giving Congress the power to regulate commerce. The meeting made no progress on the issue, but the attendees recommended that the states elect delegates to another convention, to be held in Philadelphia in May 1787, which would "devise such further provisions as shall appear to them necessary to render the constitution of the federal government adequate to the exigencies of the Union." When Virginia's legislature elected its delegates for the Constitutional Convention, Henry received the second-greatest number of votes after George Washington, with James Madison fifth in the balloting—an order reflecting Henry's relative position in Virginia politics, one rivaled only by Washington. The delegation was mixed in its views of the need for stronger national government.[3]

Edmund Randolph's letter of invitation made clear why legislators were asking Henry to participate, even though many recognized he was not inclined to afford the government major new powers. Randolph (Henry's successor as governor) knew that Henry's experience in leading the state had shown him how deeply dysfunctional the national government had become. Randolph also realized that the political crisis of the 1780s raised the prospect that a newly independent America might forget the lessons of the Revolution, chief among them the danger of centralized government. Americans needed the wisdom of "those who first kindled the Revolution," Randolph wrote, who could be trusted to protect its legacy.[4]

But Henry remained home. Although delegates from many states made major contributions to the convention, Virginians took the lead, thanks in part to George Washington's formidable and essential presence. Washington had retired from the army in 1783 with great flourish, styling himself as an American Cincinnatus, willingly surrendering military power to return to his beloved farm. "I meditate to pass the remainder of my life in a state of undisturbed repose," he told his grateful countrymen. But once Washington became convinced that the new nation would not survive without major adjustments to the Articles of Confederation, he reluctantly agreed to reenter politics. Washington was simultaneously the most important delegate at the Constitutional Convention and the one least involved in the debates. His presence lent invaluable credibility to Madison and Hamilton's audacious plans, especially when charges mounted during the ratification debates that the proceedings were illegitimate. Henry's archenemy, Jefferson, was not at the convention; he remained in Paris as ambassador to France.[5]

The thirty-six-year-old Madison wielded the most influence over the details of the new document that began to emerge from the Philadelphia negotiations. He brought to the delegates a plan for a federal government that would be stronger than the Confederation, but that he claimed would respect individual and states' rights. After intense debate and much compromise, Madison and the nationalists—who would become known as Federalists—succeeded in getting the convention to endorse a vigorous government to replace the Confederation. The new Congress would have the powers to tax and to regulate interstate commerce. The executive power, the president, would command the armed forces, appoint executive and judicial officers, and conduct diplomacy. The federal judiciary's powers were less clear. But while the Confederation had no clearly defined executive or judicial authority, the new Constitution placed the executive and judicial powers in branches of the government separate from the legislative.

The Constitution also reduced the relative strength the states enjoyed under the Articles. Numerical majorities, not the states, would rule in the House of Representatives. No longer could states so easily stop new legislation. The states also lost much of their power to regulate interstate commerce. Moreover, ratifying the new Constitution only required nine states' approval to go into effect in the states that had ratified, whereas the Confederation had required all thirteen even to agree on amendments.

Madison and the nationalists did concede on some of the most extreme aspects of the government's political power. For example, Madison had to give up on the concept that the national government could veto state legislation. But overall, the polity hammered together by the delegates was much more like the British system (a national government with balanced powers and a strong executive) than the Articles were. Although it did not become widely known until years after the Constitution was adopted, the archnationalist Alexander Hamilton frankly stated at the convention that he thought the recently rejected British system of government—in which the Parliament and king reigned over local interests—was the ideal model for America.

Signs of opposition to this accrual of national authority appeared among Virginians, even at the convention. As the meetings ended, Virginia delegates George Mason and Edmund Randolph refused to sign the document. Mason had unsuccessfully sought to mandate a two-thirds majority on any navigation acts, which would have given southerners extra protection against northern economic interests. Shortly after the convention adjourned in September 1787, Mason published a list of reasons why he could not support the Constitution. He predicted that because of the simple majority required for navigation acts, the "five southern states (whose produce and circumstances are totally different from that of the eight northern and eastern states) will be ruined." Mason also lamented the absence of a bill of rights, and the dangerous powers afforded to the Senate and president. He forecast that the new government would become either a monarchy or a "corrupt oppressive aristocracy."[6]

Madison and Washington actually thought they might yet convince Henry to support the Constitution. Madison knew a lot was at stake. "Much will depend on Mr. Henry," Madison wrote. As soon as Washington returned home, he began appealing to Henry and other possible opponents to support the Constitution, despite the defects they would identify in it. It is not entirely clear what Washington found deficient in the Constitution, because he intended to support it publicly and remained silent on its faults. Nevertheless, he sent a copy of the document to Henry, telling him that "your experience of the difficulties which have ever arisen when attempts have been made to reconcile such variety of interests, and local prejudices as pervade the several states will render explanation unnecessary. I wish the Constitution which is offered had been made more perfect, but I sincerely believe it is the best that could be obtained at this time—and as a constitutional door is opened for amendment hereafter."[7]

Henry was not convinced. He wrote back to Washington, saying, "I have to lament that I cannot bring my mind to accord with the proposed Constitution. The concern I feel on this account, is really greater than I am able to express. Perhaps mature reflection may furnish me reasons to change my present sentiments into a conformity with the opinion of those personages for whom I have the highest reverence." Opposing Washington was not something Henry relished, but on this occasion he would make that choice.[8]

As with his opposition to disestablishment of the Anglican Church, some have found Henry's hostility toward the Constitution perplexing. Americans' devotion to their system of government is a doctrine of their civil spirituality. After its ratification, they would not typically question the essential value of the Constitution, much less condemn it in the harsh terms that Henry did. Yet in 1787 Henry was in good company as an anti-federalist, both within and outside of Virginia. Benjamin Harrison, a signer of the Declaration of Independence and former governor of Virginia, told Washington that although America had its problems, this constitutional "remedy will prove worse than the disease." Like Mason, he feared that the Constitution would make the southern states forever subservient to the North.[9]

Even Thomas Jefferson expressed doubts about the Constitution, writing to Madison from France that "I am not a friend to a very energetic government. It is always oppressive." He shared Henry and Mason's concerns about the government's clout, especially the authority assigned to the president. But Jefferson's personal attachment to Madison led him to mute his concerns, reserving his efforts to advocate for the adoption of a Bill of Rights after ratification— amendments he hoped would sufficiently restrain the national government's powers. Unlike Jefferson, Henry was hardly inclined to do Madison any political favors. His opposition to the Constitution was surely influenced by his rivalry and animosity with these other Founders, but ultimately it arose from a deep political conviction that the new government did not honor the spirit of the Revolution.[10]

IN VIRGINIA, THE FIRST ORDER of business was considering Congress's request for the states to hold conventions to ratify the Constitution. No one, including Henry, opposed such a convention, but Henry insisted that the meeting have the option of proposing amendments to the Constitution before a final vote on ratification. A report in the House of Delegates (Henry had been elected a delegate from Prince Edward County in summer 1787) recorded his perspective: "No man, [Henry] said, was more truly federal than himself. But he conceived that if this resolution was adopted, the convention would only have it in their power to say, that the new plan should be adopted, or rejected; and that, however defective it might appear to them, they would not be authorized to propose amendments." Defenders of the Constitution opposed the call for amendments, wanting instead an up-or-down vote on the government, because they felt allowing individual states to propose amendments would turn into a quagmire. How could the states possibly consider all the amendments that would likely be offered? The only way would be a second constitutional convention, a scenario Madison desperately wanted to avoid.[11]

In the debate over how to handle ratification, the Federalists spoke in favor of a resolution calling for a convention "according to the recommendation of Congress," to which Henry offered an amendment authorizing the convention to propose constitutional amendments. John Marshall—then a thirty-two-year-old lawyer from Richmond—intervened and proposed that the House call a ratifying convention which would allow "free and ample discussion" of the Constitution, a motion the House approved unanimously. Whether that discussion would allow the suggestion of amendments prior to final approval was left ambiguous.[12]

In a letter to Jefferson in December 1787, Madison set forth the three parties in Virginia that would debate the Constitution. One, led by Washington and himself, included those who wanted to adopt the Constitution with no amendments. The second group, among them Governor Edmund Randolph and George Mason, favored the Constitution but sought amendments protecting the rights of the states and of individuals. The third party advocated for amendments but did not really want to adopt the Constitution. Their leader was Henry. "Mr. Henry is the great adversary who will render the event precarious," Madison wrote. "He is I find with his usual address, working up every possible interest, into a spirit of opposition." Madison believed that Henry and his allies wanted to preserve the existing

Confederation government, or perhaps even break up the American union into sectional confederacies.[13]

Madison and his colleagues Alexander Hamilton and John Jay had already begun campaigning for ratification by publishing their *Federalist* essays in New York in October 1787, making a compelling case for the new Constitution. Madison fully conceded the dangers of consolidated federal authority, but he argued that the Constitution accounted for the threat of tyranny in government by separating the powers of the government vertically (between states and the nation) and horizontally (among the government's branches). He called the new government a "compound republic," in which authority was "first divided between two distinct governments [state and national], and then the portion allotted to each subdivided among distinct and separate departments. Hence a double security arises to the rights of the people," Madison concluded.[14]

Patrick Henry, who remained at Leatherwood through most of late 1787 and the first half of 1788, waged nothing like the public campaign of Madison and Hamilton in *The Federalist*. Nevertheless, Prince Edward County elected him as a delegate to the Virginia ratifying convention, and his opponents feared that he was working behind the scenes to defeat the Constitution. John Blair Smith, a Presbyterian pastor in Prince Edward County, president of Hampden-Sydney College, and supporter of the Constitution, wrote to Madison accusing Henry of leading a dirty political campaign against the new government. "That gentleman has descended to lower artifice and management upon the occasion than I thought him capable of. . . . It grieves me to see such great natural talents abused to guilty purposes," Smith wrote. He believed that Henry was stirring up the people of the southern and western counties with rumors that the Constitution would finalize the surrender of the Mississippi River to Spain and that it would allow the Federalists to implement a national establishment of religion. Smith considered the latter assertion particularly ironic, given Henry's support for Virginia's general assessment for religion.[15]

Some Federalists heard that Henry was proposing that Virginia go it alone as an independent nation. While this might seem an unlikely prospect in retrospect, Virginia was the largest state in the Union (with about 750,000 people, including slaves), and it commanded great influence in the world agricultural trade. Edward Carrington, a Virginia delegate to the Continental Congress, told Thomas Jefferson in April 1788 that Henry was implying that a breakup of the Union was possible. Henry ostensibly proposed dividing the country into three confederacies. Carrington hoped that Henry's plan would go nowhere and that Virginians would fear the consequences of disunion more than any undesirable features of the new government.[16]

When Henry departed for the ratifying convention in Richmond in late May 1788, eight states had already approved the Constitution, just short of the nine required for adoption. (Unlike most states that elected delegates to ratifying conventions, obstreperous Rhode Island had overwhelmingly rejected the Constitution by a popular referendum in March.) Most of the states had ratified by strong majorities, but Massachusetts had only narrowly voted for the Constitution and had recommended a slate of amendments to Congress. The eight states voting prior to Virginia had given momentum to ratification, and Henry and the other anti-federalists at the convention believed they were the last defense against unconditional acceptance of this powerful government.

Henry was convinced that a large majority of Virginians opposed the unamended Constitution, and that in his beloved adopted home of Southside Virginia, as many as nine in ten were opposed. But he worried about the composition of the ratifying convention, for "the friends and seekers of power, have, with their usual subtlety wriggled themselves into the choice of the people." Federalists and anti-federalists were in roughly equal numbers at the meeting.[17]

Madison, surprisingly, had to be convinced to participate in the Virginia convention. He thought that perhaps propriety dictated that the framers of the Constitution should not take part in the ratification assemblies. He also did not like the idea of traveling back from New York, where Congress was in session, to Virginia. But Washington and others succeeded in impressing upon him that he simply had to be at the convention and that he might not even be elected as a delegate if he did not return to Virginia immediately. Washington's secretary, Tobias Lear, expressed the sentiments of many Federalists when he wrote that Madison was "the only man in this state who can effectually combat the influence of Mason and Henry." The stage was set for the great confrontation between Henry and Madison that had been brewing for years.[18]

This was to be the last political battle of Patrick Henry's career. It required him to defend the American Revolution by opposing the Constitution. Americans had fought for their independence from an abusive political regime—the British monarchy—and now James Madison and Alexander Hamilton meant to put Americans back under a strong executive, only four years after the peace treaty with Britain. To Henry this was a repudiation of all the liberties he and other patriots had fought for. America had many problems following the Revolution, he acknowledged, but Henry hardly believed that creating a monstrous national government was the solution. Many had died to free them from such a regime. Going back represented a betrayal of the Revolution.[19]

RICHMOND, STILL A RELATIVELY new town, had about 2,000 residents—under normal circumstances. But people flooded into Richmond that June, some to participate in the convention, others looking to hawk their goods or just to be part of the excitement. "Richmond is exceedingly crowded and many of no principle and desperate fortunes are attending there," wrote one worried Federalist, James

Duncanson. The convention quickly relocated from the statehouse to the more capacious New Theatre to accommodate the throngs of people. "A great proportion of them [are] Antifederalists," wrote Duncanson, "and clamorous in their opposition out of doors, ready to pursue any desperate step countenanced by their party." Patrick Henry and George Mason were doing all they could to stoke the fears of this rabble, the Federalist writer declared; they would readily sacrifice the American union to their "wicked and ambitious views."[20]

Henry may have refused to attend the Philadelphia convention, but at the Virginia ratifying assembly, his personality blazed in all its power and glory. He became the "master of ceremonies," as one recent historian put it. Thankfully, the Virginia convention appointed a good stenographer; its records may provide the most accurate accounts of any of Henry's major speeches. Although supporters and opponents both agreed that they should examine the Constitution point by point, proceeding through the document in sequence, Henry would repeatedly commandeer the floor for epic speeches about an array of concerns. George Mason insisted that the convention not try to rush ratification, for "the curse denounced by the divine vengeance, will be small, compared to what will justly fall upon us, if from any sinister views we obstruct the fullest inquiry." Mason and Henry would prove a formidable duo at the convention.[21]

George Nicholas, a delegate from Albemarle County, opened the proceedings by asserting that under the Constitution, Virginians would have "all the security which a people sensible and jealous of their liberties can wish for." Nicholas and Henry had worked together in 1781 to initiate the investigation of Thomas Jefferson's behavior as governor, but now they could not have been further apart, as indicated by Henry's opening speech, which followed Nicholas's. He countered by saying that the proposed Constitution was not simply wrongheaded but a threat to the republic itself. He was willing to stake his reputation on opposing this change, for he was the chief defender of Virginia's liberty. "I consider myself as the servant of the people of this commonwealth, as a sentinel over their rights, liberty, and happiness," he reminded the convention. "I conceive the republic to be in extreme danger. If our situation be thus uneasy, whence has arisen this fearful jeopardy? It arises from this fatal system—it arises from a proposal to change our government:—a proposal that goes to the utter annihilation of the most solemn engagements of the states. . . . A wrong step made now will plunge us into misery, and our Republic will be lost."[22]

Why, he demanded, did the Philadelphia convention presume to speak as "We, the People, instead of We, the States?" This Constitution ignored the role of the states, Henry believed. Diffuse, state-based political power was an essential safeguard of liberty. "States are the characteristics, and the soul of a confederation. If the states be not the agents of this compact, it must be one great consolidated national government of the people of all the states." The word "consolidated" appeared repeatedly in anti-federalist attacks on the Constitution. Too much power in too few hands was by definition dangerous to republican liberty. Madison, of course, denied that the new government entailed a total consolidation of power, avowing he had carefully framed checks and balances within the government to prevent the rise of tyranny. But Henry disagreed. Only a small group of men, not "the people," had forged this dubious frame of government, Henry cautioned. They had no popular or legal authority to do what they had done, far surpassing their assigned duty to amend the Articles of Confederation.[23]

A number of speakers argued against Henry's characterization of the Constitution, and one of them challenged the ethics of Henry's strategy in fighting it. Henry Lee, known as "Light Horse Harry" for his work as a cavalry officer during the Revolution, threw aside Virginia's reverence for its aging patriot hero. Henry, he suggested, was a fearmonger. "The éclat and brilliancy which have distinguished [Henry], the honors with which he has been dignified, and the brilliant talents which he has so often displayed, have attracted my respect and attention. On so important an occasion and before so respectable a body, I expected a new display of his powers of oratory: But instead of proceeding to investigate the merits of the new plan of government, the worthy character informed us of horrors which he felt, of apprehensions in his mind, which make him tremblingly fearful of the fate of the commonwealth: Mr. Chairman, was it proper to appeal to the fear of this House?"[24]

Indignant, Henry shot to his feet and gave his longest speech at the convention. Fear for the republic's fate was justified, he warned. America's liberty was tenuous, at risk of being sacrificed in the name of national power. His voice booming over the packed galleries ringing the "spacious and airy" wooden hall, he reminded the convention of his long experience in such matters, summoning them to the days of the Stamp Act: "Liberty [is] the greatest of all earthly blessings—give us that precious jewel, and you may take every thing else. . . . The time has been, when every pulse of my heart beat for American liberty, and which, I believe, had a counterpart in the breast of every true American: But suspicions have gone forth—suspicions of my integrity—publicly reported that my professions are not real—23 years ago I was supposed a traitor to my country: I was then said to be a bane of sedition, because I supported the rights of my country: I may be thought suspicious when I say our privileges and rights are in danger: But, Sir, a number of people of the people of this country are weak enough to think these things are too true." Throughout his career, Henry would be attacked and ridiculed for opposing national government authority—both British and American.[25]

Central to the debate over governmental power was the issue of a strong national military. The promoters of the Constitution made much of the ostensible threat posed by Shays' Rebellion in Massachusetts in 1786–87. This uprising of poverty-stricken farmers against foreclosure courts, while relatively minor in scale, had become a symbol of America's need for a more robust military to protect it from domestic and foreign enemies. Washington lamented the chaos spawned by Shays and concluded from the episode that "mankind left to themselves are unfit for their own government." But Henry doubted the significance of the rebellion, reminding the convention that the Confederation government had possessed sufficient strength to defeat the British during the Revolution. One admirer wrote that Henry "obviated the mighty bugbears raised to frighten and intimidate the weak and wavering into a speedy and implicit adoption." Shays was chief among those bugbears.[26]

Henry believed that the convention's quest for a more powerful military reflected no real insecurity, but revealed instead the Federalists' nationalistic dream of American glory. History showed that the search for glory often cost a people their rights, Henry declared. "Those nations who have gone in search of grandeur, power and splendor, have also fallen a sacrifice, and been the victims of their own folly: While they acquired those visionary blessings, they lost their freedom. My great objection to this government is, that it does not leave us the means of defending our rights." The Constitution's defenders had taken America's independence as a license to forge an empire, according to Henry. The Federalists, he warned, believed that "some way or other we must be a great and mighty empire; we must have an army, and a navy, and a number of things: When the American spirit was in its youth, the language of America was different: Liberty, Sir, was then the primary object." Empire building required power, but leaders possessed of consolidated power could not be trusted to preserve liberty.[27]

Challenging Madison's claim that the separate branches of government and the federated combination of national and state authority would safeguard against an aggregation of power, Henry averred that the Constitution allowed the government to control the governed, with little hope of controlling itself. The Philadelphia convention foolishly assumed that all politicians would be virtuous men, and to a Christian republican like Henry, who was well aware of the human capacity to sin, this was a fatal error. "Such a government is incompatible with the genius of republicanism: there will be no checks, no real balances, in this government: what can avail your specious imaginary balances, your rope-dancing, chain-rattling, ridiculous ideal checks and contrivances?" Nothing could check a national government entrusted with vast military might and the unlimited authority to tax.[28]

Indeed, Henry declaimed, the Constitution represented an outright repudiation of the Revolution: "Here is a revolution as radical as that which separated us from Great Britain. It is as radical, if in this transition, our rights and privileges are endangered, and the sovereignty of the states be relinquished: and cannot we plainly see, that this is actually the case? The rights of conscience, trial by jury, liberty of the press, all your immunities and franchises, all pretensions to human rights and privileges, are rendered insecure, if not lost, by this change."[29]

TO HENRY, THE PROBLEMS within the Constitution did not simply require the addition of a Bill of Rights but a tangible weakening of the proposed national government. The office of president particularly worried Henry. The Articles of Confederation provided no executive office, and the Revolution had ostensibly rejected the principle of monarchy. Yet in the Constitution, Americans were asked to accept a strong executive office that, to Henry, smacked of a kingship. "The Constitution is said to have beautiful features," he proclaimed, "but when I come to examine these features, sir, they appear to me horribly frightful: among other deformities, it has an awful squinting; it squints towards monarchy: and does not this raise indignation in the breast of every true American? Your President may easily become King."[30]

Alexander Hamilton and the Federalists sneered at this kind of accusation. "Calculating upon the aversion of the people to monarchy," Hamilton wrote in *The Federalist*, "they have endeavoured to enlist all their jealousies and apprehensions in opposition to the intended president of the United States; not merely as the embryo, but as the full grown progeny of that detested parent." Hamilton reminded opponents that the president was fundamentally unlike a king in his accountability to the people and to the other branches of government. Kings were not elected to four-year terms, and they did not face the threat of impeachment for criminal behavior. The president could veto legislation, but Congress could override his vetoes. His senior appointments required the approval of the Senate. He could not dominate the government or neglect the wishes of the people, the Federalists argued.[31]

Henry did not trust these assurances. His primary concern was the president's command of the armed forces. Inevitably, a person elected president would use the military to run roughshod over the republic. "The President, in the field, at the head of his army, can prescribe the terms on which he shall reign master, so far that it will puzzle any American ever to get his neck from under the galling yoke." (At this point, the stenographer apparently began struggling to keep up with Henry's torrent of criticism against the president, finally noting in parenthesis that "Mr. Henry strongly and pathetically expatiated on the probability of the President's enslaving America.") Henry could not fathom why Americans, having just rejected the British king, would replace him with a president, a king in everything but name.[32]

The Federalists saw the Constitution as the only way to save the American Union, but Henry saw it as the primary threat to that union. He went so far as to suggest that since the majority of American states had already accepted the Constitution, secession might be Virginia's only remaining option. Not that he opposed a union of the states: Henry recognized the advantages of a properly confederated country. But a unified nation was not his top priority. "The first thing I have at heart is American liberty; the second thing is American Union." So Henry flatly declared that unless the Constitution was radically amended, Virginians should never accept it, and they should consider leaving the Union unless their concerns were addressed.[33]

Henry was not alone among Americans in considering secession from the Union an option in the face of a tyrannical government, either in the Revolutionary era or in the future. (The patriots had, after all, just seceded from the British Empire because they believed that the king and Parliament had become oppressive.) He raised the prospect of secession even before the Constitution's adoption. Seven decades later, acting on similar anxieties, the leaders of the South would follow through on this long-standing principle.

As THE CONVENTION WORE ON, Henry became rambling and slightly desperate. Henry probably knew he was fighting a losing battle, at least on the question of ratification. He was also personally distracted. Reportedly he received news in the middle of a long address that Dorothea had given birth to Alexander, their sixth child together. In a rare glimpse of his personal feelings during the summer of 1788, Henry wrote to his daughter Elizabeth Aylett on June 11, telling her that personal and political matters were filling him with turmoil. The birth of his child and the proceedings at the convention deprived him of "any peace of mind 'til I can get home." Another mouth to feed! thought the fifty-two-year-old Henry. Yet here he was battling again in the legislative arena, instead of making money and taking care of his family.[34]

Although the sentiment at the convention was clearly turning toward ratification, the Federalists remained alarmed by Henry's vehement and eloquent opposition. A letter published in northern newspapers claimed that Henry was only trying to "move the passions of the ignorant." Governor Randolph complained that if the convention allowed Henry's loquacious speeches to continue, it would take six months to decide the question instead of six weeks. As the supporters of the Constitution sought to counter Henry's arguments, Randolph played an essential role; for even though he had refused to sign the Constitution at the convention, he now believed that Virginia had no choice but to ratify it and trust that the Congress would amend it. Refusing to ratify would mean disunion, according to Randolph, a price that he—unlike Henry—was not willing to pay.[35]

James Madison listened to Henry and seethed. This plan of government, so carefully wrought in Philadelphia, did not deserve these kinds of gratuitous attacks, he thought. But Madison found that he could not say much more than what he had already said in *The Federalist*, especially because he was quite ill. What he called a "bilious attack" rendered him weak and mostly silent. He did occasionally reply directly to Henry's fulminations, as on June 6, when he lamented to the delegates that Henry was only appealing to fear: "We ought not to address our arguments to the feelings and passions, but to those understandings and judgments which were selected by the people of this country, to decide this great question, by a calm and rational investigation." Madison also challenged Henry's contention that there was no crisis under the Articles of Confederation; the calling of the Constitutional Convention reflected a consensus that major modifications were needed in the national government.[36]

Henry was not persuaded. He asserted that the Constitution represented a betrayal of the people of Virginia. He bristled at Edmund

Randolph, who in an earlier speech had spoken of the common people as a "herd," not capable of ruling themselves, rebuking Randolph for his incautious statement denigrating the citizens whom Henry believed he championed. Randolph did not try to defend himself, saying instead that he used the term "herd" only to describe the very multitude of people in the state. His was a common use of the term at the time, but to Henry, its disrespectful tone spoke of the dangers of this Constitution, which he feared would reduce common Virginians "from respectable independent citizens, to abject, dependent subjects or slaves." Once again, Henry clamored only for the freedom and independence of white citizens, making no public association between the enslavement he feared for his fellow free Virginians and the slavery they practiced; he intimately knew but did not mention the awful realities of the slavery already in Virginia's midst.[37]

Once again he raised the question of the Mississippi River, saying that a breakup of the Union would not happen "unless a Constitution be adopted which will enable the government to plant enemies on our backs." Approving the Constitution would mean losing the Mississippi, because a majority of northern states would be willing to cede control of the river to the Spanish. He firmly believed that the northern states would not protect the navigation rights of southerners, to whom it mattered most. (On this point, Henry was soon proven wrong, as the national Congress passed resolutions in September repudiating Jay's Mississippi treaty and asserting America's right to navigate the river. This was part of Congress's effort to garner support for the Constitution from southerners.) He cited the Mississippi debate as a prime example of the danger of trusting in the benevolence of politicians. "Did we not know of the fallibility of human nature, we might rely on the present structure of this government" to protect the interests of the southern states, he warned. "But the depraved nature of man is well known."[38]

Henry also warned that the government would become more and more bloated, wasteful, and extravagant over time. "The splendid maintenance of the President and of the members of both Houses; and the salaries and fees of the swarm of officers and dependents on the government will cost this continent immense sums." Under the Confederation, the states could hold the national government in check because they gave financial support in response to requests from the national legislature, but no such protection would exist under the Constitution, and nothing would keep taxes and federal expenditures from skyrocketing.[39]

From the potential abuse of the southern states to the wasteful taxing and spending by the new government, all of Henry's concerns were ultimately rooted in his Christian republican ideals and his preference for limited, local government. In Christian theology, sin required salvation through Christ, but in political theory, the best kind of government accounted for sin by pitting people's desires for gain, survival, and self-protection against one another. "The real rock of political salvation is self-love perpetuated from age to age in every human breast, and manifested in every action," Henry declared. It was not good enough to hope for benevolent leaders. "Virtue will slumber. The wicked will be continually watching: Consequently you will be undone."[40]

Henry's views on virtue and national power were more morally complex than he admitted: he was also concerned that the expanded national power under the Constitution might be used to attack southern slavery. He feared the taxing authority of the Congress partly because he suspected northern congressmen might eventually concoct a tax on slaves so onerous that it would force slave masters to emancipate them. Northern politicians, he feared, would not heed the violent effects of abolition and could potentially impose a rash program of emancipation. Madison (like Henry, a slave owner) denied that the Constitution gave Congress any such option, assuring the convention that with regard to government-forced abolition, "I believe such an idea never entered into any American breast, nor do I believe it ever will."[41]

Like many Virginia politicians and slave masters, Henry's views on slavery remained in conflict. He professed revulsion against slavery but said at the convention that "as much as I deplore slavery, I see that prudence forbids its abolition. I deny that the General Government ought to set them free, because a decided majority of the states have not the ties of sympathy and fellow-feeling for those whose interest would be affected by their emancipation. The majority of Congress is to the North, and the slaves are to the South. In this situation, I see a great deal of the property of the people of Virginia in jeopardy, and their peace and tranquility gone away." As much as he might like to see the slaves freed, Henry declared, the reality of abolition would unleash destruction—a race war between whites and blacks—and there was no practical or safe way for the government to mandate emancipation.[42]

Thanks partly to the assertions and rebuttals between Henry and the Constitution's defenders, the ratification convention dragged on, with many speeches repeating essentially the same points. Inevitably the long meetings became tense. George Nicholas, formerly Henry's ally against Jefferson, rose on June 23 to say that Henry apparently opposed every part of the proposed Constitution and went on to imply that certain delegates had a vested interest in restricting the power of the federal courts, because they might rule unfavorably on suspicious land deals made in Kentucky. Atypically, Henry interrupted Nicholas and demanded to know if he was attacking him personally. Nicholas bluntly replied, "I mean what I say, Sir." Both men backed off, however, when the chair asked that they refrain from any personal comments during the debate.[43]

Recognizing that his arguments likely would not persuade a majority of delegates to vote his way, Henry decided that if the anti-federalists could not defeat the Constitution outright, they might be able to amend the worst features of it. Indeed, the anti-federalists would win their greatest victory in the fight for amendments. Initially, the Federalists thought that constitutional amendments, which ultimately would take form in the Bill of Rights, were an unnecessary distraction to the business of ratification. Madison also argued that a Bill of Rights would imply that the national government had powers beyond those enumerated in the text of the Constitution. For example, an amendment forbidding the government from violating freedom of speech might suggest that it had the power to do so unless the Constitution expressly prohibited it. It would be much simpler, Madison thought, just to agree that the national government had only the powers enumerated in the Constitution and no others. But the anti-federalists did not accept Madison's assurances about the national government's limited authority. Their relentless pressure at the states' ratifying conventions helped ensure the adoption of those ten amendments that now form the basis for Americans' most treasured rights under the law. Without Henry and the anti-federalists' strident opposition, the Federalists would never have included provisions protecting freedom of religion, speech, the press, the right to bear arms, trial by jury, and other essential liberties. These amendments explicitly limited the power of the national government. Henry demanded that the Constitution clarify that all powers not expressly given to the national government were retained by the states, because otherwise, the national government would absorb powers by default. Henry noted that the Constitution did limit certain powers of Congress, such as its ability to suspend the writ of habeas corpus (the right of relief from unlawful detention). What about Americans' other rights? Was the national government restricted with regard to those? "The fair implication is, that they can do everything they are not forbidden to do," Henry concluded.[44]

As the convention debate drew to a close, Henry and his fellow anti-federalists attempted to introduce amendments to the Constitution prior to ratification. Again, Madison and the Federalists vehemently opposed this idea. How could the states consider amendments proposed by other states, when eight states had already ratified without amendments? When George Wythe moved that the convention ratify the Constitution and then recommend amendments, Henry offered a declaration of rights and a slate of structural amendments that he called on the delegates to consider before they voted on ratification. These included an amendment, designed with Jay's Mississippi treaty in mind, that would have required a three-fourths majority vote of the House and Senate to approve any treaty that ceded American territory, or navigation rights to American rivers. A majority at the convention approved Henry's amendments and called on the new Congress and the other states to consider them, but he could not convince a majority to delay ratification until the amendments received national consideration.[45]

In a final attempt to postpone ratification, Henry gave a speech that would secure his legendary reputation as a speaker. Madison, he said, "tells you of important blessings which he imagines will result to us and mankind in general, from the adoption of this system." Henry, however, saw not blessings but curses at hand. Heaven, he proclaimed, was watching: "I see the awful immensity of the dangers with which it is pregnant.—I see it—I feel it.—I see *beings* of a higher order, anxious concerning our decision. When I see beyond the horizon that binds human eyes, and look at the final consummation of all human things, and see those intelligent beings which inhabit aetherial mansions, reviewing the political decisions and revolutions which in the progress of time will happen in America, and consequent happiness or misery of mankind—I am led to believe that much of the account on one side or the other, will depend on what we now decide." As Henry spoke, a terrible storm rose outside the hall. Fierce winds and roaring thunder forced him to conclude his speech. Frightened members scurried to take cover. For Henry's biographer William Wirt, the "spirits whom he had called, seemed to have come at his bidding."[46]

Angels or not, Henry failed to stop ratification. The convention voted the next day to approve the Constitution, 89–79. One Federalist wrote that "notwithstanding Mr. Henry's declamatory powers," he was "vastly overpowered by the deep reasoning of our glorious little Madison." Just before the vote began, Henry began to adopt a conciliatory tone. He saw himself as "being overpowered in a good cause. Yet I will be a peaceable citizen! . . . I wish not to go to violence, but will wait with hopes that the spirit which predominated in the revolution, is not yet gone." He had raised the stakes of ratification to their highest level, yet when he began to realize that he would lose, he moderated his approach to retain influence under the ratified Constitution.[47]

Henry took some comfort in the fact that the convention recommended forty amendments that essentially reflected the changes he had called for earlier. The first half of the amendments composed a declaration of rights, in which the convention called for explicit affirmation of rights such as trial by jury, freedom of speech and religion, and bearing arms. The second half enumerated additions and modifications they wished to be included in the Constitution. Most important, the convention demanded a clause that stated "that each state in the Union shall respectively retain every power, jurisdiction and right, which is not by this Constitution delegated" to the national government. This restriction, so fervently promoted by Henry, eventually took form in the Tenth Amendment.[48]

Defeated except for the hope of amending a Constitution that had now gone into effect (New Hampshire had actually upstaged Virginia, becoming the ninth and deciding state to ratify on June 21), the anti-federalists met in the Virginia Senate chambers on June 27 to discuss strategy. George Mason supposedly drafted a "fiery, irritating manifesto" that would have roused opposition to the Constitution among Virginians. Most of the anti-federalist leaders were unwilling to fight on, however. One account written a few years later recalled that Henry steered the group toward reconciliation, stating that "he had done his duty strenuously, in opposing the Constitution, in the proper place,—and with all the powers he possessed. The question had been fully discussed and settled, and, that as true and faithful republicans, they had all better go home!" Despite Henry's rumblings about disunion at the convention, he vowed to cooperate with the new government. He knew he had lost in an open political process at the ratifying convention. He had made his argument, but his fellow representatives disagreed with him. From then on, Henry accepted the basic legitimacy of the Constitution. But he had not yet given up hope for amendments.[49]

Writing to Washington shortly after the convention, Madison predicted his opponent's next steps. "Mr. Henry declared previous to the final question that although he should submit as a quiet citizen, he should seize the first moment that offered for shaking off the yoke in a *constitutional way*. I suspect the plan will be to engage two-thirds of the legislatures in the task of undoing the work; or to get a Congress appointed in the first instance that will commit suicide on their own authority." Madison was correct, as Henry planned to push for a second national convention to secure amendments, and to unite Virginians against the Constitution until adequate amendments were adopted.[50]

During the fall meeting of the Virginia House of Delegates, Henry attacked Madison and helped prevent his election by the legislature to the U.S. Senate. A correspondent told Madison that "Mr. Henry on the floor exclaimed against your political character and pronounced you unworthy of the confidence of the people in the station of Senator. That your election would terminate in producing rivulets of blood throughout the land." Regardless of whether this account was exaggerated, Henry's verbal assault on Madison had its intended effect: Madison came in third in the Senate election, behind two anti-federalists. Henry also passed a plan recommending a second constitutional convention. In its message to the Confederation Congress, the Virginia legislature reminded the friends of the Constitution that their objections to the new government were "deduced from principles which have been established by the melancholy example of other nations." They would not be satisfied until major changes were made to the document.[51]

Washington and Madison remained deeply concerned about Henry's influence. Washington still thought Henry's sway in the legislature was "unpropitious to federal measures." Henry might have been the great enemy of kings, but to Washington, his power in Virginia seemed monarchical. "He has only to say let this be Law—and it is Law," Washington lamented to Madison.[52]

Despite his successes, Henry remained pessimistic. His mood was captured in a November 1788 letter to Richard Henry Lee, one of the Virginians chosen as senator over Madison. Although he believed that a majority of Virginians supported the proposed amendments, Henry did not know what fate they might meet in Congress. "I firmly believe the American union depends on the success of amendments," he told Lee. Henry hinted that if the amendments failed, he might move to North Carolina, which had refused to ratify the Constitution, a defeat probably influenced by Henry. For the time being, North Carolina remained outside the new union. That state's resistance might herald the advent of a southern confederacy, separate from the northern-dominated nation.[53]

Federalist anger at Henry surged in late 1788, when Henry faced a scathing series of editorials against him in the *Virginia Independent Chronicle*. The author, "Decius," accused Henry of all manner of chicanery, most of it centered on charges that in decrying the Constitution he had pursued a personal financial agenda cloaked in the language of republican liberty. In all his dealings, Henry's "first and fixed determination was to get money," Decius wrote, highlighting Henry's engagement in land speculation; he argued that the end of state sovereignty would also mean the end of sweetheart land deals for Henry. Decius warned Virginians not to subject themselves to this "little tyrant's despotism." As we have seen, there may have been substance to Decius's charges with regard to Henry's land speculations as governor: his motives did not always seem entirely pure. Extending that argument to his motives for opposing the Constitution was dubious, however.[54]

Though several of his sympathizers rose to his defense in the papers, Henry seems not to have taken Decius too seriously. He jokingly noted that Decius was "not lucky enough to hit upon one charge that is warranted by truth. How lucky it is that he knew me no better, for I know of many deficiencies in my own conduct." He believed that leading Federalists would publicly disown Decius's opinions, although they had probably encouraged the anonymous author. Henry classed Decius among "the political understrappers who ever follow the footsteps of power and whine and fawn or snarl a bark as they are bid."[55]

Undeterred by the growing hostility toward him, Henry focused on keeping James Madison out of not just the Senate but also the House of Representatives, believing as he did that anti-federalists could not trust Madison to promote serious amendments to the Constitution. The legislature put Madison's home county in an anti-federalist–leaning district, forcing the sickly Madison, suffering from hemorrhoids, to traverse the bumpy roads to Virginia from the capital in New York to campaign for election against James Monroe. Among the most critical groups for Madison to win over were the Baptists. They were inclined to vote for Monroe unless Madison could convince them that he would support a religious-freedom amendment as part of the Bill of Rights. Madison wrote to Baptist pastor George Eve in January 1789, assuring him that he now supported amending the Constitution. The first Congress should pursue "the most satisfactory provisions for all essential rights, particularly the rights of conscience in the fullest latitude," he said. Madison's promises helped to woo the Baptists; pastors such as Eve actively campaigned for him. Madison defeated Monroe fairly handily and returned to New York to deliver on his campaign promise.[56]

Now all Henry could do was wait for news from the first Congress convened under the new system of government. Not only had he failed to defeat the Constitution and to add amendments prior to ratification, but he had also failed even to get a second convention called to consider amendments. Still, Madison was promising that he would promote amendments as soon as the Congress gathered in New York. Henry would not be pleased with the process, or with the content of the amendments. Nevertheless, he and the antifederalists' relentless pressure against the Constitution would soon result in the Bill of Rights, where Americans find their most basic rights enshrined.

# 10

## "TO CARE FOR THE CRAZY MACHINE"

## Reconciling with the Republic

IN 1794, PATRICK HENRY ACQUIRED his final home, Red Hill, in south-central Virginia. His years there hardly resembled the peaceful retirement of a man whose life's work was nearing completion. The one-and-a-half-story farmhouse at Red Hill resonated with the voices of children. He and Dorothea—who was approaching forty—still had five boys and three girls age sixteen and younger living with them. They were a source of great happiness for Patrick and Dorothea, yet three other children had died between 1791 and 1794—two older ones from his marriage to Sarah, and seventeen-month-old Richard, who died in 1793. Like so many eighteenth-century families, Patrick and Dorothea had many children, and they knew well the pain of a child's death.

Motivated in part by his familiarity with grief, Henry was a doting, concerned father. Retirement from politics meant more time with his children. Visitors reportedly "caught him lying on the floor with a group of these little ones climbing over him in every direction, or dancing around him with obstreperous mirth to the tune of his violin, while the only contest seemed to be who could make the most noise." In the fall of 1794, Patrick notified his adult daughter Betsey that another baby, Winston, had been born earlier that year. "I must give out the law and plague myself no more with business, sitting down with what I have," he wrote. "For it will be sufficient employment to see after my little flock, and the management of my plantation." Staying out of debt, and staying out of politics, meant freedom to be with his family in the idyll of Red Hill, which he called "one of the garden spots of the world."[1]

Henry always struggled to maintain income to cover his expenses. For his family's sake, he dreaded insolvency. Despite his reference to the "plague" of business, he still quietly dreamed of striking it rich in western land deals. Although Henry remained in the Virginia assembly until 1791, in 1789 his attention returned to law and land speculation. But as his letter to Betsey indicated, he also wished to be clear of his legal practice and land deals altogether.

Some thought that as Henry tried to gain financial security, he descended into corruption. A hostile Federalist passed near Henry's home in Prince Edward County in 1791 and noted that Henry "is now making a great deal of money by large fees of £50 or £100 for clearing horse thieves and murderers, which has lost him much of the great reputation he enjoyed in his neighborhood. . . . I am told that he will travel hundreds of miles for a handsome fee to plead for criminals, and that his powers of oratory are so great he generally succeeds." Regardless of whether this critic exaggerated Henry's work with known criminals, there is no doubt that Henry spent his final decade bolstering his finances—as well as contending with repeated illnesses and fevers. Henry had retired as the most influential leader in Virginia at a time when George Washington's influence was moving to the national stage, yet he still did not consider himself a professional politician or lifelong government official. He had plenty of opportunities to jump back into state or national government, but he chose not to, except in one instance at the very end of his life.[2]

EVEN IN HIS ABSENCE, Henry exerted a powerful influence on the politics of Virginia and the emerging nation. James Madison still feared that Henry would stir up opposition to the new Constitution, if it were to remain unamended. Madison's colleague in the House, Theodore Sedgwick of Massachusetts, thought Madison was "constantly haunted with the ghost of Patrick Henry." Instead of stubbornly resisting the anti-federalist critique of the Constitution, Madison wisely decided to preempt Henry by promoting a slate of amendments in the first Congress. These new articles did not seriously reduce the power of the national government, as Henry desired, but instead primarily articulated rights upon which the government should not infringe.[3]

His opponents continually believed Henry was plotting to obstruct every step of the formation of the new government. Rumors briefly circulated that the anti-federalists would try to elect Henry president, with New York's anti-federalist leader George Clinton as vice president. (Under the original system for electing the president, state-appointed electors would cast two votes for president. The top vote-getter would become president, and the second-place finisher would become vice president.) A Connecticut newspaper lamented that "although the grateful voice of Americans cries aloud—Our beloved WASHINGTON shall be the first President of our rising empire;—yet it is lamentably affirmed, that the anti-federal party . . . have secretly combined to oppose his election to the President's chair: His Excellency's competitor, proposed by these dukes of the rueful countenance, is Patrick Henry!!!" But any thoughts of Henry becoming president were quickly abandoned, with all sentiment pointing to the election of George Washington.[4]

If Washington's victory was a foregone conclusion, John Adams's selection as vice president was not. Although Adams was an old friend, Henry preferred George Clinton as a counterweight to Washington. A worried Madison wrote to Jefferson in December 1788, telling him that the "enemies to the government, at the head and the most inveterate of whom, is Mr. Henry, are laying a train for the election of Governor Clinton." As a presidential elector from Virginia, Henry cast his presidential votes for Washington and Clinton, but Adams received the second-most votes to Washington and became vice president.[5]

In the first Congress, Madison kept his word and introduced a slate of amendments that, in revised form, would become the Bill of Rights. His primary motive was to soothe the fears of anti-federalists, such as Henry. "It will be a desirable thing to extinguish from the bosom of every member of the community any apprehensions," he said when he proposed the amendments in June 1789, "that there are those among his countrymen who wish to deprive them of the liberty for which they valiantly fought and honorably bled." Madison reminded the House that certain patriotic, respected Americans opposed the Constitution because of an understandable zeal for liberty. The Congress should take their concerns to heart and specifically state those rights the Constitution was meant to protect. Both sides believed that Madison was only trying to throw "a tub to the whale," a saying that referred to a tactic of sailors trying to distract a whale that threatened their ship. Henry was Madison's whale.[6]

Madison's amendments borrowed from the statements of rights proposed in the ratifying conventions, especially Virginia's. His original nineteen amendments were revised into twelve, which passed in Congress. In 1791, ten of them were ratified in the states. These amendments focused on the rights of Americans and restrictions of the national government's activities. Henry was not satisfied with the Bill of Rights, however. It made no serious structural modifications in the government itself. Henry was especially disappointed that the president's power was not constrained. Writing to his ally Richard Henry Lee in August 1789, he said the amendments proposed "will tend to injure rather than to serve the cause of liberty— provided they go no further. . . . See how rapidly power grows. How slowly the means of curbing it! That the President is to be accountable for the general success of government is precisely the principle of every despotism." The amendments sounded good, but to Henry, without significant reductions in the government's strength, they only masked the political monstrosity the Constitution had created.[7]

Henry was not the only one disappointed with the Bill of Rights. Richard Henry Lee wrote back to Henry from Congress in September to report that the anti-federalists had been outmaneuvered. Trying to get Virginia's more substantive, government-limiting amendments adopted was futile: "We might as well have attempted to move Mount Atlas upon our shoulders. In fact, the idea of subsequent amendments was delusion altogether. . . . Some valuable rights are indeed declared, but the powers that remain are very sufficient to render them nugatory at pleasure." Virginia's other senator, William Grayson, wrote to say proposed amendments were "good for nothing."[8]

Agreeing that they should generate opposition to the amendments in Virginia, Lee and William Grayson wrote to the state legislature in September 1789 expressing frustration at the amendments' limitations. "It is impossible for us not to see the necessary tendency to consolidated empire in the natural operation of the Constitution if no further amended than now proposed," they warned. Henry advocated for a legislative resolution detailing the deficiencies of the Constitution and proposed amendments. But his momentum had faltered. Henry's rival Edward Carrington, a former Continental army officer and staunch Federalist, told Madison that Henry "made a speech to the House, but it not appearing to take well, it was never stirred again." The Virginia House and Senate struggled to agree on the proper approach to the amendments and postponed deliberations. When Virginia finally ratified the amendments in 1791, the Bill of Rights became part of the Constitution.[9]

The weary Henry actually left the House before the debates on the amendments were over. In one case, this absence resulted in an anti-federalist defeat on a question decided by one vote. Edmund Randolph believed that Henry had returned to Prince Edward County "in discontent, that the present Assembly is not so pleasant as the last." Henry knew he had lost his battle with Madison and that continued resistance was pointless. As he told Betsey (his twenty-year-old daughter, to whom he often confided his inner thoughts in his later years), he was also not physically well, and continued to feel the pressures of family obligations.[10]

AFTER 1789, HENRY BEGAN to accept the reality of the new government. He knew the ratification process had given it popular legitimacy. But he also entertained occasional visions of another republic, separate from Madison's new creation. Perhaps he could find a refuge in the distant reaches of the South. Ever the land speculator, Henry remained involved with schemes to purchase western lands. In late 1789, Henry and other Virginians received a grant from the state of Georgia giving them ownership of eleven million acres, an area encompassing what would become northern Mississippi. This "Yazoo" grant, so named for the river that flowed through it, was intended primarily as a moneymaking endeavor. But Henry and his colleagues, many of them angry about the new national government, also quietly speculated that Yazoo might combine with other disaffected areas of the new Southwest to create an independent republic. Joseph Martin, Henry's old friend and western agent, remarked in late 1788 that he intended to leave the United States and recruit hundreds of families to the Tombigbee River, the eastern border of the Yazoo grant, creating a population that might be the nucleus of a new nation.[11]

In early 1790, Henry wrote in remarkably frank terms to Richard Henry Lee about his separatist intentions for the Yazoo settlements. Assuming that Lee had heard of the purchase, he asked, "If our present system grows into tyranny is not a frontier possession most eligible? And a central one most to be dreaded? . . . A comfortable prospect of the issue of the new system would fix me here for life. A contrary one sends me southwestward." Henry saw the new Southwest as a potential sanctuary for anti-federalists, should their worst fears about the new government come to pass. Virginia's anti-federalist Congressman Theodorick Bland congratulated Henry for the purchase, calling it "an asylum from tyranny whenever it may arise."[12]

Henry also believed that the white settlers already living in the frontier Southwest should be able to organize on their own terms. Congress should not decide for them. So Henry recoiled when he received word that North Carolina's legislature had ceded to Congress its far western lands—the area known as Franklin, in the future state of Tennessee—for the purpose of turning it into a new state. Giving the land to Congress instead of ceding political control to the citizens of the western territory, North Carolina's action seemed like a capitulation to federal authority, and a fulfillment of his predictions about the encroaching power of Congress. By accepting the cession, the Congress would "sanction the most manifest violation of rights that can be committed," Henry wrote. It was one thing for popular assemblies to ratify the Constitution, but another for the settlers of the unorganized west to be forced into the centralized American republic.[13]

Henry would meet a major setback in his plans for the Yazoo grants when President Washington negotiated a treaty with Creek Indians in August 1790 that returned the Yazoo lands to them and invalidated the agreement between Georgia and Henry's consortium. Henry was incensed. This treaty confirmed his fear that the national government would trample the states and the people. "It is a deception to urge," he wrote, "that encroachments from the American government are not dangerous. In fact they are the more to be dreaded at this particular time in our own government than from any other quarter. No foreign power can annoy us. Therefore from our own rulers only can usurpation spring." He understandably saw the negation of the Yazoo land grant as a political power grab and an early validation of his fears about the power of the government, but it was also one more failed opportunity to make money on western investments. The line between political principle and personal enrichment did sometimes blur, unfortunately, in Henry's career. But there was nothing he could do to retain control of these lands, which he and his colleagues only really owned in principle. The Yazoo grants would later degenerate into notorious corruption; in the mid-1790s, speculators procured the Yazoo territory again via bribery of Georgia legislators, but by that time Henry's stake in the region had evaporated.[14]

Land speculation remained in Henry's blood even after the Yazoo debacle. Into the late 1790s, he was involved in deals in Virginia and North Carolina—bargains that often involved the sale not only of land but also of slaves. His 1798 negotiations for the Seven Islands plantation, just across the Staunton River from his Red Hill estate, were complicated by his attempts to buy slaves working there. Henry was concerned that they were too expensive, but in a magnanimous tone he wrote that "they are so extremely desirous of staying with me, I consent to take them." Henry's early flirtations with antislavery advocacy would never fundamentally alter his attitude about trafficking in slaves.[15]

Land and slaves were Henry's means of securing his financial security. But because of the swiftly changing fortunes in the land deals, the uncertainties of personal income from crop sales, and his own periodic episodes of extravagance, Henry occasionally fell into debt. His most severe bout of indebtedness occurred in the mid-1780s, when Henry apparently abandoned his normally modest spending habits to keep up with the stylish expectations of the governor's office. His son-in-law Spencer Roane recalled that in those years Henry never appeared in public without fine clothes, including a scarlet cloak and powdered wig. Members of his family "were furnished with an excellent coach, at a time when these vehicles were not so common as at present. They lived as genteelly, and associated with as polished society, as that of any governor before or since has ever done. He entertained as much company as others, and in as genteel a style; and when, at the end of two years, he resigned the office, he had greatly exceeded the salary, and [was] in debt, which was one cause that induced him to resume the practice of the law." Henry recognized he had brought this liability on himself and his family and vowed to rectify it. By 1785, he had begun to fear that if he died early, he would leave his family vulnerable to his creditors, to whom he owed money as late as 1791, when he wrote Betsey from Richmond telling her that he was "obliged to be very industrious and to take on me great fatigue to clear myself of debt." He said that he aimed to get out of arrears within a couple years, and by 1794, he had achieved his goal. Roane noted that "for a great part of his life (tho' he died rich) he was struggling in debt and difficulties," but it seems that toward the end of his life he regained the financial independence he had so valued and striven for.[16]

Practicing law not only buttressed Henry's finances but also allowed him to advocate for the economic liberty of Virginians by protecting them from the continuing claims of the British. The most famous case of his life (aside from the Parsons' Cause of 1763) came in his 1791 defense of Virginia debtors against lawsuits brought by British creditors. The Treaty of Paris maintained that Americans had to pay their outstanding individual and business debts to Britain, but many Virginians had refused. Even Henry himself insisted that he would not pay any outstanding British debts he owed, although his cluttered records made it difficult for him to discern exactly how much he might owe to British lenders—very little, he approximated hopefully in a 1785 memorandum to himself.[17]

When British creditors sued Virginians to collect the debts, Henry seized the opportunity to argue that the war had voided the Americans' obligations. Defending his clients before a panel of judges, he poignantly appealed to the sacrifices Americans had made in the Revolution and reminded the legal board of the deprivations they would have faced if the British had won. Even Henry's critics admitted that he had lost little of his persuasive powers; his old enemy Edmund Pendleton grudgingly told James Madison that "Mr. Henry was truly great, and for the first time I ever heard him, methodical and connected for two days and a half." His argument carried the day, both in the initial hearing and on appeal in 1793. The Supreme Court overturned these rulings in 1796, but Henry was no longer involved with the case by then.[18]

Henry loved to turn complaints filed by British citizens and Loyalists into occasions to revisit the glorious cause of American liberty. In one notable 1789 case in New London, Virginia, an aggrieved Loyalist named John Hook sued an American army commissary who in 1781 had seized two of Hook's cows without permission. Henry defended the commissary by recalling the sufferings of Washington's troops in the late stages of the war. What kind of man, he asked, would refuse to feed these destitute freedom fighters? He reminded the jury of the great victory at Yorktown, evoking the patriots' shouts of elation there. Henry then bellowed, "But hark! What notes of discord are these which disturb the general joy, and silence the acclamations of victory—they are the notes of John Hook, hoarsely bawling through the American camp, *beef! beef!*

*beef!*" Not only did Hook lose the case, but angry locals almost tarred and feathered him.[19]

Henry participated in more scandalous trials as well, which might have signaled a willingness on his part to engage ethically dubious clients in exchange for financial gain. The most famous of these cases was his 1793 defense of young Richard Randolph against the charge of infanticide. Randolph had married his cousin Judith in 1789, but within a few years he apparently became sexually involved with Judith's younger sister Nancy. When the affair produced a child, prosecutors claimed, Randolph murdered the baby and disposed of the body. Randolph claimed that Nancy had not been pregnant, and the witnesses who had seen the most—plantation slaves who saw Randolph on the day in question—were barred from testifying under Virginia law. Henry, along with future chief justice John Marshall, argued that Richard Randolph was the victim of rumor-mongering. They got him acquitted.[20]

BY THE EARLY 1790s, Henry had reconciled himself to the new American government and abandoned (for the most part) notions of resistance or forming a separate republic. Henry expressed his feelings to James Monroe in a January 1791 letter, in which he suggested that in the interest of American unity, the anti-federalists should cooperate with the government: "Although the form of government into which my countrymen determined to place themselves, had my enmity, yet as we are one and all embarked, it is natural to care for the crazy machine, at least so long as we are out of sight of a port to refit." If Americans were out at sea on a defective boat, then Henry thought they should make the best of it until time presented an opportunity to dock and rebuild the ship.[21]

Even as he acquiesced, however, Henry worried that the government was already fulfilling his worst fears. He particularly loathed Alexander Hamilton's plans for bolstering the nation's public credit.

Under his plan, outlined in 1790, Hamilton wanted the federal government to assume state debts incurred during the Revolution, which would significantly expand the national government's financial burden and disproportionately benefit the northern states, which had paid off less of their debts than those in the South, including Virginia. For Henry, the plan was "a consistent part of a system which I ever dreaded. Subserviency of southern to northern interests are [sic] written in capitals on its very front." He called Hamilton and his supporters "advocates of oppression."[22]

Having feared that the Constitution, as originally written, would not adequately restrict the actions of the national government, Henry now became an advocate for its strict interpretation—the only hope if the states were to maintain their power. As one of his last acts in the legislature, Henry sponsored a resolution in late 1790 protesting Hamilton's debt financing plan, arguing that it violated the Constitution because it claimed a power not expressly granted to the national government. The resolution ended ominously with the warning that the plan would "alienate the affections of the good citizens of this Commonwealth, from the government of the United States, will lessen their confidence in its wisdom and justice, and finally tend to produce measures extremely unfavourable to the interests of the union." The threat of secession yet loomed.[23]

The debt assumption plan caused a major split between the great defenders of the Constitution, James Madison and Alexander Hamilton. This division led to the organization of Madison and Jefferson's Republican Party, which opposed Hamilton and the Federalists' financial program. Henry ideologically sympathized with Madison and Jefferson's hostility to Hamilton's economic scheme, but he was never a likely candidate to join the ranks of the Republicans. Jefferson's animosity toward him ran too deep, and Henry's respect for Washington inclined him to support the administration and the Federalist Party. Henry's political alignments in the 1790s reflected both his pragmatism and the perpetuation of his decade-old feud with Jefferson.

As for his relationship with Washington, it had cooled during the debates over the Constitution. Their disagreement even risked becoming clouded with the sort of bitterness that already separated Henry and Jefferson. Henry had heard rumors that Washington had made disparaging comments about him being a "factious, seditious character." By 1794, however, Washington and Henry began to patch up their alliance, and Washington made several attempts to have Henry serve in his administration. Governor Henry Lee of Virginia brokered the rapprochement between the two men. "Light Horse Harry" was quickly becoming one of Henry's closest friends, even though they had engaged in nasty debates at the Virginia ratifying convention. Washington told Lee that he had never made any insulting remarks about Henry even when they profoundly disagreed. "On the question of the constitution, Mr. Henry and myself, it is well known, have been of different opinions, but personally I have always respected and esteemed him." Washington considered himself indebted to Henry because of Henry's loyalty during the dark times of 1778, when some patriots tried to remove him from command of the army, and Henry refused to participate in the plot, instead alerting the general to the campaign against him.[24]

Harry Lee offered Henry an appointment to the U.S. Senate in 1794. (James Monroe had just vacated his seat to become an envoy to France.) Lee knew Henry might be reluctant to leave retirement, but he cited "our conviction of your preferential love of country" and a growing crisis over relations with France and Britain as grounds for his request. Many Virginians were delighted when news of the offer broke, with a Lynchburg editorial heralding the prospect of the appointment of "this veteran defender of the rights and liberties of the people." But Henry refused, explaining that personal circumstances and his distance from Philadelphia prevented him from accepting.[25]

Henry also declined an offer to become ambassador to Spain. President Washington was eager to put someone in the position who had a national reputation and deep roots in Kentucky, where the issue of Spanish relations historically had mattered most. This diplomat would negotiate navigation rights to the Mississippi, the very issue that had helped galvanize Henry's resistance to the new Constitution. Eight years earlier, Henry might have jumped at such an opportunity, but now he refused, citing again the difficulties of leaving his retirement. Henry may have felt confident that the Americans and Spanish would eventually work out the favorable terms he had sought in the 1780s, and indeed, in 1795, the man sent in Henry's stead, Thomas Pinckney of South Carolina, settled with Spain on an agreement that allowed free navigation of the Mississippi and access to the port of New Orleans.[26]

Henry's repeated refusals to assume national office resulted not only from his financial fears, but also from a growing concern over his family's health. He felt like he was constantly dodging death, and of course it was constantly stalking his children. Each summer, Virginia would be ravaged by dysentery (or "the flux"), a malady that could cause violent, bloody diarrhea and was often fatal. "The flux has been very near us, but, it has pleased God, we escaped it," Henry told Betsey in 1793. Shortly after declining the Senate seat and ambassadorship, he informed his daughter that the flux was again plaguing the area and that many of his slaves were suffering from the "ague," or malarial fever, an illness he knew well from his frequent bouts in the past. Henry feared leaving his family behind for long durations when mortal illnesses could seize any of them at any moment.[27]

The offers from Lee and Washington reveal how much political influence Patrick Henry retained even in retirement. By 1794–95, both Washington's Federalists and the emerging Republican Party of Jefferson dreamed of enticing him out of his repose to support their side. Because of the instability caused by the French Revolution as well as growing tension with Britain, America had entered its most dire international crisis since the Revolution. Bitterness that lingered after the Revolution, along with the British navy's seizure of ostensibly neutral American ships, led Republicans to clamor for war. But Washington and the Federalists loathed both the idea of war with Britain and any renewed alliance with a France that had descended into murderous chaos, with former King Louis XVI and Marie Antoinette among the tens of thousands guillotined. Federalists warned that another war with Britain would wreck the fledgling American economy just as it was finding its strength. America depended on Britain for three-quarters of its foreign trade.

Henry had a personal stake in peace; he feared that war would create an economic catastrophe that would ruin his chances of getting out of debt through land sales. Once again, the line between Henry's personal finance and his politics blurred. Washington dispatched John Jay—notorious for his role in the negotiations with Spain over the Mississippi in the mid-1780s—to London in 1794 to avert a military clash. In this situation, Henry's endorsement of the Federalists or the Republicans would carry a great deal of political weight, as he maintained his national reputation as an independent-minded patriot. Even Jefferson briefly tried to reconcile with Henry in early 1795, asking a common friend to assure Henry that he harbored no bad feelings toward him.[28]

It was Washington, however, who made the most strenuous efforts to recruit Henry. The offers of a Senate seat and ambassadorship were followed, finally, by an invitation in 1795 to become secretary of state. Washington knew that if Henry accepted the post, it would facilitate the nation's reception of the Jay Treaty, which the Senate approved in mid-1795, granting America favorable trade status with Britain and aligning the new nation diplomatically with the kingdom from which it had so recently won its freedom. Yet it failed to address some of the key grievances remaining from the Revolution, such as British compensation for slaves they took from Americans during the war. The treaty was sure to alienate the French, Britain's inveterate enemies. It led to a final break in the relationship between George Washington and James Madison, and further energized Madison's Republican Party. Although early reaction to the treaty was mixed in the North, it sparked general outrage in the South. One poem printed in a Virginia newspaper recommended that Americans "spurn the base born child, the imp of slavery begot in hell." Rumors swirled that the treaty might yet again lead Virginia to consider seceding from the Union.[29]

Throughout the uproar about the Jay Treaty, Henry maintained silence. His reticence explains Washington's interest in making him secretary of state. If Henry was not opposed to the Jay Treaty, then recruiting him to the cabinet would be a major coup. One adviser told Washington that bringing Henry on board would devastate the Republican movement: "a more deadly blow could not be given to the faction in Virginia, and perhaps elsewhere, that that gentleman's acceptance of the office in question, convinced as we are of the sentiments he must carry with him. So much have the opposers of the government held him up as their oracle, even since he has ceased to respond to them, that any event, demonstrating his active support to government, could not but give the party a severe shock." That October, Washington made the offer, stating his case as forcefully as possible, in language he knew Henry would understand. The crisis at hand, Washington wrote, would "decide whether order and good government shall be preserved, or anarchy and confusion ensue." He assured Henry that he did not intend to pursue an alliance with Britain or any other European nation beyond the limited bonds the treaty set forth, and that all he sought was America's continued independence and welfare.[30]

Henry was flattered by Washington's offer, but he still did not accept. He gave the usual reasons: he and Dorothea had eight children of their own, with yet another on the way, and he feared going to Philadelphia, then the nation's capital, where his family would be exposed to smallpox and yellow fever. Henry himself was in relatively poor health, and recent crop losses added to the "derangement" of his finances. Ever since he was a young man, the necessity of boosting his finances often had taken him out of the public arena, but never had personal contingencies distracted him from a more significant role. On the other hand, Henry was hardly alone: he was the fourth of five men who refused Washington's offer before Washington finally found a taker in Timothy Pickering, his secretary of war. One of the others who declined, Massachusetts's Rufus King, professed that he had no interest in becoming another object of the "foul and venomous shafts of calumny" increasingly directed at the government.[31]

Henry insisted to the president that his refusal had nothing to do with any animosity between him and Washington. Nor did he harbor continuing resentment toward the government under the new Constitution. "Believe me sir, I have bid adieu to Federal and Antifederal ever since the adoption of the present government, and in the circle of my friends [I] have often expressed my fears of disunion amongst the states from [a] collision of interests, but especially from the baneful effects of faction. In that case the most I can say is that if my country is destined in my day to encounter the horrors of anarchy, every power of mind and body which I possess will be exerted in support of the government under which I live and which has been fairly sanctioned by my countrymen. I should be unworthy [of] the character of a republican or an honest man, if I withheld my best and most zealous efforts, because I opposed the Constitution in its unaltered form."[32]

Henry hinted at his resistance to the Jay Treaty with Britain only at the end of the letter. He told Washington that if "evil, instead of good, grows out of the measures you adopt," he hoped people would judge Washington's motives fairly. Although Henry had opposed Washington on the Constitution, and although he clearly had doubts about the Jay Treaty, his respect for Washington would never allow him to break publicly with the president.[33]

The Jay Treaty was harmful to the nation, Henry thought, but its negotiation and adoption accorded with the tenets Madison had set out in the Constitution. In a 1796 letter to Betsey, Henry made clear that although he did not approve of the treaty—"a very bad one indeed"—he thought it hypocritical for Madison and supporters of the Constitution to deny the president and Senate's exclusive right to make treaties. Republicans in Congress were trying to stop the House of Representatives from funding appropriations required to enforce the treaty, which would effectively give the House a voice in its ratification. But Henry had no sympathy for such intrigues; Madison, he believed, was simply reaping what he had sown.[34]

Despite Henry's repeated refusals, offers for public service persisted. Harry Lee continued to tell Washington that Henry might be willing to accept some kind of appointment. In December 1795, Lee invited Henry to become chief justice of the Supreme Court, an office recently made vacant by John Jay's resignation. (Jay, remarkably, had served simultaneously as chief justice and special envoy to Great Britain.) Henry hesitated to respond, to the growing irritation of George Washington, who did not like offering positions to people not certain to accept. After waiting two weeks for a response, Washington scolded Lee and told him that the delay was "embarrassing in the extreme." He had other appointments waiting to be made, and the Supreme Court's meeting was only weeks away. Henry ultimately declined. Amazingly, he still crossed Washington's mind as a possible successor to James Monroe as ambassador in Paris in July 1796, although he was sure Henry would never accept the position.[35]

Thomas Jefferson was convinced that Washington was offering these positions even though he knew Henry would refuse. The Federalists, he thought, wanted to create the impression that Henry was on their side. "Most assiduous court is paid to P.H.," Jefferson wrote to James Monroe. "He has been offered every thing which they knew he would not accept." As Washington's frustration with Lee showed, however, the president actually wanted Henry in the administration and was not much interested in making symbolic job offers. He saw Henry as a relatively nonpartisan figure on foreign affairs, neither strongly anti-French nor pro-French, who would not jeopardize the administration's official policy of neutrality. Of course, Henry had no fondness for the British. He expected that the British would renew their oppression of the United States whenever the opportunity presented itself. [36]

BUT THE FRENCH WERE HARDLY an acceptable ally, either. Henry was increasingly worried about the emerging anti-Christian implications of the French Revolution, as well as the deistic attacks on Christianity that many of that revolution's friends championed. Increasingly serious about his own faith, Henry believed more fervently than ever that a strong republic needed robust religion to preserve it from corruption, turmoil, and violence.

Many traditional Christians in the United States had initially welcomed the French Revolution as a movement akin to their own, and one that would undermine the long-despised Catholic Church. But the French Revolution began to take an ugly anti-Christian turn in 1792, with the massacre of hundreds of priests and the conversion of some churches into Temples of Reason.

To many observers, the anti-Christianism of the French Revolution coincided with the rise of a militant new deism in America, a surge symbolized and incited by the 1794 publication of Thomas Paine's *The Age of Reason*. This book by the former hero of the American Revolution attacked traditional Christianity as a tool of political oppression. Here was Paine's deistic creed:

> I believe in one God, and no more: and I hope for happiness beyond this life.
>
> I believe in the equality of man; and I believe that religious duties consist in doing justice, loving mercy, and endeavoring to make our fellow creatures happy.
>
> But, lest it should be supposed that I believe many other things in addition to these, I shall, in the progress of this work, declare the things I do not believe, and my reasons for not believing them.
>
> I do not believe in the creed professed by the Jewish church, by the Roman church, by the Greek church, by the Turkish church, by the Protestant church, nor by any church that I know of. My own mind is my own church.

Paine's assault found an eager audience in the United States. Although it was originally published in France, where Paine had gone to support the Revolution, *The Age of Reason* appeared in seventeen American editions between 1794 and 1796.[37]

The rising anti-Christian spirit of the French Revolution and the threat of deism confirmed that Henry could never align with America's pro-French Jeffersonian party. Aside from his personal history with Jefferson, and his political battles with Madison, Henry increasingly believed that he needed to defend traditional Christianity against Francophile deism. That meant keeping his distance from Jefferson's party, if not openly siding with the Federalists. His deepening concern for Christian fidelity was reflected in a lengthy 1796 letter to Betsey:

> The view which the rising greatness of our country presents to my eyes is greatly tarnished by the general prevalence of Deism which with me is but another name for vice and depravity. I am however much consoled by reflecting, that the religion of Christ has from its first appearance in the world, been attacked in vain by all the wits, philosophers, and wise ones, aided by every power of man and its triumph has been complete. What is there in the wit or wisdom of the present Deistical writers or professors that can compare them with Hume, Shaftsbury, Bolingbroke, and others? And yet these have been confuted and their fame decaying, insomuch that the puny efforts of Paine are thrown in to prop their tottering fabrick, whose foundations cannot stand the test of time.

Despite his occasionally inconsistent application of virtue in his land deals and legal practice, Henry continued to believe that the success of the republic depended upon the power of virtue, which he saw as rooted in traditional religion. For Henry, the publication of Paine's *Age of Reason* was troubling because it essentially encouraged public sinfulness. Once freed from the restraints of the Bible and morality, he believed, skeptical Americans would naturally pursue selfishness and immorality. As he said in his letter to Betsey, Henry worried that he had not sufficiently identified himself as a practicing, traditional Christian:

> Amongst other strange things said of me, I hear it is said by the Deists that I am one of their number, and indeed that some good people think I am no Christian. This thought gives me much more pain than the appellation of Tory, because I think religion of infinitely higher importance than politics, and I find much cause to reproach myself

that I have lived so long and have given no decided and public proofs of my being a Christian. But indeed my dear child this is a character which I prize far above all this world has or can boast.[38]

Some have suggested that religion might have become more important to Henry as he grew older (at the time of the publication of *The Age of Reason*, Henry was fifty-eight). He seemingly had become more reflective about his faith, and about his country's religious commitments. We might also speculate that he was concerned that his personal business had not always reflected spotless Christian character. But Henry also believed that with Paine's writings and Jefferson's well-known skepticism challenging the nation's spiritual foundations, Americans could no longer take their religious heritage for granted. He feared that without fidelity to long-established religious precepts, the United States would spin apart in an atheistic whirlwind, just like Revolutionary France.

Henry might have wished he had shown himself to be more of a Christian leader, but in the 1790s his fellow Americans increasingly honored him as an exemplar of virtue. His reluctance to enter national politics only enhanced his popularity. Some newspapers even began calling him "Saint Patrick." Just as they admired Washington for his resignation from military service in 1783, Americans loved Henry's willingness to give up power to pursue the private life. Both Washington and Henry, in the popular view, fulfilled the ancient ideal of Cincinnatus, the Roman leader who wielded power only so long as it took to defeat Rome's enemies, then returned to his simple life on the farm. Henry's withdrawal from the public arena charmed the American people, buttressing his image as a classic hero.[39]

Henry may never have been so admired nationally as in 1796, when some Federalists tried to convince him to run for president to replace the retiring Washington. Despite their old differences over the Constitution and debt financing plan, even Alexander Hamilton briefly pursued the idea of supporting Henry. John Marshall and Harry Lee spoke with Henry in Richmond in May 1796 about whether he would be willing to run. Unsurprisingly, he was not. Hamilton quickly decided "to be rid of P.H." and moved on to Thomas Pinckney of South Carolina as his preferred candidate. Nationally circulated editorials made the case for Henry as president well into the fall. One Virginia writer promoted Henry as a better candidate than Jefferson because of Henry's courage and patriotism, recalling his leadership during the Revolution, his excellent service as Virginia governor, and his "praise-worthy conduct since the adoption of the federal constitution" (apparently this person did not approve of Henry's opposition to the Constitution). Conversely, the writer denounced Jefferson primarily because of the notorious episode in 1781 when he abandoned his office in the face of British invasion.[40]

In a letter circulated just before the election, Henry reiterated his unwillingness to serve as president. He did not explain why he would not accept the office, but we may assume that the same reasons as before guided his choice: his health, debts, and desire to stay out of politics. He also had watched with disgust how Washington had been treated like an ordinary politician in his last years in office. "If he whose character as our leader during the whole war was above all praise is so roughly handled in his old age, what may be expected to men of the common standard of character?" he wondered. If he entered national politics, Henry suspected that he would face the same kind of opprobrium when public opinion turned against him. He concluded his letter with the hope that "wisdom and virtue may mark the choice about to be made of a President." Henry certainly approved of the election of his old friend John Adams over his rival Thomas Jefferson.[41]

Attempts to bring Henry back into office remained relentless. In November the Virginia legislature voted to make Henry the governor for a sixth term. It is difficult to know whether Henry grew tired of these invitations, or whether he was flattered by the unceasing attention. In any case, he declined the governorship, just as he had refused the other enticements, writing that his "advanced age and decayed faculties" made acceptance impossible. He wrote bluntly that he could not see "any important political good in reach of the office of governor," noting that Virginia's chief executive could make little difference in confronting the gravest crisis of the day, which was in foreign affairs.[42]

Henry averred that regardless of who was serving in public office, the United States' most important ally should be virtue. Without that trait, the nation would not last long. Selfishness would ruin the country, and factional squabbling would lead to disunion. Part of Henry's reluctance about serving in office lay in his doubts about the efficacy of politics itself. Government could suppress vice and encourage morality, but it could never change the hearts of people. France was not America's real enemy. "The enemy we have to fear," Henry wrote, "is the degeneracy, luxury, and vices of the present times. Let us be allied against these and we secure the happiness and liberty of our country."[43]

Henry's commitment to the Federalists was tested by the adoption of the Alien and Sedition Acts in 1798. Fears about the French immigrant population in America, and anger over Republican attacks on the Federalists, led to these controversial, suppressive laws. The Alien Act allowed the president to summarily expel noncitizen foreigners deemed dangerous to the safety of the country. This ominous law was never enforced, but the Sedition Act was, which made it illegal to say or publish anything of a "false, scandalous, or malicious" nature against the government. Fourteen people were eventually prosecuted under the law, and one Republican congressman from Vermont was actually jailed for sedition. The Sedition Act revealed how fragile the First Amendment's protection of free speech was and exacerbated sectional tensions, with almost all southern congressmen opposing the measure. Just as Henry had contemplated the possibility of secession a decade earlier, some southern political leaders again discussed the viability of a separate southern republic that would remove itself from a tyrannical national government intent on suppressing dissent. Led by Thomas Jefferson and James Madison, respectively, Kentucky and Virginia passed resolutions against the Alien and Sedition Acts. (Even though Jefferson was Adams's vice president, the state legislature of Kentucky recruited him to pen its resolution. He agreed to do so anonymously.) The resolutions argued that the acts represented an unconstitutional confiscation of power by the national government and that the Sedition Act violated the First Amendment. Asserting states' right to check usurpations by the national government, Jefferson's resolution declared the acts void.

The Sedition Act showed that the Federalist-dominated government could indeed run roughshod over the First Amendment's protection of free speech. Henry's predictions about the national government's unstoppable power seemed to be coming true. Given this outrageous intrusion on the people's rights, it would seem likely that Henry would issue a self-satisfied, cautionary "I told you so." But by 1798, the nation's political alignments had changed so dramatically that Henry chose to maintain circumspection. Although he could never bring himself to support the Alien and Sedition Acts, he did endorse the Virginia Federalist candidate John Marshall for Congress, convinced that for all its avowal of the power of national government, the party of Washington still represented the path of political virtue.

As a fellow Virginia Federalist, Henry found John Marshall a sympathetic character. Twenty years younger than Henry, Marshall was a cousin of Thomas Jefferson, but he had opposed Jefferson on most major issues. He had returned in 1798 from service as an envoy to France, where his delegation found themselves subject to demands for bribes from French agents dubbed W, X, Y, and Z in the newspapers. The affair worsened tensions with the French and positioned Marshall for a run for Congress from the Richmond district, which included Henry's old home of Hanover County. Despite the Federalists' growing unpopularity in the South, Marshall made it known that he would not have supported the Alien and Sedition Acts had he been in Congress, a stance that elicited the ire of New England Federalists. But Marshall also came out against the Kentucky and Virginia Resolutions, because he believed that the Alien and Sedition Acts were simply bad laws, not unconstitutional ones. Having stood against both French corruption and the Alien and Sedition Acts, Marshall was the only kind of Federalist who could win election in Virginia in 1799. Yet he would still have a hard time winning, thanks to his lack of support for the Kentucky and Virginia Resolutions. Some Republicans even circulated the rumor that Henry opposed Marshall. Doubting the truth of these reports, and looking to tip the balance in their candidate's favor, Virginia Federalists approached Henry about endorsing Marshall.[44]

Wishing to crush the rumor, Henry publicly recommended Marshall for Congress. In his endorsement—in the form of a letter to the Virginia Federalist Archibald Blair—Henry explained that his support for Marshall turned upon the Federalists' advocacy for American union and traditional virtue. He said he suspected that certain Republicans (Jefferson and Madison?) were seeking to either overturn the government or dissolve the Union. (This was an ironic charge, given the identical accusations of antinationalism leveled against Henry for the past decade.) He expressed perplexity about the state of foreign affairs but agreed that the French government had behaved intolerably. France's intrigues were dangerous, but not as dangerous as its anti-Christianism. The French Revolution, he wrote, was "destroying the great pillars of all government and of social life; I mean virtue, morality, and religion. . . . Infidelity in its broadest sense under the name of philosophy is fast spreading and that under the patronage of French manners and principles." In light of the French threat, and Marshall's calm resolve in the face of their insults and requests for bribes, Henry gave him his highest endorsement: "tell Marshall I love him because he felt and acted as a Republican, as an American." In the end, Marshall won by a thin margin. Patrick Henry's support was essential to the victory.[45]

For Virginia Federalists, the crisis over France and the Union warranted more from Henry than an endorsement of Marshall. The times called for Henry to return from retirement and to fight the friends of France as a legislator. Archibald Blair told Henry that his services were desperately needed, as "your presence alone in our assembly, would put opposition to flight, and save us from impending misery." To Blair, the Republicans' actions augured the possibility not just of secession, but of civil war. Only someone of Henry's stature could hope to make a difference in this impasse.[46]

Real pressure to reenter public life came when George Washington wrote to him, expressing deep concern for the fate of the Union and lamenting that the harshest critics of the government came from Virginia. He saw the Republicans as fanatics who charged the government with the worst crimes at every turn. Behind every action of the Federalists, the Republicans saw attempts to ally with Britain and to destroy the Constitution. In such a crisis, the nation could not afford to have leaders such as Henry remain in retirement, the former president said. Washington then pointedly asked him to run for the state legislature again. "Your weight of character and influence in the House of [Delegates] would be a bulwark against such dangerous sentiments as are delivered there at present. It would be a rallying point for the timid, and an attraction of the wavering. In a word, I conceive it to be of immense importance at this crisis that you should be there."[47]

Ever devoted to Washington, Henry could not refuse this request. At least this job would require little travel far from home, he reasoned, and by returning to public office, he would honor his old friend Washington. He agreed to run. Writing to Washington, he commended the president's long-standing resistance to a deeper alliance with France, an entanglement that even Henry had supported in the early stages of the French Revolution. He now saw the error of this position, he said, and saluted Washington for saving the country, once from Britain, and once from France. Henry went on to blame atheistic French principles for undermining Americans' morality and their devotion to Washington's and Adams's administrations. Henry accepted Washington's challenge—he did not want to lose his reputation as the first among patriots. "I am ashamed to refuse the little boon you ask of me, when your example is before my eyes—my children would blush to know, that you and their father were contemporaries, and that when you asked him to throw in his mite for the public happiness, he refused to do it. In conformity with these feelings, I have declared myself a candidate for this county at the next election."[48]

News of Henry's return sent his Republican enemies into apoplexy. John Taylor of Caroline, a Republican in the House of Delegates, wrote frantically to James Madison, begging him to run for the Virginia legislature. Only someone like Madison could be an effective counterweight to Henry, Taylor said. (Madison had retired from the U.S. Congress in 1797.) Taylor believed that Henry was running only out of spite toward Madison and Jefferson and that he was ultimately positioning himself for a run for president in 1800. "What other motive can he have, but a desire to gratify hatred or ambition, for joining a party [the Federalists], who have carried a constitution, which he pronounced bad, even under the construction of its friends, beyond the worst construction of its enemies, and of himself its greatest enemy?" For Taylor, the fate of liberty, Virginia, and the Union all relied on the outcome of the contest between Federalists and Republicans in Virginia.[49]

Even before he could open his campaign for the statehouse, Henry was nominated—yet again—for a diplomatic position, this time as envoy to France under the Adams administration. Henry's friend Joseph Martin wrote, "With heartfelt pleasure I see your appointment as one of our plenipotentiaries to France but am in doubt whether you will accept or not." Martin's doubts were correct, because nominating Henry for an international posting was silly at this point in his life. He had refused such positions many times, and his health was in massive decline. In his letter turning down the appointment, Henry told President Adams that he was almost too sick to write.[50]

Increasingly unwell in recent years, Henry had grown sicker in early March, before the offer of the French appointment arrived, when he had taken a twenty-mile trip to the Charlotte County courthouse to deliver a speech supporting his election to the legislature. The records of that speech are not very reliable, but it seems certain that the feeble Henry denounced the Kentucky and Virginia Resolutions and the peril to the Union. It is less clear what he said regarding the Alien and Sedition Acts; he probably expressed regret over their adoption but advised the audience that disunion was not the solution, at least not at that time. One source records Henry as saying that "the Alien and Sedition Laws were only the fruit of that Constitution the adoption of which he opposed." Henry won the election because of the strength of his personal popularity, and his mediating position on the Virginia Resolution and the Alien and Sedition Acts.[51]

Thomas Jefferson, who only a few years before had tried to reconcile with his old nemesis, was disgusted with Henry's election and his affiliation with the Federalists. Henry's "apostasy must be unaccountable to those who do not know all the recesses of his heart," he wrote. Jefferson must have counted himself as among those who understood Henry's heart. His characterization of Henry's election as "apostasy" has framed the historical discussion of Henry's views in the 1790s. If we accept Jefferson's view that Henry's election as a Federalist represented an embrace of that party's national crusade against free speech and the campaign against America's former allies in France, then Henry had turned his back on states' rights, even tacitly accepting the Alien and Sedition Acts.[52]

Although Henry's journey from anti-federalist to Federalist might have appalled Jefferson, it is important to remember that the political alignments of 1799 were completely different from those of 1788. In the intervening decade, Henry accepted the process by which the Constitution had been adopted, and he was inclined to embrace stronger national government as part of the price Virginia should pay for having ratified the Constitution. His change of view was partly motivated also by personal feeling; Henry's old battles with Madison and Jefferson colored his political opinions. Since the early 1780s, if Thomas Jefferson was in favor of something, Henry was likely to be against it. And the feeling was mutual. Beyond such considerations, however, we have to remember that Henry was a pragmatist. His 1799 position was not the first permutation in his stance toward the role and strength of government; he had supported a more powerful governor's office in Virginia during the Revolution.

For Henry, the biggest change of circumstances since ratification was the pressing threat of French anti-Christianism. Henry had come to see French deism and atheism as the greatest menaces to the republic, and if fighting the advocates of France meant tolerating the more dubious policies of the Washington and Adams administrations, so be it. Henry was not an ideological purist, but neither was he an apostate. For him, local government best cultivated the virtuous republic, which was his ultimate priority. To Henry in the late 1780s, the greatest threat to republican government was the Constitution, but once the new form of government was adopted, he believed he should work within its framework to maintain the nation's liberty. Madison had promised that the government possessed sufficient balance among its branches, and between state and national sovereignty, to preserve liberty, insisting to his anti-federalist critics that the powers of the national government were strictly limited. Madison also delivered on his promise to add the Bill of Rights, which further restrained the national government. Ironically, by the late 1790s, Henry seemed more willing to accede to the power of the national government, while Madison and Jefferson were pursuing radical actions to check governmental might. Madison, then, had changed course as dramatically as Henry. Madison was the person most responsible for crafting the formidable new government; now he was doing all he could to impede it.

By the late 1790s, Henry had turned his attention away from the threat of the national government to the assault on traditional virtue and religion associated with the French Revolution. For Henry, a broadly construed Constitution was a structural hazard to liberty, but French heresy was a moral poison that would ruin the republic. The Constitution, as amended, represented a potential risk, but Paine's and Jefferson's skepticism was a clear and present danger. Henry could countenance expanded national power under Washington and Adams, if they kept the French menace at bay. But Henry's ideal republic still featured strong local government and a virtuous people: those twin priorities always anchored Henry's political principles.

Henry hoped to defend those beliefs one last time in the Virginia legislature, but he never got his chance. His chronic illnesses and fevers escalated when he suffered an intestinal disruption that may have been associated with kidney stones, or "the gravel." Dorothea recalled that when Henry died on June 6, 1799, "he met death with firmness, and in full confidence that through the merits of a bleeding Savior that his sins would be pardoned."

Patrick Henry preceded Washington in death by seven months. The political lives of Jefferson and Madison, on the other hand, still had a long course to run: in just a year and a half they would begin a combined sixteen-year tenure in the president's office, with Jefferson's triumph over John Adams. In a last jab at his great nemesis, Dorothea wrote, "I wish the great Jefferson and all the heroes of the deistical party could have seen my ever dear and honored husband pay his last debt to nature." Henry was sixty-three years old.[53]

EPILOGUE

# "Mourn Virginia Mourn!"
## *The Legacy of Patrick Henry*

P ATRICK HENRY REMAINED a controversial figure literally
until the day he died. Even as Henry was passing from
this life, the rabidly Republican *Vermont Gazette* published
an attack accusing him of being in thrall to the Federalists. Responding to rumors that Henry might replace Adams as the Federalist
candidate for president in the 1800 election, the writer suggested
that Federalists had manipulated the great patriot in his old age:
"his mind no longer quick to the apprehension of worldly deceit,
the insuspicious temper of his dotage, or second childhood has
made him a dupe." To the end, the mere possibility of Henry's return to the national political stage made news and caused consternation across the country.[1]

Along with his critics, Henry still had many friends and admirers,
as revealed in his obituary in the *Virginia Gazette*:

Mourn Virginia Mourn! Your Henry is gone! Ye friends to liberty in every clime, drop a tear. No more will his social feelings spread delight through his happy house. No more will his edifying example dictate to his numerous offspring the sweetness of virtue and the majesty of patriotism. . . .

Farewell, first-rate patriot, farewell! As long as our rivers flow, or mountains stand—so long will your excellence and worth be the theme of homage and endearment, and Virginia, bearing in mind her loss, will say to rising generations, imitate my HENRY.[2]

This eulogy captured the great themes in Henry's career: liberty, virtue, and patriotism.

Henry's death might have been expected to cool political animosity toward him among Virginia Republicans, but even months later, at the end of 1799, the bitterness lingered. In the Virginia House of Delegates, a resolution honoring Henry for his unsurpassed eloquence in the cause of liberty and virtue, and sanctioning the placement of a marble bust of Henry in the legislative hall, was tabled by a significant majority.[3]

Time and Republican ascendancy did soothe some bad feelings toward Henry. By the early nineteenth century, he had begun to develop his now-familiar posthumous reputation as the greatest orator of the Revolution. This portrait was definitively painted by William Wirt's admiring 1817 biography, *Sketches of the Life and Character of Patrick Henry*, which focused much more on Henry's natural brilliance as a speaker than the content of his thought. Wirt's Henry was a wondrous phenomenon, the "Orator of Nature" who spurred the Revolution by his prodigious talents alone. The book was hugely successful, with twenty-five editions published by 1871.[4]

Wirt corresponded extensively with Henry's old nemesis Jefferson about the biography. Jefferson was exceedingly frank in his assessment. Jefferson admitted that the two men had been friends until

1781, when they parted ways politically and personally. Jefferson commended Henry as the "greatest orator that ever lived." He credited Henry for being "the man who gave the first impulse to the ball of revolution." But his negative views of Henry were blistering. He considered Henry "avaricious and rotten hearted. His two great passions were the love of money and of fame, but when these came into competition the former predominated." Wirt latched on to Jefferson's admiring quotations for the biography, but he omitted the bad ones. The posthumous exaltation of such Founders as Henry and Washington often meant that bitter feelings and questions about character had to be excised from the historical record. (No one, until recently, received as whitewashed biographical treatments as Jefferson himself.) But Jefferson was deeply irritated with Wirt's hagiographic treatment of Henry; the former president was still complaining about the book among guests at Monticello as late as 1824.[5]

Americans have always revered Henry for his brilliant oratory. The focus on Henry's speeches, especially the "Liberty or Death" speech, resulted from the unanimous testimony that he was an unequaled political speaker. But the celebration of Henry's oratory may have also resulted from a certain discomfort with the content of his thought, especially his opposition to the Constitution.

Americans did not entirely forget about Henry's ideas, however. Especially in the era of the Civil War, partisans on both sides of the conflict employed Henry and his beliefs to support their own causes. Hinton Rowan Helper, a native North Carolinian and celebrated antislavery author, cited Henry to open a chapter on southern antislavery sentiment in his best-selling *Impending Crisis of the South* (1857). Helper noted that Henry and the other major Virginia Founders lamented the immorality of slavery. If those patriots were living in 1857, Helper speculated that there was "scarcely a slaveholder between the Potomac and the mouth of the Mississippi, that would not burn to pounce upon them with bludgeons, bowie-knives and pistols!" He believed the new southern slave masters were so blindly devoted to what had become euphemized as "the peculiar institution" that they had turned their backs on the antislavery tradition of Henry and the other southern Founding Fathers. One could certainly find antislavery statements from early in Henry's career, but Helper exaggerated the extent of Henry's revulsion, which never took hold in action against slavery.[6]

Conversely, Confederate apologists used Henry's memory to highlight what they saw as the deficiencies of the Constitution and its disempowerment of the states. Especially after the war, southerners pointed to Henry's speeches at the Virginia ratifying convention to demonstrate that potential for the national government's domination was built into the Constitution itself. Alexander Stephens, vice president of the Confederacy, wrote admiringly of Henry in his *Constitutional View of the Late War Between the States*. Henry "possessed one of those wonderful minds which, by a sort of instinct or supernatural faculty, scents the approaches of power, even in the distance. This instinct, or far-seeing superhuman endowment, prompted him to sound the alarm when the Constitution was at first presented to him." Stephens asserted, however, that Henry feared future misapplications of the Constitution, rather than its original intent. But other Confederates took a more negative view of the Constitution itself. Their perspective was probably closer to Henry's than Stephens's was. Henry's descendant Patrick Henry Fontaine, writing in the pro-southern *DeBow's Review* in 1870, argued that all of Henry's predictions about the Constitution's dangers had come true. To Fontaine, Henry had spoken prophetically at the ratifying convention: "He saw clearly that the Constitution was artfully framed to place the sovereign power of the United States in the hands of a majority of the people of the great consolidated government, which would absorb the rights of the several states." Fontaine believed that Henry, more than any other prominent southerner, grasped the way the Constitution imperiled the principles of the Revolution. In his estimation, Henry was the greatest statesman of all the Founders, certainly above Madison, Jefferson, and Hamilton, and even above the beloved Washington. To Fontaine, Henry had won primacy in that pantheon precisely because he maintained ideological consistency as both a patriot and an anti-federalist.[7]

Fontaine's opinions of Henry as an anti-federalist were those of an unvarnished Confederate, yet he was right to say that Henry did indeed oppose the Constitution because he perceived the new government as a betrayal of the Revolution. However, most observers—even sympathetic biographers—have agreed with the historian and U.S. senator from Indiana, Albert J. Beveridge, who in 1900 said that although Henry was sincere in his opposition to the Constitution, his sincerity did not make him right. To Beveridge, Henry was struggling against America's national destiny, "the onward forces which were making of the American people the master nation of the world." For many Americans who were aware of the entire trajectory of his public life, the Henry of historical memory became a great patriot who briefly lost his way in the late 1780s.[8]

Beginning in the late nineteenth century, a series of authors tried to expand or modify Wirt's admiring portrait of Henry. This patriotic trend began with Henry's grandson, a man tellingly named William Wirt Henry. A prominent historian, lawyer, and Confederate veteran, Henry published in 1891 a three-volume set titled *Patrick Henry: Life, Correspondence, and Speeches*, which, while imperfect, remains the best published collection of Henry's papers. Since William Wirt Henry's compilation, scholars and popular writers have fought back and forth, with the academics seeking to deconstruct myths about Henry that the popularizers promptly restore. The historian Bernard Mayo noted fifty years ago that of all the major Founders,

Henry presented the most perplexing disjunction between popular and scholarly interpretations.[9]

In recent years, both the political Left and Right have appropriated the image of Henry as a radical dissenter. Much of this use of Henry, of course, is based only on current applications of the ringing phrase "Give me liberty or give me death." Henry is a favorite of the contemporary Tea Party, a movement that reacted against President Barack Obama's massive increases in domestic spending and became the biggest news story of the 2010 election cycle. One sign at a 2009 Tea Party rally in Columbus, Ohio, read "Give me liberty, not debt."

No matter how much they venerate Henry's defense of American liberty, few Americans today, Tea Partiers or otherwise, take seriously Henry's fundamental criticisms of the Constitution. Unlike Henry, the conservatives who cite him would defend the Constitution and Bill of Rights—at least as they were originally intended, if not as they have been interpreted—as the best guarantees of our liberties. Certainly, after ratification, Henry came to advocate a strict interpretation of the Constitution as the only hope for restraining the national government. But he always worried that in establishing such a strong national authority, Madison and Hamilton had created a kind of Frankenstein's monster, destined to grow uncontrollably and eventually to become tyrannical. As welcome as the Bill of Rights was to anti-federalists such as Henry, those amendments did not address the fundamental issue of the national government's expansive powers.

Henry has also become a hero to many Christian conservatives, who see him as a defender of both Christian virtue and liberty. In 2000, the conservative activist and homeschooling advocate Michael Farris founded Patrick Henry College in Purcellville, Virginia. One of the college's dorms is even named Red Hill, after Henry's last home. Many homeschoolers see Patrick Henry as one of their own, because he was tutored by his Christian family at home and yet achieved great heights in the public sphere. Henry is an attractive figure to those Christian conservatives interested in sustaining the image of America as a Christian nation, because among the major Founders, he probably held some of the most committed Christian beliefs. Certainly as compared to Washington, Madison, and especially Jefferson, Henry made his sympathy toward traditional Christianity widely known. A serious Anglican with stirring memories of the Great Awakening, he possessed religious beliefs that were orthodox for his time. Although he was not an evangelical (in the sense that he did not emphasize the need for a conversion experience), he had abundant sympathy for the dissenting Protestants of Virginia, with his oratory profoundly influenced in style and substance by the evangelical preachers of his era.

At times, advocates of a Christian perspective on America's founding have gone to extremes in recruiting Henry to their cause. In particular, a widely circulated quotation erroneously attributed to Henry has him declaring, "It cannot be emphasized too strongly or too often that this great nation was founded, not by religionists, but by Christians; not on religions, but on the gospel of Jesus Christ!" David Barton of the WallBuilders organization once used this quote regularly in writings and speeches, but in 2000 he issued a statement in which he described this and a number of other Founders' quotes as "unconfirmed." Barton's retraction has hardly slowed the use of the quotation; it still appears all over the Internet and in books such as David Limbaugh's *Persecution: How Liberals Are Waging War Against Christianity.*[10]

We do not need such apocryphal quotes to establish that Henry's political thought was based on Christian principles. If anything, Henry's faith seems to have become even stronger and more heartfelt over time. In his will, drafted in 1798, he wrote of his bequests that "this is all the inheritance I can give to my dear family. The religion of Christ can give them one which will make them rich indeed." But we should also remember that Henry was very much a man of his time, and he had his shortcomings. He struggled with issues common to those who function as private individuals and public figures, such as the tension between political service and personal gain, and the typical ethical conundrums of lawyers who defend clients who are almost certainly guilty. Like many other Christians of his time, Henry worked to reconcile his religious principles with owning slaves. In the same will in which he prayed for his family's eternal inheritance, Henry did not manumit his slaves; instead, he declared that his slaves should be divided equally among his remaining family. In the inventory of Henry's estate, taken a year later, we see his sixty-seven slaves: men, women, and children with names like Tom, Pegg, and Anny.[11]

ASSESSING WHAT THE FOUNDERS would think about contemporary issues is always a difficult, if not foolhardy, enterprise. Academic historians normally refuse to engage in such speculation. But it is no great leap to imagine that Patrick Henry would fundamentally object to nearly every feature of today's titanic national government. This statement is not to place Henry on either side of today's political spectrum: he would disapprove equally of the massive, top-down social programs championed by the Left, the globetrotting military power championed by the Right, and the bailouts of financial companies championed by a majority of national politicians in 2008. Unlike many of his Christian conservative admirers today, he would not approve of America's recent ventures associated with the War on Terrorism, both in Iraq and in Afghanistan, a conflict that has become America's longest war. Henry would probably find that today's America has almost nothing in common with the republic of liberty he envisioned in 1776. On one hand, the national government has seemingly burst all bounds of power on the domestic and international stages, and on the other, the notion of a virtuous republic has been almost entirely abandoned in favor of what people of Henry's age would have called "license." To him, consolidated political power and ethical license historically triggered the loss of true liberty and the rise of moral and political tyranny.

If Henry were to travel through time to ascend the rostrum in the Virginia House of Delegates, or to address Philadelphia's Independence Hall, or to let his voice resound again into the rafters of St. John's Church, where he demanded liberty or death, he would no doubt exhort us to reconsider the value of public morality. He would caution us not just about the usual hot-button social and cultural issues, but also regarding matters such as greed and financial deception, issues that lay at the heart of America's financial meltdown that began in 2008. True freedom, he might warn us, lies not in doing whatever we want. Freedom is doing what we should do, for the sake of community and the republic.

Of course, Henry was not a perfect model of the virtues he trumpeted, even in the specific area of personal finances. (We might well imagine Henry, ever the speculator, investing in the infamous credit default swaps that helped cause our recent recession.) But if he did not always live up to his own lofty standards, we should remember that an inconsistency between the utterly laudable principles espoused and the life actually lived is an ethical problem common among mere mortals, including the leading Founders.

Surveying our country's current state of affairs, Henry might also advise us to consider the ways in which we have traded the accountability and responsiveness of diffuse, local governments for the intrusive might of national government. He might warn us that national power makes for an effective empire, not good government. A big government does not tend to safeguard our liberty, either, as we have witnessed on the ragged edges of the Bush and Obama administrations' prosecution of the War on Terrorism. Intrusive body scanning at airports, warrantless wiretapping, rendition of terrorism suspects to secret prisons, and torture are only examples of the sorts of misdeeds to be expected from a mammoth government and military that seemingly can do whatever it wants. What James Madison called the Constitution's "parchment barriers," intended to restrict the government's growth, seem ever more feeble against the power of our massive federal system.[12]

In America, Henry's memory has taken on a vague, patriotic cast that fails to capture his fractious yet exemplary life. The "real" Henry was branded a traitor and apostate on multiple occasions by his many enemies, including Thomas Jefferson. His vision of the American republic was not a matter of sentiment and grand words and gestures; it was grounded in virtue, religious faith, and responsive local government. Standing against his fellow Founders James Madison and Thomas Jefferson at almost every turn in the 1780s and '90s, and steadfastly opposing the adoption of the Constitution, he was the boldest of patriots. As a country, we may have chosen national power over decentralized government and individualistic freedom over virtue. But in 1776, Patrick Henry's ideals of liberty, religion, a moral society, small government, and local politics were essential principles upon which America was built.

# ACKNOWLEDGMENTS

Thanks to my colleagues and friends in Baylor University's history department and Baylor's Institute for Studies of Religion, including David Bebbington, Jeff Hamilton, Barry Hankins, Philip Jenkins, Byron Johnson, and Rodney Stark; at Basic Books/Perseus Books Group, including Lara Heimert, Alex Littlefield, Caitlin Graf, Katy O'Donnell, Michelle Welsh-Horst, Antoinette Smith, and Adam Eaglin; and my agent and friend Giles Anderson. Thanks to David Groff for his stellar editing work; to Thomas Buckley, Jeff Polet, and my Baylor assistant Thomas DeShong for reading the manuscript and saving me from a host of errors; to Karen Gorham at the Patrick Henry Memorial Foundation for research assistance, as well as the staffs at the Library of Congress, the University of Virginia Special Collections, the Library of Virginia, and other repositories of Henry papers; and to the Earhart Foundation for supporting the project with a summer stipend. As always, I am so thankful for the unfailing love and support from my wife, Ruby Kidd; my sons, Jonathan and Josh; and my mother, Nancy Kidd. I am dedicating the book to my father, Michael Kidd, who passed away unexpectedly before the book's completion. I hope that this small gesture conveys my gratefulness for his legacy in my life.

# NOTES

## Introduction: "The Nefarious and Highly Criminal" Patrick Henry: Patrick Henry in American Memory

1. William Wirt, *Sketches of the Life and Character of Patrick Henry*, 15th ed. (New York, 1857), 140–42.

2. Edmund Randolph, *History of Virginia*, ed. Arthur H. Shaffer (Charlottesville, VA, 1970), 212.

3. Patrick Henry, speech of June 24, 1788, in *Documentary History of the Ratification of the Constitution*, ed. John P. Kaminski and Gaspare J. Saladino (Madison, WI, 1993), 10:1506.

4. St. Jean de Crèvecoeur to William Short, June 10, 1788, in ibid., 10:1592.

5. Ibid., 9:952.

6. "The Virginia Convention, June 24, 1788," in ibid., 10:1506, 1511.

## Chapter 1: "If Your Industry Be Only Half Equal to Your Genius": Patrick Henry and Backcountry Virginia

1. George Willison, *Patrick Henry and His World* (Garden City, NY, 1969), 31–35.

2. Jefferson quoted in William Wirt Henry, *Patrick Henry: Life, Correspondence, and Speeches* (New York, 1891), 1:18; Lauren F. Winner, *A Cheerful and Comfortable Faith: Anglican Religious Practice in the Elite Households of Eighteenth-Century Virginia* (New Haven, CT, 2010), 130. I have silently modernized the spelling and punctuation of eighteenth-century prose throughout the book.

3. Jefferson quoted in Henry, *Patrick Henry*, 1:18; Richard R. Beeman, *Patrick Henry: A Biography* (New York, 1974), 7.

4. James Horn, "Tobacco Colonies: The Shaping of English Society in the Seventeenth-Century Chesapeake," in *The Origins of Empire: British Overseas Enterprise to the Close of the Seventeenth Century*, ed. Nicholas Canny (New York, 1998), 183.

5. Nicholas Spencer to Lord Culpeper, August 6, 1676, quoted in Edmund S. Morgan, *American Slavery, American Freedom: The Ordeal of Colonial Virginia* (New York, 1975), 236.

6. "Rabble Crue" quote from Morgan, *American Slavery*, 258.

7. Jack P. Greene, "Society, Ideology, and Politics: An Analysis of the Political Culture of Mid-Eighteenth-Century Virginia," in Jack P. Greene, *Negotiated Authorities: Essays in Colonial Political and Constitutional History* (Charlottesville, VA, 1994), 262; Jacob Price, "The Rise of Glasgow in the Chesapeake Tobacco Trade, 1707–1775," *William and Mary Quarterly* 3rd series, 11, no. 2 (April 1954): 179.

8. William Feltman, *The Journal of Lieut. William Feltman* (Philadelphia, 1853), 10; Jack P. Greene, *Pursuits of Happiness: The Social Development of Early Modern British Colonies and the Formation of American Culture* (Chapel Hill, NC, 1988), 85–86; Anthony S. Parent Jr., *Foul Means: The Formation of a Slave Society in Virginia, 1660–1740* (Chapel Hill, NC, 2003), 186.

9. Robert Douthat Meade, *Patrick Henry: Patriot in the Making* (Philadelphia, 1957), 44–45.

10. Narrative of Col. Samuel Meredith, Patrick Henry Papers, Library of Congress, 1; also in Henry, *Patrick Henry*, 1:8–9; David A. McCants,

*Patrick Henry, The Orator* (Westport, CT, 1990), 12. For Henry's reading and intellectual world, see Kevin J. Hayes, *The Mind of a Patriot: Patrick Henry and the World of Ideas* (Charlottesville, VA, 2008).

11. Philip Vickers Fithian to Enoch Green, December 1, 1773, in *Philip Vickers Fithian Journal and Letters, 1767–1774*, ed. John R. Williams (Princeton, NJ, 1900), 278.

12. Henry, *Patrick Henry*, 1:9–10.

13. *Virginia Gazette*, November 26, 1736, p. 4; *Virginia Gazette*, October 7, 1737, p. 3.

14. Ibid., October 7, 1737, p. 3.

15. T. H. Breen, *Tobacco Culture: The Mentality of the Great Tidewater Planters on the Eve of Revolution*, 2nd ed. (Princeton, NJ, 2001), xiii.

16. Quoted in T. H. Breen, *The Marketplace of Revolution: How Consumer Politics Shaped American Independence* (New York, 2004), 124; Breen, *Tobacco Culture*, 38.

17. Narrative of Col. Samuel Meredith, 3; William Wirt, *Sketches of the Life and Character of Patrick Henry* (New York, 1857), 29.

18. Robert Douthat Meade, *Patrick Henry: Practical Revolutionary* (Philadelphia, 1969), 79–82.

19. Ulrich B. Phillips, *American Negro Slavery* (New York, 1918), 83–84.

20. James Reid, "The Religion of the Bible and Religion of King William County Compared," in *The Colonial Virginia Satirist: Mid-Eighteenth-Century Commentaries on Politics, Religion, and Society*, ed. Richard Beale Davis (Philadelphia, 1967), 56.

21. *Journal of the House of Burgesses* (Williamsburg, VA, 1736), 27; Virginia Assembly, "An Act Concerning Servants and Slaves," 1705, at www2.vcdh .virginia.edu/xslt/servlet/XSLTServlet?xsl=/xml_docs/slavery/documents /display_laws2.xsl&xml=/xml_docs/slavery/documents/laws.xml&lawi =1705–10–03. Thanks to Charles Irons for help with this reference.

22. Breen, *Tobacco Culture*, 92–93; Ron Chernow, *Washington: A Life* (New York, 2010), 107.

23. Breen, *Tobacco Culture*, 153–158.

24. Chernow, *Washington*, 107.

25. Beeman, *Patrick Henry*, 7; George Morgan, *Patrick Henry* (Philadelphia, 1929), 43.

26. Fred Anderson, *Crucible of War: The Seven Years' War and the Fate of Empire in British North America, 1754–1766* (New York, 2000), 5–7.

27. Samuel Davies, *Religion and Patriotism: The Constituents of a Good Soldier* (Philadelphia, 1755), 4–5.

28. Davies, *Religion and Patriotism*, 5, 22.

29. Meade, *Practical Revolutionary*, 86–87.

30. Beeman, *Patrick Henry*, 7–8.

31. Meade, *Patriot in the Making*, 98.

32. "Journal of a French Traveller in the Colonies, 1765, I," *American Historical Review* 26, no. 4 (July 1921): 742–743.

33. Governor Alexander Spotswood quoted in Morgan, *American Slavery*, 360.

34. Meade, *Patriot in the Making*, 39.

35. Wirt, *Sketches*, 34–36. The account of Randolph's interview is based on a second-hand report of Judge John Tyler to Wirt.

## Chapter 2: "The Infatuation of New Light": The Great Awakening and the Parsons' Cause

1. James Maury to John Camm, December 12, 1763, in James Maury letterbook, in Sol Feinstone Collection of the American Revolution, microfilm, reel 2; Richard R. Beeman, *Patrick Henry: A Biography* (New York, 1974), 15–20.

2. Thomas S. Kidd, *The Great Awakening: The Roots of Evangelical Christianity in Colonial America* (New Haven, CT, 2007), 235–36.

3. "Tutored" quote in Jack P. Greene, "Society, Ideology, and Politics: An Analysis of the Political Culture of Mid-Eighteenth Century Virginia," in Jack P. Greene, *Negotiated Authorities: Essays in Colonial Political and Constitutional History* (Charlottesville, VA, 1994), 264.

4. William Wirt Henry, *Patrick Henry: Life, Correspondence, and Speeches* (New York, 1891), 1:15.

5. King James I quoted in Perry Miller, "Religion and Society in the Early Literature of Virginia," in *Errand into the Wilderness*, ed. Perry Miller (Cambridge, MA, 1956), 101; H. J. Eckenrode, *Separation of Church and State in Virginia: A Study in the Development of the Revolution* (1910; New York, 1971), 5–6.

6. Charles F. James, *Documentary History of the Struggle for Religious Liberty in Virginia* (Lynchburg, VA, 1900), 18–20.

7. William H. Foote, *Sketches of Virginia Historical and Biographical* (Philadelphia, 1850), 44–45; Chris Beneke, *Beyond Toleration: The Religious Origins of American Pluralism* (New York, 2006), 34–36.

8. Jonathan Edwards, "A Faithful Narrative of the Surprising Work of God," in *A Jonathan Edwards Reader*, ed. John Smith, et al. (New Haven, CT, 1995), 63.

9. Robert H. Bishop, *An Outline of the History of the Church in the State of Kentucky* (Lexington, KY, 1824), 40.

10. Kidd, *Great Awakening*, 234–36.

11. Patrick Henry to William Dawson, October 14, 1745, in "Letters of Patrick Henry, Sr., Samuel Davies, James Maury, Edwin Conway and George Trask," *William and Mary Quarterly* 2nd series, 1, no. 4 (October 1921): 266–67.

12. Patrick Henry to William Dawson, June 8, 1747, in "Letters," *William and Mary Quarterly*, 273.

13. Samuel Davies to the Bishop of London, January 10, 1752, in Foote, *Sketches of Virginia*, 183–84; Rhys Isaac, "Religion and Authority: Problems of the Anglican Establishment in Virginia in the Era of the Great Awakening and the Parsons' Cause," *William and Mary Quarterly* 3rd series, 30, no. 1 (January 1973): 26.

14. Kidd, *Great Awakening*, 290.

15. Soame Jenyns, *A View of the Internal Evidence of the Christian Religion*, 10th ed. (Richmond, VA, 1787), 28; Narrative of Colonel Samuel Meredith, Patrick Henry Papers, Library of Congress, 2.

16. Narrative of Meredith, 2–3; Philip Doddridge, *The Rise and Progress of Religion in the Soul*, 6th ed. (Boston, 1749), 9.

17. Narrative of Meredith, 3.

18. James Maury to John Fontaine, June 15, 1756, in Ann Maury, trans. and comp., *Memoirs of a Huguenot Family* (New York, 1853), 402; Isaac, "Religion and Authority," 11–13.

19. Governor Dinwiddie to the Bishop of London, September 12, 1757, in *Historical Collections Relating to the American Colonial Church*, ed. William Stevens Perry (1870; New York, 1969), 455; Isaac, "Religion and Authority," 13–14.

20. John Camm, "The Humble Representation of the Clergy," in *Pamphlets of the American Revolution, 1750–1776*, ed. Bernard Bailyn (Cambridge, MA, 1965), 1:353; Landon Carter, *A Letter to the Right Reverend Father in God* (Williamsburg, VA, 1759), 8.

21. William Kay to the Bishop of London, June 14, 1752, quoted in Isaac, "Religion and Authority," 8.

22. Carter, *Letter*, 14.

23. Bailyn, *Pamphlets*, 1:295; "turbulent" quote from Jack P. Greene, *The Quest for Power: The Lower Houses of Assembly in the Southern Royal Colonies, 1689–1776* (Chapel Hill, NC, 1963), 359; Fauquier quote in Thomas J. Wertenbaker, *Give Me Liberty: The Struggle for Self-Government in Virginia* (Philadelphia, 1958), 214.

24. Richard Bland, *A Letter to the Clergy of Virginia* (Williamsburg, VA, 1760), 16, 20.

25. Leonard W. Labaree, *Royal Government in America: A Study of the British Colonial System Before 1783* (New Haven, CT, 1930), 264–65.

26. William Robinson to the Bishop of London, 1763, in Perry, *Historical Collections*, 482.

27. Maury to Camm, December 12, 1763.

28. Carl R. Loundsbury, *The Courthouses of Early Virginia: An Architectural History* (Charlottesville, VA, 2005), 88–89, 151–52.

29. Maury to Camm, December 12, 1763.

30. Ibid.

31. John Camm, *A Review of the Rector Detected* (Williamsburg, VA, 1764), 23; Robert Douthat Meade, *Patrick Henry: Patriot in the Making* (Philadelphia, 1957), 136–37.

32. Meade, *Patriot in the Making*, 141–42.

33. Charles S. Sydnor, *Gentlemen Freeholders: Political Practices in Washington's Virginia* (1952; Westport, CT, 1984), 51–54.

34. John Pendleton Kennedy, ed., *Journals of the House of Burgesses of Virginia, 1761–1765* (Richmond, VA, 1907), 271–72.

35. Beeman, *Patrick Henry*, 25, 30.

## Chapter 3: "If This Be Treason": The Stamp Act Crisis

1. "Journal of a French Traveler in the Colonies, 1765," *American Historical Review* 26, no. 4 (July 1921): 745.

2. "Line of treason" quote in Edmund Pendleton to James Madison, April 21, 1790, in *The Letters and Papers of Edmund Pendleton, 1734–1803*, ed. David John Mays (Charlottesville, VA, 1967), 2:565; Richard R. Beeman, *Patrick Henry: A Biography* (New York, 1974), 37–38.

3. "Heard" quote in Thomas Jefferson, "Autobiography," 1821, at www.yale.edu/lawweb/avalon/jeffauto.htm; "baffled" quote in Thomas Jefferson to William Wirt, August 14, 1814, in *The Writings of Thomas Jefferson*, ed. Albert E. Bergh (Washington, DC, 1907), 13:169.

4. Edmund S. Morgan and Helen M. Morgan, *The Stamp Act Crisis: Prologue to Revolution*, rev. ed. (New York: 1962), 36–37; Fred Anderson, *Crucible of War: The Seven Years' War and the Fate of Empire in British North America, 1754–1766* (New York, 2000), 547–48.

5. John Pendleton Kennedy, ed., *Journals of the House of Burgesses of Virginia, 1761–1765* (Richmond, VA, 1907), 303; Morgan and Morgan, *Stamp Act*, 58, 87–88; Walter Isaacson, *Benjamin Franklin: An American Life* (New York, 2003), 223.

6. Morgan and Morgan, *Stamp Act*, 93–94.

7. *Boston Evening Post*, May 27, 1765.

8. Kennedy, *Journals*, 345. On the qualities of the most powerful House members in the eighteenth century, Jack P. Greene, "Foundations of Political Power in the Virginia House of Burgesses, 1720–76," in Jack P. Greene, *Negotiated Authorities: Essays in Colonial Political and Constitutional History* (Charlottesville, VA, 1994), 238–58.

9. Thomas Jefferson to William Wirt, in S. V. Henkels, ed., "Jefferson's Recollections of Patrick Henry," *Pennsylvania Magazine of History and Biography* 34, no. 4 (1910): 388; T. H. Breen, *Tobacco Culture: The Mentality of the Great Tidewater Planters on the Eve of Revolution*, 2nd ed. (Princeton, NJ, 2001), 189–90.

10. George Morgan, *The True Patrick Henry* (Philadelphia, 1907), 100; Kennedy, *Journals*, 360.

11. Morgan and Morgan, *Stamp Act*, 125; Kennedy, *Journals*, lxviii.

12. *Maryland Gazette*, July 4, 1765, in Morgan and Morgan, *Stamp Act*, 128–29.

13. *Boston Gazette*, July 8, 1765; Morgan and Morgan, *Stamp Act*, 135.

14. Morgan and Morgan, *Stamp Act*, 142–44.

15. Ibid., 161–64.

16. James Mercer Garnett, "James Mercer," *William and Mary College Quarterly Historical Magazine* 17, no. 2 (October 1908): 88.

17. Francis Fauquier to the Lords of Trade, November 3, 1765, in Kennedy, *Journals*, lxix–lxx.

18. Ibid., lxx–lxxi.

19. Morgan and Morgan, *Stamp Act*, 330–31.

20. House of Commons, *The Examination of Doctor Benjamin Franklin* (Philadelphia, 1766), 3–4; Isaacson, *Benjamin Franklin*, 229–31.

21. Morgan and Morgan, *Stamp Act*, 347–48.

22. George Mason to the Committee of Merchants in London, June 6, 1766, in *The Papers of George Mason*, ed. Robert A. Rutland (Chapel Hill, NC, 1970), 1:65–66; Jeff Broadwater, *George Mason: Forgotten Founder* (Chapel Hill, NC, 2006), 38–39.

23. "Journal of a French Traveler," 747.

24. William Robinson to the Bishop of London, August 12, 1765, in *Historical Collections Relating to the American Colonial Church*, ed. William Stevens Perry (1870; New York, 1969), 515.

25. Morgan, *True Patrick Henry*, 100.

## Chapter 4: "The First Man Upon This Continent": Boycotts and the Growing Crisis with Britain

1. John Pendleton Kennedy, ed., *Journals of the House of Burgesses of Virginia, 1761–1765* (Richmond, VA, 1907), 218.

2. George Washington to George Mason, April 5, 1769, in *The Papers of George Washington: Digital Edition*, ed. Theodore Crackel (Charlottesville, VA, 2007); Jeff Broadwater, *George Mason: Forgotten Founder* (Chapel Hill, NC, 2006), 50–51.

3. "Circular Letter to the Governors in America," April 21, 1768, at www.yale.edu/lawweb/avalon/amerrev/amerdocs/circ_let_gov_1768.htm.

4. Kennedy, *Journals*, 214–16.

5. Richard R. Beeman, *Patrick Henry: A Biography* (New York, 1974), 22–23.

6. Frank L. Dewey, "Thomas Jefferson and a Williamsburg Scandal: The Case of Blair v. Blair," *Virginia Magazine of History and Biography* 89, no. 1 (January 1981): 57; Andrew Burstein and Nancy Isenberg, *Madison and Jefferson* (New York, 2010), 16.

7. Beeman, *Patrick Henry*, 25–27; "Kinney v. Clark (1844)," in *Cases Argued and Decided in the Supreme Court of the United States*, ed. Stephen K. Williams (Rochester, NY, 1911), 11:89.

8. Patrick Henry to William Fleming, June 10, 1767, in Thomas Perkins Abernathy, *Western Lands and the American Revolution* (New York, 1937), 61–62; Patrick Griffin, *American Leviathan: Empire, Nation, and the Revolutionary Frontier* (New York, 2007), 101.

9. Robert Douthat Meade, *Patrick Henry: Patriot in the Making* (Philadelphia, 1957), 278–79.

10. "Notice of Sale of All of the John Robinson Estate," December 28, 1769, in *The Letters and Papers of Edmund Pendleton, 1734–1803*, ed. David John Mays (Charlottesville, VA, 1967), 53–54.

11. Ron Chernow, *Washington: A Life* (New York, 2010), 483; David Waldstreicher, ed., *Notes on the State of Virginia, by Thomas Jefferson, with Related Documents* (Boston, 2002), 199; T. H. Breen, *Tobacco Culture: The Mentality of the Great Tidewater Planters on the Eve of Revolution*, 2nd ed. (Princeton, NJ, 2001), 204–06.

12. Patrick Henry, Memorandum of September 5, 1785, in *Henry Family Papers, Records of the Ante-Bellum Southern Plantations from the Revolution Through the Civil War*, ed. Kenneth Stampp, Series M, Selections from the Virginia Historical Society, Part 5: Southside Virginia; Robert Douthat Meade, *Patrick Henry: Practical Revolutionary* (Philadelphia, 1969), 151–52, 315–16.

13. Jackson Turner Main, "The One Hundred," *William and Mary Quarterly* 3rd series, 11, no. 3 (July 1954): 376–77; "Journal of a French Traveler in the Colonies," *American Historical Review* 26, no. 4 (July 1921): 745.

14. Anthony S. Parent Jr., *Foul Means: The Formation of a Slave Society in Virginia, 1660–1740* (Chapel Hill, NC, 2003), 124–25; Meade, *Patriot in the Making*, 294.

15. William Waller Hening, ed., *The Statutes at Large; Being a Collection of All the Laws of Virginia* (Richmond, VA, 1821), 8:358; Kennedy, *Journals*, 259.

16. Parent, *Foul Means*, 161–62.

17. "A Hanover County, Virginia, Uprising, Christmas, 1769," in *American Negro Slavery*, ed. Michael Mullin (Columbia, SC, 1976), 95.

18. Robert L. Scribner, ed., *Revolutionary Virginia: The Road to Independence* (Charlottesville, VA, 1973), 1:87–88.

19. Pauline Maier, *American Scripture: Making the Declaration of Independence* (New York, 1997), 239.

20. Patrick Henry to Robert Pleasants, January 18, 1773, in Meade, *Patriot in the Making*, 299–300.

21. Lacy K. Ford, *Deliver Us from Evil: The Slavery Question in the Old South* (New York, 2009), 23.

22. Robert Pleasants to Anthony Benezet, August 20, 1774, in "Letters of Robert Pleasants, of Curles," *William and Mary Quarterly* 2nd series, 1, no. 2 (April 1921): 107, 108 n2.

23. Samuel Allinson to Patrick Henry, October 17, 1774, in Allinson Family Papers, Rutgers University Special Collections; Robert Pleasants to Patrick Henry, March 28, 1777, in William Wirt Henry, *Patrick Henry: Life, Correspondence, and Speeches* (New York, 1891), 3: 49–51.

24. Meade, *Practical Revolutionary*, 168–69.

25. Waldstreicher, *Notes on the State of Virginia*, 195–96; Peter S. Onuf, "'To Declare Them a Free and Independant People': Race, Slavery, and National Identity in Jefferson's Thought," *Journal of the Early Republic* 18, no. 1 (Spring 1998): 1–6.

26. George Mason quoted in *The Founders' Constitution*, ed. Philip B. Kurland and Ralph Lerner (Chicago, 1987), at http://press-pubs.uchicago .edu/founders/documents/a1_9_1s3.html; Broadwater, *George Mason*, 191–92; Beeman, *Patrick Henry*, 97.

27. Kennedy, *Journals*, 233.

28. "Nonimportation Association of Burgesses and Merchants," June 22, 1770, in Scribner, *Revolutionary Virginia*, 82; Beeman, *Patrick Henry*, 48.

29. Dumas Malone, *Jefferson and His Time: Jefferson the Virginian* (Boston, 1948), 1:121.

30. Thomas Jefferson, "Autobiography," at www.yale.edu/lawweb /avalon/jeffauto.htm; "Extracts from the Journal of the Proceedings of the House of Burgesses, of Virginia," March 13, 1773, in Scribner, *Revolutionary Virginia*, 91.

31. Richard Henry Lee to John Dickinson, July 25, 1768, in *The Letters of Richard Henry Lee*, ed. James Curtis Ballagh (1911; New York, 1970), 1:29.

32. George Mason to Martin Cockburn, May 26, 1774, in *The Papers of George Mason*, ed. Robert A. Rutland (Chapel Hill, NC, 1970), 1:190.

33. Jefferson, "Autobiography."

34. "An Association, Signed by 89 Members of the Late House of Burgesses," May 27, 1774, in Scribner, *Revolutionary Virginia*, 97.

35. Jefferson, "Autobiography"; Scribner, *Revolutionary Virginia*, 103–04.

36. "At a Meeting of the Freeholders of Hanover County," July 20, 1774, in Henry, *Patrick Henry*, 1:191–93.

37. "Convention Association," August 6, 1774, in Scribner, *Revolutionary Virginia*, 231–32.

38. Edmund Randolph, *History of Virginia*, ed. Arthur H. Shaffer (Charlottesville, VA, 1970), 206.

39. George Washington, diary, August 30–31, 1774, in Crackel, *Papers of George Washington*.

## Chapter 5: "Liberty or Death": Arming for Revolution

1. Joseph Jackson, "Washington in Philadelphia," *Pennsylvania Magazine of History and Biography* 56, no. 2 (1932): 124.

2. Richard R. Beeman, *Plain, Honest Men: The Making of the American Constitution* (New York, 2009), 73–75.

3. Mark David Hall, "Roger Sherman: An Old Puritan in a New Nation," in *The Forgotten Founders on Religion and Public Life*, ed. Daniel L. Dreisbach, Mark David Hall, and Jeffry H. Morrison (Notre Dame, IN, 2009), 248–49; John Adams to Patrick Henry, June 3, 1776, in *Papers of John Adams*, ed. Robert J. Taylor (Cambridge, MA, 1979), 4:234.

4. John Adams, *The Works of John Adams, Second President of the United States: With a Life of the Author, Notes and Illustrations* (Boston, 1850–1856), 2:366–67; Richard R. Beeman, *Patrick Henry: A Biography* (New York, 1974), 60.

5. Adams, *Works of John Adams*, 2:367; Beeman, *Patrick Henry*, 61.

6. *At a Meeting of the Delegates of Every Town and District in the County of Suffolk* (Boston, 1774), 1; Adams, *Works of Adams*, 2:380.

7. Adams, *Works of Adams*, 2:390, 396; Robert Douthat Meade, *Patrick Henry: Patriot in the Making* (Philadelphia, 1957), 331.

8. Edmund C. Burnett, ed., *Letters of Members of the Continental Congress* (Washington, DC, 1921), 1:28–29.

9. Anne Christian to her sister, October 15, 1774, in William Fleming Papers, Washington and Lee University; Beeman, *Patrick Henry*, 63–64.

10. www.redhill.org/descendants_genealogy.html.

11. Meade, *Patriot in the Making*, 280–282; Priscilla Hart, "The Madhouse of Colonial Williamsburg: An Interview with Shomer Zwelling," *History News Network*, October 5, 2009, at http://hnn.us/articles/117164.html.

12. "Recommendations and Instructions to Hanover County Delegates," March 4, 1775, in *Revolutionary Virginia: The Road to Independence*, ed. Robert L. Scribner (Charlottesville, VA, 1975), 2:311–12.

13. "Humble Petition and Memorial of the Assembly of Jamaica," December 28, 1774, in Scribner, *Revolutionary Virginia*, 2:363–66; "Proceedings of the Second Virginia Convention," March 23, 1775, in Scribner, *Revolutionary Virginia*, 2:366.

14. Charles L. Cohen, "The 'Liberty or Death' Speech: A Note on Religion and Revolutionary Rhetoric," *William and Mary Quarterly* 3rd series, 38, no. 4 (October 1981): 710–14.

15. William Wirt, *Sketches of the Life and Character of Patrick Henry*, 15th ed. (New York, 1857), 138–39, 141; Cohen, "'Liberty or Death' Speech," 706.

16. Wirt, *Sketches*, 138–39.

17. Ibid., 140–42.

18. Edmund Randolph, *History of Virginia*, ed. Arthur H. Shaffer (Charlottesville, VA, 1970), 212; James Parker to Charles Steuart, April 6, 1775, in Robert Douthat Meade, *Patrick Henry: Practical Revolutionary* (Philadelphia, 1969), 36.

19. Joseph Addison, *Cato, A Tragedy* (Boston, 1767), 37; H. Trevor Colbourn, *The Lamp of Experience: Whig History and the Intellectual Origins of the American Revolution* (Chapel Hill, NC, 1965), 153; Kevin J. Hayes, *The Mind of a Patriot: Patrick Henry and the World of Ideas* (Charlottesville, VA, 2008), 72–73.

20. Wirt, *Sketches*, 141.

21. James Parker quoted in Meade, *Practical Revolutionary*, 43.

22. "Proceedings," March 25, 1775, in Scribner, *Revolutionary Virginia*, 2:374–75; "Lieutenant George Gilmer to the Albemarle County First Independent Company," in Scribner, *Revolutionary Virginia*, 3:52.

23. Robert L. Scribner, "Introductory Note," in Scribner, *Revolutionary Virginia*, 4:3–5; Michael A. McDonnell, *The Politics of War: Race, Class, and Conflict in Revolutionary Virginia* (Chapel Hill, NC, 2007), 49–50.

24. "An Humble Address," April 21, 1775, in Scribner, *Revolutionary Virginia*, 4:54–55; Woody Holton, *Forced Founders: Indians, Debtors, Slaves, and the Making of the American Revolution in Virginia* (Chapel Hill, NC, 1999), 141–45.

25. Scribner, *Revolutionary Virginia*, 3:52 n2; Holton, *Forced Founders*, 147.

26. Charles Dabney to William Wirt, December 21, 1805, in Patrick Henry Papers, Library of Congress; George Dabney to William Wirt, May 14, 1805, in Patrick Henry Papers, Library of Congress; Beeman, *Patrick Henry*, 70.

27. "Hanover County Committee," May 9, 1775, in Scribner, *Revolutionary Virginia*, 3:111.

28. "A True Patriot," in *Virginia Gazette* (Pinkney), May 11, 1775, in Scribner, *Revolutionary Virginia*, 3:117; Lord Dunmore, "A Proclamation," May 6, 1775, in Scribner, *Revolutionary Virginia*, 3:100–01.

29. Orange County Committee, "An Endorsement of Violence and Reprisal," in Scribner, *Revolutionary Virginia*, 3:112–13.

30. Patrick Henry to Francis Lightfoot Lee, May 8, 1775, in Lee Family Papers, University of Virginia Library.

31. William Wirt Henry, *Patrick Henry: Life, Correspondence, and Speeches* (New York, 1891), 1:290.

32. Thomas Jefferson to William Wirt, August 4, 1805, in "Jefferson's Recollections of Patrick Henry," *Pennsylvania Magazine of History and Biography* 34, no. 4 (1910): 393.

33. George Washington to John Washington, June 20, 1775, in *The Papers of George Washington: Digital Edition*, ed. Theodore Crackel (Charlottesville, VA, 2007); Beeman, *Patrick Henry*, 72.

## Chapter 6: "To Cut the Knot": Independence

1. William Waller Hening, ed., *The Statutes at Large* (Richmond, VA, 1821), 9:36; "Patrick Henry's Commission," *American Historical Record* 2, no. 13 (January 1873): 32–33.

2. "Form of a Commission for the Colonel of the First Regiment, and Commander in Chief of the Regular Forces," August 26, 1775, in *Revolutionary Virginia: The Road to Independence*, ed. Robert L. Scribner (Charlottesville, VA, 1978), 3:498.

3. Lord Dunmore, "A Proclamation," November 7, 1775, and Patrick Henry to the County Lieutenant of Westmoreland, November 20, 1775, in Scribner, *Revolutionary Virginia*, 4:334, 435–36.

4. Robert W. Carter to Landon Carter, quoted in Michael McDonnell, *The Politics of War: Race, Class, and Conflict in Revolutionary Virginia* (Chapel Hill, NC, 2007), 101; "Commission for the Colonel of the First Regiment," August 26, 1775, in Scribner, *Revolutionary Virginia*, 3:498.

5. Virginia Committee of Safety, "Orders for Colonel William Woodford," October 24, 1775, in Scribner, *Revolutionary Virginia*, 4:270; Virginia Committee of Safety, Vice President John Page to Patrick Henry, November 4, 1775, in Scribner, *Revolutionary Virginia*, 4:321.

6. E. C. Branchi, "Memoirs of the Life and Voyages of Doctor Philip Mazzei," *William and Mary Quarterly* 2nd series, 9, no. 3 (July 1929): 173.

7. "A Few Anonymous Remarks on Lord Dunmore's Proclamation," *Virginia Gazette*, November 23, 1775, in Scribner, *Revolutionary Virginia*, 4:459–62.

8. McDonnell, *Politics of War*, 135–40; Goochland County Committee, *Virginia Gazette*, November 29, 1775, in Scribner, *Revolutionary Virginia*, 4:491–92.

9. Letter from Richard Meade, December 18, 1775, in *The Bland Papers, Being a Selection from the Manuscripts of Colonel Theodorick Bland, Jr.*, ed. Charles Campbell (Petersburg, VA, 1840), 1:39; William Woodford quoted in John E. Selby, *The Revolution in Virginia, 1775–1783* (Williamsburg, VA,

1988), 73–74; Fourth Virginia Convention Proceedings, January 17, 1776, in Scribner, *Revolutionary Virginia*, 5:423.

10. Patrick Henry to William Woodford, December 6, 1775, Newberry Library; Virginia Committee of Safety, "Instruction to Colonel Woodford," in Scribner, *Revolutionary Virginia*, 5:221.

11. Edmund Pendleton to William Woodford, December 24, 1775, in *The Letters and Papers of Edmund Pendleton, 1734–1803*, ed. David John Mays (Charlottesville, VA, 1967), 1:141; George Washington to Joseph Reed, February 26, 1776, in *Papers of George Washington: Digital Edition*, ed. Theodore Crackel (Charlottesville, VA, 2007).

12. John Adams to Abigail Adams, February 13, 1776, in *Letters of Delegates to Congress, 1774–1789*, ed. Paul H. Smith (Washington, DC, 1978), 3:241.

13. Virginia Committee of Safety Proceedings, February 28, 1776, in Scribner, *Revolutionary Virginia*, 6:149; McDonnell, *Politics of War*, 181–83.

14. *Virginia Gazette* (Purdie), March 1, 1776, 3.

15. Ibid., March 15, 1776, supplement, 2.

16. Richard Henry Lee to John Page, March 19, 1776, in Smith, *Letters of Delegates to Congress*, 3:408n.

17. *Virginia Gazette* (Purdie), February 2, 1776, 2; Lincoln MacVeagh, ed., *The Journal of Nicholas Creswell, 1774–1777* (New York, 1924), 136; McDonnell, *Politics of War*, 198–99.

18. George Washington to Joseph Reed, April 1, 1776, in Crackel, *Papers of George Washington: Digital Edition*.

19. Richard Henry Lee to Patrick Henry, April 20, 1776, in *The Letters of Richard Henry Lee*, ed. James Curtis Ballagh (1911; New York, 1970), 1:176.

20. *A Proclamation for a Continental Fast*, March 16, 1776, Philadelphia, broadside; Robert Douthat Meade, *Patrick Henry: Practical Revolutionary* (Philadelphia, 1969), 102.

21. Charlotte County Committee, "A Public Letter of Instructions," in Scribner, *Revolutionary Virginia*, 6:447.

22. John Adams to James Warren, July 24, 1775, in *Warren-Adams Letters*, ed. Worthington Chauncey Ford (Boston, 1917), 1:89; Charles Lee to

Patrick Henry, May 7, 1776, in *Collections of the New York Historical Society* 5 (1872): 1–3.

23. Edmund Randolph, *History of Virginia*, ed. Arthur H. Shaffer (Charlottesville, VA, 1970), 250; Resolution of Patrick Henry, in Scribner, *Revolutionary Virginia*, vol. 7, part 1: 145–46.

24. Randolph, *History of Virginia*, 250.

25. Fifth Virginia Convention, May 15, 1776, in Scribner, *Revolutionary Virginia*, 7, part 1:142–43.

26. Patrick Henry to John Adams, May 20, 1776, in *Papers of John Adams*, ed. Robert J. Taylor (Cambridge, MA, 1979), 4:201.

27. *Virginia Gazette* (Purdie), May 17, 1776, 3; *Virginia Gazette* (Dixon and Hunter), May 18, 1776, 3.

28. John Adams to Patrick Henry, June 3, 1776, in Taylor, *Papers of John Adams*, 4:235.

29. Ibid., 4:234; "Political cooks" quote in Andrew Burstein and Nancy Isenberg, *Madison and Jefferson* (New York, 2010), 34.

30. Virginia Declaration of Rights (1776), at http://avalon.law.yale.edu /18th_century/virginia.asp; Randolph, *History of Virginia*, 253.

31. Jeff Broadwater, *George Mason: Forgotten Founder* (Chapel Hill, NC, 2006), 81.

32. Patrick Henry, undated fragment, in William Wirt Henry, *Patrick Henry: Life, Correspondence, and Speeches* (New York, 1891), 1:116; Thomas J. Buckley, S.J., "Patrick Henry, Religious Liberty, and the Search for Civic Virtue," in *The Forgotten Founders on Religion and Public Life*, ed. Daniel L. Dreisbach, Mark David Hall, and Jeffry H. Morrison (Notre Dame, IN, 2009), 131–32.

33. Third Virginia Convention, August 16, 1775, in Scribner, *Revolutionary Virginia*, 3:450–51, 453 n3; Thomas O'Gorman, *A History of the Roman Catholic Church in the United States* (New York, 1902), 252.

34. Fifth Virginia Convention, "Petition of Baptists of Prince William County," May 19, 1776, in Scribner, *Revolutionary Virginia*, 188–89; Patrick Henry to the Ministers and Delegates of the Baptist Churches, August 13, 1776, *Dunlap's Pennsylvania Packet*, September 3, 1776.

35. Virginia Declaration of Rights, http://avalon.law.yale.edu/18th _century/virginia.asp; Randolph, *History of Virginia*, 254; Thomas E. Buckley, *Church and State in Revolutionary Virginia, 1776–1787* (Charlottesville, VA, 1977), 17–19.

36. Randolph, *History of Virginia*, 255.

37. Ibid., 255–56.

38. Patrick Henry to the President and House of Convention, June 29, 1776, in Patrick Henry papers, Pierpont Morgan Library, New York City.

39. Fifth Virginia Convention, June 29, 1776, in Scribner, *Revolutionary Virginia*, 654–55; McDonnell, *Politics of War*, 243–44.

## Chapter 7: "Our Worthy Governor": Patrick Henry in Wartime

1. "Diary of Col. Landon Carter," *William and Mary Quarterly* 1st series, 20, no. 3 (January 1912): 180, 184.

2. "Address of the First and Second Virginia Regiment to Patrick Henry, on His Appointment of Governour, Answer of the Governour," July 1, 1776, in *American Archives: Documents of the American Revolution, 1774–1776*, at http://dig.lib.niu.edu/amarch.

3. Michael A. McDonnell, *The Politics of War: Race, Class, and Conflict in Revolutionary Virginia* (Chapel Hill, NC, 2007), 250–51.

4. *Virginia Gazette* (Purdie), August 2, 1776, 2; Brent Tarter and Robert L. Scribner, eds., *Revolutionary Virginia: The Road to Independence* (Charlottesville, VA, 1983), vol. 7, part 2: 669 n.3; George F. Willison, *Patrick Henry and His World* (Garden City, NY, 1969), 329.

5. Patrick Henry to George Washington, September 20, 1776, in *The Papers of George Washington: Digital Edition*, ed. Theodore Crackel (Charlottesville, VA, 2007).

6. George Washington to Patrick Henry, October 5, 1776, also on militias, George Washington to John Hancock, September 2, 1776, in Crackel, *Papers of George Washington*; Robert Douthat Meade, *Patrick Henry: Practical Revolutionary* (Philadelphia, 1969), 141–42.

7. Thomas Paine, "The American Crisis," December 19, 1776, in Thomas Paine, *Common Sense and Related Writings*, ed. Thomas P. Slaughter (Boston, 2001), 126.

8. Journal of the House of Delegates, December 21, 1776, in *Official Letters of the Governors of the State of Virginia*, ed. H. R. McIlwaine (Richmond, VA, 1926), 1:82–83.

9. David Waldstreicher, ed. *Notes on the State of Virginia by Thomas Jefferson with Related Documents* (Boston, 2002), 165.

10. Patrick Henry to Richard Henry Lee, March 28, 1777, in William Wirt Henry, *Patrick Henry: Life, Correspondence and Speeches* (New York, 1891), 1:515; Elizabeth A. Fenn, *Pox Americana: The Great Smallpox Epidemic of 1775–82* (New York, 2001), 85, 94–95.

11. Patrick Henry to George Washington, March 29, 1777, in Crackel, *Papers of George Washington*.

12. George Washington to Patrick Henry, April 13, 1777, Patrick Henry to George Washington, September 5, 1777, in Crackel, *Papers of George Washington*; Patrick Henry to Charles Lewis, February 21, 1777, and March 15, 1777, in Patrick Henry papers, Pierpont Morgan Library, New York City.

13. McDonnell, *Politics of War*, 284–88; Patrick Henry to George Washington, October 30, 1777, in Crackel, *Papers of George Washington*.

14. Patrick Henry to George Wythe, October 22, 1777, Bancroft Library, University of California-Berkeley; McDonnell, *Politics of War*, 295–96.

15. Articles of Confederation, Article I, at http://press-pubs.uchicago .edu/founders/documents/v1ch1s7.html.

16. Ibid., Article VII.

17. *Virginia Gazette* (Dixon and Hunter), October 31, 1777, 2.

18. Ibid., November 7, 1777, 2.

19. Richard R. Beeman, *Patrick Henry: A Biography* (New York, 1974), 109–10.

20. Patrick Griffin, *American Leviathan: Empire, Nation, and Revolutionary Frontier* (New York, 2007), 142; Secret instructions to Clark, January 2, 1778; George Wythe, George Mason, and Thomas Jefferson to George

Rogers Clark, January 3, 1778, in *George Rogers Clark Papers, 1771–1781*, ed. James A. James (1912; New York, 1972), 34.

21. Patrick Henry to George Rogers Clark, January 24, 1778; Patrick Henry to Virginia Delegates in Congress, November 16, 1778; and Patrick Henry to George Rogers Clark, December 12, 1778, in James, *Clark Papers*, 72, 75; Griffin, *American Leviathan*, 142–43.

22. Patrick Henry to Benjamin Harrison, May 19, 1779, in James, *Clark Papers*, 322; Griffin, *American Leviathan*, 143–45.

23. George Rogers Clark to Patrick Henry, February 3, 1779, and March 9, 1779, in James, *Clark Papers*, 97, 304.

24. Thomas Jefferson to George Rogers Clark, November 26, 1782, in *The Papers of Thomas Jefferson*, ed. Julian P. Boyd (Princeton, NJ, 1952), 6:205; John E. Selby, *The Revolution in Virginia, 1775–1783* (Charlottesville, VA, 1988), 202–03.

25. [Benjamin Rush] to Patrick Henry, January 12, 1778, in L. H. Butterfield, *Letters of Benjamin Rush* (Princeton, NJ, 1951), 1:182–83.

26. Patrick Henry to George Washington, February 20, 1778, and Henry to Washington, March 5, 1778, in Crackel, *Papers of Washington*.

27. George Washington to Patrick Henry, March 27, 1778, and Washington to Henry, March 28, 1778, in ibid; Alyn Brodsky, *Benjamin Rush: Patriot and Physician* (New York, 2004), 246, 377 n.2.

28. George Washington to Henry Lee, August 26, 1794, and Henry to Washington, February 20, 1778, n.1, in Crackel, *Papers of Washington*.

29. Patrick Henry to Benjamin Harrison, May 27, 1778, in McIlwaine, *Official Letters*, 1:283.

30. Patrick Henry to Richard Henry Lee, June 18, 1778, in Henry, *Patrick Henry*, 1:564.

31. Colonel William Preston to Patrick Henry, November 25, 1778, in "Preston Papers," ed. R. B. Marston, *John P. Branch Historical Papers of Randolph-Macon College* 4, no. 3 (June 1915): 297–98; Emory G. Evans, "Trouble in the Backcountry: Disaffection in Southwest Virginia During the American Revolution," in *An Uncivil War: The Southern Backcountry during the*

*American Revolution*, ed. Ronald Hoffman, Thad W. Tate, and Peter J. Albert (Charlottesville, VA, 1985), 190.

32. Henry to Lee, June 18, 1778, in Henry, *Patrick Henry*, 1:564–55.

33. Patrick Henry to Henry Laurens, November 23, 1778, in Henry, *Patrick Henry*, 3:205.

34. Continental Congress, *Proclamation* (Hartford, CT, 1779); Patrick Henry recommendation, April 6, 1779, in McIlwaine, *Official Letters*, 364–65.

35. St. George Tucker to Theodorick Bland Jr., June 6, 1779, in Henry, *Patrick Henry*, 2:34–35.

36. House of Senators resolution, June 1, 1779, in McIlwaine, *Official Letters*, 379.

## Chapter 8: "Virtue Has Taken Its Departure": The War's End and a New Virginia

1. Patrick Henry to Thomas Jefferson, February 15, 1780, in William Wirt Henry, *Patrick Henry: Life, Correspondence, and Speeches* (New York, 1891), 2:48–49.

2. John Parke Custis to George Washington, January 9, 1779, in *The Papers of George Washington: Digital Edition*, ed. Theodore J. Crackel (Charlottesville, VA, 2007).

3. George Washington to John Augustine Washington, November 26, 1778, in ibid.

4. Henry to Jefferson, February 15, 1780, in Henry, *Patrick Henry*, 2:49.

5. Patrick Henry to Adam Stephen, June 10, 1779, Virginia Historical Society; Robert Douthat Meade, *Patrick Henry: Practical Revolutionary* (Philadelphia, 1969), 224–25.

6. John E. Selby, *The Revolution in Virginia, 1775–1783* (Charlottesville, VA, 1988), 248–50.

7. Meade, *Practical Revolutionary*, 228; John Ferling, *Almost a Miracle: The American Victory in the War of Independence* (New York, 2007), 421.

8. Michael Kranish, *Flight from Monticello: Thomas Jefferson at War* (New York, 2010), 162.

9. Ibid., 166–67.

10. Ibid., 188–90.

11. Quotes from Ferling, *Almost a Miracle*, 497–99; Meade, *Practical Revolutionary*, 234–35.

12. Henry, *Patrick Henry*, 2:118–19.

13. Thomas Jefferson to George Washington, May 28, 1781, in *The Papers of Thomas Jefferson*, ed. Julian P. Boyd (Princeton, NJ, 1952), 6:33.

14. Kranish, *Flight from Monticello*, 278, 295–96.

15. Archibald Stuart to Thomas Jefferson, September 8, 1818, in Henry, *Patrick Henry*, 148; David Waldstreicher, ed., *Notes on the State of Virginia with Related Documents* (Boston, 2002), 165–66; Richard Henry Lee to [James Lovell], June 12, 1781, in *The Letters of Richard Henry Lee*, ed. James Curtis Ballagh (1911; New York, 1970), 2:237; Michael A. McDonnell, *The Politics of War: Race, Class, and Conflict in Revolutionary Virginia* (Chapel Hill, NC, 2007), 465–66.

16. McDonnell, *Politics of War*, 469–70; Henry, *Patrick Henry*, 2:154.

17. Thomas Jefferson to Isaac Zane, December 24, 1781, in Boyd, *Papers of Thomas Jefferson*, 6:143; Richard R. Beeman, *Patrick Henry: A Biography* (New York, 1974), 132.

18. Thomas Jefferson to James Monroe, May 20, 1782, in Boyd, *Papers of Thomas Jefferson*, 6:185; Andrew Burstein and Nancy Isenberg, *Madison and Jefferson* (New York, 2010), 92.

19. Elizabeth A. Fenn, *Pox Americana: The Great Smallpox Epidemic of 1775–82* (New York, 2001), 129–31.

20. Horatio Gates to Patrick Henry, May 10, 1782, in Henry, *Patrick Henry*, 2:173.

21. Ibid., 174; McDonnell, *Politics of War*, 487, 490; Eva Sheppard Wolf, *Race and Liberty in the New Nation: Emancipation in Virginia from the Revolution to Nat Turner's Rebellion* (Baton Rouge, LA, 2006), 44, 125; Bureau of the Census, *A Century of Population Growth* (Washington, DC, 1909), 132.

22. Beeman, *Patrick Henry*, 120–21.

23. George Mason to Patrick Henry, May 6, 1783, in *The Papers of George Mason*, ed. Robert A. Rutland (Chapel Hill, NC, 1970), 2:770–71; Emory G. Evans, "Private Indebtedness and the Revolution in Virginia, 1776 to 1796," *William and Mary Quarterly* 3rd series, 28, no. 3 (July 1971): 368–69.

24. William Wirt, *Sketches of the Life and Character of Patrick Henry* (New York, 1857), 254–55.

25. Wirt, *Sketches*, 252–53; John A. George, "Virginia Loyalists, 1775–1783," in *Richmond College Historical Papers* 1, no. 2 (June 1916): 219.

26. Thomas Jefferson to James Madison, May 7, 1783, in Boyd, *Papers of Thomas Jefferson*, 6:266; J. Kent McGaughy, *Richard Henry Lee of Virginia: A Portrait of an American Revolutionary* (Lanham, MD, 2004), 171–72; Richard Henry Lee to Patrick Henry, December 18, 1784, in Ballagh, *Letters of Richard Henry Lee*, 2:314.

27. Jefferson to Madison, May 7, 1783, in Boyd, *Papers of Thomas Jefferson*, 6:266; Beeman, *Patrick Henry*, 124–26; Ron Chernow, *Alexander Hamilton* (New York, 2004), 176.

28. William Short to Thomas Jefferson, May 14, 1784, in Beeman, *Patrick Henry*, 126–27.

29. Charles F. James, *Documentary History of the Struggle for Religious Liberty in Virginia* (Lynchburg, VA, 1900), 129.

30. Thomas E. Buckley, S.J., "Patrick Henry, Religious Liberty, and the Search for Civic Virtue," in *The Forgotten Founders on Religion and Public Life*, ed. Daniel L. Dreisbach, Mark David Hall, and Jeffry H. Morrison (Notre Dame, IN, 2009), 125–27.

31. Richard Henry Lee to James Madison, November 26, 1784, in Ballagh, ed., *Letters of Richard Henry Lee*, 2:304; George Washington to George Mason, October 3, 1785, in Crackel, *Papers of George Washington*.

32. James Madison to Thomas Jefferson, July 3, 1784, in *The Papers of James Madison*, ed. Robert A. Rutland and William M. E. Rachal (Chicago, 1973), 8:94; Thomas E. Buckley, S.J., *Church and State in Revolutionary Virginia, 1776–1787* (Charlottesville, VA, 1977), 86–88. Thanks to Tom Buckley

for helping me understand, via e-mail, the legal details of the incorporation bill.

33. James Madison to James Monroe, November 27, 1784, in Rutland and Rachal, *Papers of James Madison*, 8:158; Meade, *Practical Revolutionary*, 280–83.

34. James Madison, "Memorial and Remonstrance," June 20, 1785, document 43 in Philip B. Kurland and Ralph Lerner, *The Founders' Constitution* (Chicago, 1987), at http://press-pubs.uchicago.edu/founders/documents/amendI_religions43.html; William Fristoe, *A Concise History of the Ketocton Baptist Association* (Staunton, VA, 1808), 94.

35. "A Bill for Establishing Religious Freedom," (1786), in *The Sacred Rights of Conscience: Selected Readings on Religious Liberty and Church-State Relations in the American Founding*, ed. Daniel L. Dreisbach and Mark David Hall (Indianapolis, 2009), 251.

36. Thomas Jefferson to James Madison, December 8, 1784, in Boyd, *Papers of Thomas Jefferson*, 7:558; Kevin R. C. Gutzman, *Virginia's American Revolution: From Dominion to Republic, 1776–1840* (Lanham, MD, 2007), 64.

37. Mary V. Thompson, *"In the Hands of a Good Providence": Religion in the Life of George Washington* (Charlottesville, VA, 2008), 69–71.

38. James Jay to Patrick Henry, December 20, 1784; Countess of Huntingdon to Governor of Virginia, April 8, 1784; Outlines of Countess of Huntingdon's Plan, April 8, 1784, in Henry, *Patrick Henry*, 3:248–61; Patrick Henry to Virginia Delegates in Congress, February 3, 1785, in Henry, *Patrick Henry*, 2:273–74; Patrick Henry to Joseph Martin, February 4, 1785, Patrick Henry Papers, Library of Congress.

39. George Washington to Richard Henry Lee, February 8, 1785, in Crackel, *Papers of George Washington*; Richard Henry Lee to George Washington, February 27, 1785, in Ballagh, *Letters of Richard Henry Lee*, 2:338–39.

40. Edwin S. Gaustad, *Sworn on the Altar of God: A Religious Biography of Thomas Jefferson* (Grand Rapids, MI, 1995), 101.

41. Patrick Henry to the County Lieutenant and Commanding Officer of Greenbrier County, June 23, 1785, in *Calendar of Virginia State Papers*,

ed. William P. Palmer (Richmond, VA, 1884), 4:39; Patrick Henry to Joseph Martin, April 16, 1785, Samuel Brown to Patrick Henry, July 29, 1785, and Henry to Brown, August 11, 1785, in Henry, *Patrick Henry*, 3:294–95, 312–13; Daniel Boone to Patrick Henry, August 16, 1785, in *Southern Literary Messenger*, January 1, 1860, 52; John Mack Faragher, *Daniel Boone: The Life and Legend of an American Pioneer* (New York, 1992), 250.

42. St. George Tucker to Patrick Henry, January 6, 1786, in McDonnell, *Politics of War*, 512; Patrick Henry to the Speaker of the House of Delegates, October 17, 1786, in Harrison Ethridge, "Governor Patrick Henry and the Reorganization of the Virginia Militia, 1784–1786," *Virginia Magazine of History and Biography* 85 (1977): 438.

43. Patrick Henry to the Speaker of the House of Delegates, November 17, 1785, in Henry, *Patrick Henry*, 337; William Foushee to Patrick Henry, December 6, 1785, in Palmer, *Virginia State Papers*, 4:71.

44. Richard Henry Lee to Patrick Henry, February 14, 1785, in Ballagh, *Richard Henry Lee*, 332.

45. George Rogers Clark to Patrick Henry, May [?], 1786, in Palmer, *Virginia State Papers*, 122.

46. Patrick Henry to the President of Congress, May 16, 1786, in Henry, *Patrick Henry*, 353.

47. William Grayson, et al., to Patrick Henry, June 8, 1786, and Patrick Henry to Edward Carrington, et al., July 5, 1786, in *The Papers of James Monroe*, ed. Daniel Preston (Westport, CT, 2006), 2:309, 316.

48. Eli Merritt, et al., "Sectional Conflict and Secret Compromise: The Mississippi River Question and the United States Constitution," *American Journal of Legal History* 35, no. 2 (April 1991): 132.

49. James Monroe to Patrick Henry, August 12, 1786, in Preston, *Papers of James Monroe*, 2:333–34.

50. Patrick Henry to Anne Christian, October 20, 1786, in Henry, *Patrick Henry*, 3:380.

51. James Madison to George Washington, December 7, 1786, in Crackel, *Papers of George Washington*.

52. Patrick Henry to Anne Christian, October 20, 1786, in Henry, *Patrick Henry*, 3:380; Meade, *Practical Revolutionary*, 318–19; www.redhill.org /descendants_genealogy.html.

53. Patrick Henry to Edmund Randolph, February 13, 1787, in Henry, *Patrick Henry*, 2:311.

## Chapter 9: "I Smelt a Rat": Defending the Revolution by Opposing the Constitution

1. *Independent Gazetteer* (Philadelphia), December 21, 1786, 3; Hugh Blair Grigsby, *The History of the Virginia Federal Convention of 1788* (Richmond, VA: 1890), 1:32 n.36.

2. William Wirt Henry, *Patrick Henry: Life, Correspondence, and Speeches* (New York, 1891), 2:301; James Madison to Thomas Jefferson, March 19, 1787, in *The Papers of James Madison*, ed. Robert A. Rutland and William M. E. Rachal (Chicago, 1975), 9:319; James Madison to George Washington, March 18, 1787, in ibid., 9:316.

3. Jack N. Rakove, *Original Meanings: Politics and Ideas in the Making of the Constitution* (New York, 1996), 32–33; Richard R. Beeman, *Patrick Henry: A Biography* (New York, 1974), 140–41.

4. Edmund Randolph to Patrick Henry, December 6, 1786, in Henry, *Patrick Henry*, 2:310–11.

5. Joseph J. Ellis, *His Excellency: George Washington* (New York, 2004), 177.

6. George Mason, "Objections to the Constitution of Government Formed by the Convention," in *The Complete Anti-Federalist*, ed. Herbert J. Storing (Chicago, 1981), 2:11–13.

7. George Washington to Patrick Henry, Benjamin Harrison, and Thomas Nelson, September 24, 1787, in *The Papers of George Washington: Digital Edition*, ed. Theodore J. Crackel (Charlottesville, VA, 2007); James Madison to George Washington, October 18, 1787, in *The Documentary History of the Ratification of the Constitution*, ed. John P. Kaminski and Gaspare J. Saladino (Madison, WI, 1990), 8:77; Robert Middlekauff, *The Glorious Cause: The American Revolution, 1763–1789* (New York, 1982), 646–48.

8. Patrick Henry to George Washington, October 19, 1787, in Crackel, *Papers of George Washington*.

9. Benjamin Harrison to George Washington, October 4, 1787, in ibid.

10. Thomas Jefferson to James Madison, December 20, 1787, in *The Papers of Thomas Jefferson*, ed. Julian P. Boyd (Princeton, NJ, 1955), 12:442; Joseph J. Ellis, *American Sphinx: The Character of Thomas Jefferson* (New York, 1996), 122–24.

11. "Petersburg, (Virginia), Nov. 1," *Pennsylvania Packet*, November 10, 1787.

12. Ibid.; Kaminski and Saladino, *Documentary History*, 8:110.

13. James Madison to Thomas Jefferson, December 9, 1787, in Boyd, *Papers of Thomas Jefferson*, 12:410.

14. James Madison, *Federalist #51*, in *The Federalist*, ed. George W. Carey and James McClellan (Indianapolis, 2001), 270.

15. John Blair Smith to James Madison, June 12, 1788, in *The Papers of James Madison*, ed. Robert A. Rutland, et al. (Charlottesville, VA, 1977), 11:120; Pauline Maier, *Ratification: The People Debate the Constitution, 1787–1788* (New York, 2010), 231–32; 1790 Census figures, at www2.census.gov /prod2/decennial/documents/1790m-02.pdf.

16. Edward Carrington to Thomas Jefferson, April 24, 1788, in Kaminski and Saladino, *Documentary History*, 9:755.

17. Patrick Henry to John Lamb, June 9, 1788, in Henry, *Patrick Henry*, 2:342–43.

18. Tobias Lear to John Langdon, April 3, 1788, in Kaminski and Saladino, *Documentary History*, 9:699; Pauline Maier, *Ratification*, 216, 225–26.

19. "The Virginia Convention, June 5, 1788," in Kaminski and Saladino, *Documentary History*, 9:951.

20. James Duncanson to James Maury, June 7 and 13, 1788, in Kaminski and Saladino, *Documentary History*, 10:1582–84; Maier, *Ratification*, 255–56.

21. "The Virginia Convention, June 3, 1788," in Kaminski and Saladino, *Documentary History*, 9:914; Andrew Burstein and Nancy Isenberg, *Madison and Jefferson* (New York, 2010), 181.

22. "The Virginia Convention, June 4, 1788," in Kaminski and Saladino, *Documentary History*, 9:929–30.

23. Ibid., 9:930.

24. "The Virginia Convention, June 5, 1788," in ibid., 9:949.

25. Alexander White to Mary Wood, June 10–11, 1788, in ibid., 10:1591; Henry speech in ibid., 9:952.

26. George Washington to Henry Lee, October 31, 1786, in Crackel, *Papers of George Washington*; "Extract of a Letter from a Gentleman at Philadelphia, Dated 16th June 1788," *Independent Gazetteer*, June 24, 1788.

27. Kaminski and Saladino, *Documentary History*, 9:954, 959.

28. "The Virginia Convention, June 5, 1788," in ibid., 9:959.

29. Ibid., 9:951.

30. Ibid., 9:963.

31. Alexander Hamilton, *Federalist #67*, in Carey and McClellan, *The Federalist*, 348.

32. "The Virginia Convention, June 5, 1788," in Kaminski and Saladino, *Documentary History*, 9:964.

33. Ibid., 9:962, 967.

34. Patrick Henry to Elizabeth Aylett, June 11, 1788, Hoxey Collection, Special Collections, University of Texas at Arlington Library; Robert Douthat Meade, *Patrick Henry: Practical Revolutionary* (Philadelphia, 1969), 357–58.

35. *Vermont Gazette*, July 7, 1788, 3; "The Virginia Convention, Friday, June 6, 1788," in Kaminski and Saladino, *Documentary History*, 9:975.

36. Ibid., 9:989–90; Maier, *Ratification*, 271.

37. Kaminski and Saladino, *Documentary History*, 9:1044–45; Gordon S. Wood, *Empire of Liberty: A History of the Early Republic, 1789–1815* (New York, 2009), 35–36.

38. "The Virginia Convention, June 7, 1788," and "The Virginia Convention, June 12, 1788," in Kaminski and Saladino, *Documentary History*, 9:1039, 10:1220; Lance Banning, *The Sacred Fire of Liberty: James Madison and the Founding of the Federal Republic* (Ithaca, NY, 1995), 268–69.

39. Kaminski and Saladino, *Documentary History*, 9:1044.

40. "The Virginia Convention, June 9, 1788," in ibid., 9:1062.

41. "The Virginia Convention, June 17, 1788,"and "The Virginia Convention, June 24, 1788," in ibid., 10:1341, 1503; Robin L. Einhorn, *American Taxation, American Slavery* (Chicago, 2006), 178–83; David Waldstreicher, *Slavery's Constitution: From Revolution to Ratification* (New York, 2009), 142–45.

42. "The Virginia Convention, June 24, 1788," in Kaminski and Saladino, *Documentary History*, 10:1476–77. A reminiscence sixty years later held that Henry burst out at one point with the crass warning that, under the Constitution, "They'll free your niggers!" Given Henry's documented sober comments about slavery at the convention, and the belated nature of the source, I do not think this quote is authentic. Robin Einhorn, "Patrick Henry's Case Against the Constitution: The Structural Problem with Slavery," *Journal of the Early Republic* 22, no. 4 (Winter 2002): 554–55, n.10.

43. "The Virginia Convention, June 23, 1788, in Kaminski and Saladino, *Documentary History*, 10:1468–69.

44. "The Virginia Convention, June 17, 1788," in ibid., 10:1345.

45. Maier, *Ratification*, 305–07.

46. "The Virginia Convention, June 24, 1788," in Kaminski and Saladino, *Documentary History*, 10:1506, 1511.

47. Extract of a Letter from Richmond, June 18," *Pennsylvania Mercury*, June 26, 1788; Burstein and Isenberg, *Madison and Jefferson*, 183; "The Virginia Convention, June 25, 1788," in Kaminski and Saladino, *Documentary History*, 10:1537.

48. "The Virginia Convention, June 27, 1788," in Kaminski and Saladino, *Documentary History*, 10:1553.

49. Maier, *Ratification*, 313; "Meeting of Antifederalist Convention Delegates, June 27, 1788," in ibid., 10:1561–62; David J. Siemers, *Ratifying the Republic: Antifederalists and Federalists in Constitutional Time* (Stanford, CA, 2002), 32.

50. James Madison to George Washington, June 27, 1788, in Crackel, *Papers of George Washington*.

51. Henry Lee to James Madison, November 19, 1788, in Rutland, et al., *Papers of James Madison*, 11:356; Henry, *Patrick Henry*, 2:423–25.

52. George Washington to James Madison, November 17, 1788, in Crackel, *Papers of George Washington*; Maier, *Ratification*, 440.

53. Patrick Henry to Richard Henry Lee, November 15, 1788, Patrick Henry Papers, Library of Congress; Beeman, *Patrick Henry*, 169.

54. *Virginia Independent Chronicle*, January 14, February 4, 1789.

55. Patrick Henry to William Grayson, March 31, 1789, in *Virginia Historical Magazine* 14, 203.

56. James Madison to George Eve, January 2, 1789, in Rutland, et al., *Papers of James Madison*, 11:405.

## Chapter 10: "To Care for the Crazy Machine": Reconciling with the Republic

1. Scene at Henry's home in William Wirt Henry, *Patrick Henry: Life, Correspondence, and Speeches* (New York, 1891), 2:518; Patrick Henry to Elizabeth Aylett, September 8, 1794, in ibid., 3:424; "garden spots" in George Morgan, *The True Patrick Henry* (Philadelphia, 1907), 396.

2. "William Loughton Smith Journal, 1790–1791," *Massachusetts Historical Society Proceedings* 51 (October 1917–June 1918): 68.

3. Theodore Sedgwick to Benjamin Lincoln, July 19, 1789, in *Creating the Bill of Rights: The Documentary Record from the First Federal Congress*, ed. Helen E. Veit, et al. (Baltimore, 1991), 263.

4. *Pennsylvania Packet*, January 7, 1789, 2; *Federal Gazette* (Philadelphia), January 14, 1789, 3; *Norwich Packet*, January 26, 1789, 3.

5. James Madison to Thomas Jefferson, December 8, 1788, in *The Papers of James Madison*, ed. Robert A. Rutland, et al. (Charlottesville, VA, 1977), 11:382.

6. James Madison, speech of June 8, 1789, in Veit, et al., *Creating the Bill of Rights*, 78; Kenneth R. Bowling, "'A Tub to the Whale': The Founding Fathers and the Adoption of the Federal Bill of Rights," *Journal of the Early Republic* 8, no. 3 (Autumn 1988): 223–24.

7. Patrick Henry to Richard Henry Lee, August 28, 1789, Patrick Henry Papers, Library of Congress.

8. Richard Henry Lee to Patrick Henry, September 14, 1789, and William Grayson to Patrick Henry, September 29, 1789, in Patrick Henry Papers, Library of Congress.

9. Richard Henry Lee to Patrick Henry, September 27, 1789, Richard Henry Lee and William Grayson to the Speaker of the House of Representatives in Virginia, September 28, 1789, in *The Letters of Richard Henry Lee*, ed. James Curtis Ballagh (1911; New York, 1970), 2:506, 508; Edward Carrington to James Madison, December 20, 1789, in Rutland, et al., *Papers of James Madison*, 12:463.

10. Henry, *Patrick Henry*, 2:449; Patrick Henry to Elizabeth Aylett, November 5, 1789, Virginia Historical Society, Richmond.

11. Thomas P. Abernathy, *The South in the New Nation, 1789–1819* (Baton Rouge, LA, 1961), 88–89.

12. Patrick Henry to Richard Henry Lee, January 29, 1790, and Theodorick Bland to Patrick Henry, March 9, 1790, in Henry, *Patrick Henry*, 3:414, 419.

13. Ibid., 3:415; Samuel Cole Williams, *History of the Lost State of Franklin* (Johnson City, TN, 1924), 243.

14. Patrick Henry to [Francis Watkins?], November 12, 1790, Patrick Henry papers, Library of Congress; Richard R. Beeman, *Patrick Henry: A Biography* (New York, 1974), 184.

15. Patrick Henry to James Townes, October 24, 1798, Patrick Henry Letters, Library of Virginia, Richmond.

16. Spencer Roane quoted in Moses Coit Tyler, *Patrick Henry* (Boston, 1894), 267–68; Patrick Henry to Elizabeth Aylett, October 30, 1791, Virginia Historical Society; Henry's son-in-law (Spencer Roane) quoted in George Morgan, *Patrick Henry* (Philadelphia, 1929), 449; Henry Mayer, *A Son of Thunder: Patrick Henry and the American Republic* (New York, 1986), 465.

17. Patrick Henry, Memorandum of September 5, 1785, Henry Family Papers, Records of the Ante-Bellum Southern Plantations from the Revolution

through the Civil War, ed. Kenneth Stampp, Series M, Selections from the Virginia Historical Society, Richmond, Part 5: Southside Virginia.

18. "Great" quote in Edmund Pendleton to James Madison, December 9, 1791, in *The Letters and Papers of Edmund Pendleton, 1734–1803*, ed. David John Mays (Charlottesville, VA, 1967), 2:582; Beeman, *Patrick Henry*, 177–80.

19. William Wirt, *Sketches of the Life and Character of Patrick Henry* (New York, 1857), 389–91.

20. Beeman, *Patrick Henry*, 180–81.

21. Patrick Henry to James Monroe, January 24, 1791, in *The Papers of James Monroe*, ed. Daniel Preston (Westport, CT, 2006), 2:493.

22. Ibid.

23. *Journal of the House of Delegates* (Richmond, VA, 1790), 36.

24. Henry Lee to George Washington, August 17, 1794, in *The Writings of George Washington*, ed. Worthington Chauncey Ford (New York, 1891), 12:456 n.1; George Washington to Henry Lee, August 26, 1794, in Jared Sparks, *The Writings of George Washington* (Boston, 1836), 10:431. (Note that as of this writing, the Papers of George Washington, Presidential Series, runs only through April 1794. Thus, several letters to or from Washington in this chapter are quoted from older sources.)

25. Henry Lee to Patrick Henry, July 11, 1794, Patrick Henry Papers, Library of Congress; Patrick Henry to Henry Lee, July 14, 1794, in Henry, *Patrick Henry*, 2:547; *Gazette of the United States* August 12, 1794, 3.

26. Edmund Randolph to Patrick Henry, n.d. [1794], Henry Family Papers, Virginia Historical Society; Patrick Henry to Edmund Randolph, September 14, 1794, Henry, *Patrick Henry*, 2:548–49.

27. Patrick Henry to Elizabeth Aylett, October 26, 1793, and Patrick Henry to Elizabeth Aylett, September 8, 1794, in Henry, *Patrick Henry*, 3:422–23.

28. Robert Douthat Meade, *Patrick Henry: Practical Revolutionary* (Philadelphia, 1969), 433; Patrick Henry to Elizabeth Aylett, May 3, 1794, Princeton University Rare Books and Special Collections; Gordon S. Wood, *Empire of Liberty: A History of the Early Republic, 1789–1815* (New York, 2009), 193–94.

29. Thomas J. Farnham, "The Virginia Amendments of 1795: An Episode in the Opposition to Jay's Treaty," *Virginia Magazine of History and Biography* 75, no. 1 (January 1967): 78, 82; *Aurora General Advertiser*, August 17, 1795, 3; Todd Estes, *The Jay Treaty Debate, Public Opinion, and the Evolution of Early American Political Culture* (Amherst, MA, 2006), 104–26; Wood, *Empire of Liberty*, 198–99.

30. Edward Carrington to George Washington, October 16, 1795, in Sparks, *Writings of George Washington*, 11:81; George Washington to Patrick Henry, October 9, 1795, in ibid., 11:82.

31. Rufus King quoted in Ron Chernow, *Washington: A Life* (New York, 2010), 735.

32. Patrick Henry to George Washington, October 16, 1795, Gratz Federal Convention papers, Historical Society of Pennsylvania, Philadelphia. Several drafts of this letter exist, and I am using the HSP copy because it is clearly in Henry's handwriting.

33. Ibid.

34. Patrick Henry to Elizabeth Aylett, August 20, 1796, in Henry Family Papers, Virginia Historical Society.

35. George Washington to Henry Lee, January 11, 1796, in *The Documentary History of the Supreme Court of the United States, 1789–1800*, ed. Maeva Marcus and James R. Perry (New York, 1985), vol. 1, part 2: 829; George Washington to Timothy Pickering, July 8, 1796, in Ford, *Writings of George Washington*, 13:236.

36. Thomas Jefferson to James Monroe, July 10, 1796, in *The Papers of Thomas Jefferson*, ed. Barbara B. Oberg (Princeton, NJ, 2002), 147–48.

37. Thomas Paine, *The Age of Reason* (New York, 1827), 5; Gary B. Nash, "The American Clergy and the French Revolution," *William and Mary Quarterly* 3rd series, 22, no. 3 (July 1965): 402.

38. Patrick Henry to Elizabeth Aylett, August 20, 1796, in Henry Family Papers, Virginia Historical Society.

39. Garry Wills, *Cincinnatus: George Washington and the Enlightenment* (New York, 1984), 13.

40. Alexander Hamilton to Rufus King, May 4, 1796, in *The Papers of Alexander Hamilton*, ed. Harold C. Syrett (New York, 1974), 20:158; *National Gazette* (Philadelphia), June 18, 1792; James Roger Sharp, *American Politics in the Early Republic: The New Nation in Crisis* (New Haven, CT, 1993), 148; Patrick Daily, *Patrick Henry: The Last Years, 1789–1799* (Bedford, VA, 1986), 155–56; Charles Simms, "To the Freeholders of the Counties of Prince William, Stafford, and Fairfax," *Federal Gazette* (Baltimore), October 4, 1796.

41. Patrick Henry to Elizabeth Aylett, August 20, 1796, in Henry Family Papers, Virginia Historical Society; Patrick Henry, "To the People of the United States," *Gazette of the United States* (Philadelphia), November 15, 1796.

42. Patrick Henry to John Preston, November 29, 1796, in Henry, *Patrick Henry*, 3:424; Patrick Henry to General Samuel Hopkins, November 29, 1796, in Rhoda Doubleday, *Atlantic Between* (New York, 1947), 621–22.

43. Patrick Henry to Wilson Cary Nicholas, November 29, 1796, Patrick Henry Letters, Library of Virginia.

44. Albert J. Beveridge, *The Life of John Marshall* (Boston, 1916–19), 2:411.

45. Patrick Henry to Archibald Blair, January 8, 1799, Patrick Henry Letters, Library of Virginia.

46. Archibald Blair to Patrick Henry, January 13, 1799, in Henry, *Patrick Henry*, 3:427–28.

47. George Washington to Patrick Henry, January 15, 1799, in *The Papers of George Washington: Digital Edition*, ed. Theodore Crackel (Charlottesville, VA, 2007).

48. Patrick Henry to George Washington, February 12, 1799, in ibid.

49. John Taylor to James Madison, March 4, 1799, in *The Papers of James Madison*, ed. David B. Mattern, et al. (Charlottesville, VA, 1991), 17:245–46.

50. Joseph Martin to Patrick Henry, April 2, 1799, in *Publications of the Southern History Association* 6 (1902): 30.

51. Henry, *Patrick Henry*, 2:607–10; Douglas Bradburn, "A Clamor in the Public Mind: The Opposition to the Alien and Sedition Acts," *William and Mary Quarterly* 3rd series, 65, no. 3 (July 2008): 593–94 n.46.

52. Thomas Jefferson to Archibald Stuart, May 14, 1799, in Oberg, *Papers of Thomas Jefferson*, 31:110.

53. Dorothea Henry to Elizabeth Aylett, [June 1799], in "Two Unpublished Henry Letters," ed. Hugh Buckner Johnston, *William and Mary Quarterly* 2nd series, 21, no. 1 (January 1941): 33–34.

## Epilogue: "Mourn Virginia Mourn!": The Legacy of Patrick Henry

1. *Vermont Gazette*, June 6, 1799, 2.

2. *Virginia Gazette*, June 11, 1799, in Richard R. Beeman, *Patrick Henry: A Biography* (New York, 1974), 190.

3. *Journal of the House of Delegates* (Richmond, VA, 1799), 22.

4. William Wirt, *Sketches of the Life and Character of Patrick Henry*, 15th ed. (New York, 1857), 442–43.

5. Thomas Jefferson to William Wirt, August 4, 1805, in "Jefferson's Recollections of Patrick Henry," ed. Stanislaus Henkels, *Pennsylvania Magazine of History and Biography* 34, no. 4 (1910): 387; Andrew Burstein, "Immortalizing the Founding Fathers: The Excesses of Public Eulogy," in *Mortal Remains: Death in Early America*, ed. Nancy Isenberg and Andrew Burstein (Philadelphia, 2003), 92; William R. Taylor, *Cavalier and Yankee: The Old South and American National Character* (New York, 1964), 68–69.

6. Hinton Rowan Helper, *Compendium of the Impending Crisis of the South* (New York, 1860), 91.

7. Alexander Stephens, *A Constitutional View of the Late War Between the States* (Philadelphia, 1868–70), 163; P. H. Fontaine, "New Facts in Regard to the Character and Opinions of Patrick Henry," *DeBow's Review* (October 1870): 824, 826.

8. Albert J. Beveridge, "The Star of Empire" (1900), at http://oll.liberty fund.org/title/2282/216471.

9. Bernard Mayo, *Myths and Men: Patrick Henry, George Washington, Thomas Jefferson* (Athens, GA, 1959), 2.

10. www.wallbuilders.com/LIBissuesArticles.asp?id=126; David Limbaugh, *Persecution: How Liberals Are Waging War Against Christianity* (New York, 2004), 347.

11. George Morgan, *The True Patrick Henry* (Philadelphia, 1907), 456–62.

12. James Madison, *Federalist #48*, in *The Federalist*, ed. George W. Carey and James McClellan (Indianapolis, 2001), 256.

# INDEX